THE SEMANTICS OF ANALOGY

THE SEMANTICS OF ANALOGY
Rereading Cajetan's *De Nominum Analogia*

JOSHUA P. HOCHSCHILD

University of Notre Dame Press

Notre Dame, Indiana

Manufactured in the United States of America

Library of Congress Cataloging-in-Publication Data

Hochschild, Joshua P., 1972–
  The semantics of analogy : rereading Cajetan's De nominum
analogia / Joshua P. Hochschild.
    p. cm.
  "This work began as a doctoral project at the University of Notre
Dame"—Acknowledgments.
  Includes bibliographical references and index.
  ISBN-13: 978-0-268-03091-9 (pbk. : alk. paper)
  ISBN-10: 0-268-03091-X (pbk. : alk. paper)
  1. Cajetan, Tommaso de Vio, 1469–1534. De nominum analogia.
  2. Analogy. 3. Semantics (Philosophy) I. Title.
  B785.C153D434 2010
  169—dc22   2010008769

∞ *The paper in this book meets the guidelines for permanence and durability of
the Committee on Production Guidelines for Book Longevity of the Council on
Library Resources.*

Contents

Acknowledgments vii

Abbreviations xi

Preface: Reinterpreting a Classic xiii

Introduction: Some Theoretical and Historical Preliminaries 1

PART 1 — CAJETAN'S QUESTION

Chapter One   Systematizing Aquinas? A Paradigm in Crisis   17

Chapter Two   Reconstructing Cajetan's Question: The
Semantic Intent of *De Nominum Analogia*   33

Chapter Three   Analogy, Semantics, and the
"Concept vs. Judgment" Critique   47

Chapter Four   Some Insufficient Semantic Rules for Analogy   65

PART 2 — CAJETAN'S ANSWER

Chapter Five   Cajetan's Semantic Principles   85

Chapter Six   The Semantics of Analogy:
Inequality and Attribution   99

Chapter Seven   The Semantics of Proportionality:
                  The Proportional Unity of Concepts   122

Chapter Eight   The Semantics of Proportionality:
                  Concept Formation and Judgment   143

Chapter Nine   The Semantics of Proportionality:
                  Syllogism and Dialectic   161

Conclusion   173

Notes   177

Bibliography   233

Index   245

Acknowledgments

This work began as a doctoral project at the University of Notre Dame, and through its gestation there and subsequent development into the present form I have incurred many debts.

I mention first Gyula Klima, who introduced me to medieval philosophy, and from whom I tried to learn as much as possible through my undergraduate and graduate studies. His own comments about Cajetan's theory of analogy were the seeds of this work, and I hope he doesn't regret trusting me to cultivate them.

At Notre Dame I also had the privilege and challenge of engaging two contemporary authorities on analogy. Fr. David Burrell allowed me to convince him that it might be worth writing on Cajetan's theory of analogy, and showed great loyalty when it was most needed. Dr. Ralph McInerny was patient and forgiving; his work and conversations sharpened my wits and improved my arguments, and he arranged for crucial material support during my last year at Notre Dame. As neither of these scholars needs to be reminded, my departures from their interpretations of Cajetan in no way diminish my respect for their work, and only increase my appreciation for their generosity.

In researching this study I benefited from correspondence with E. J. Ashworth, Angel d'Ors, William McMahon, and Jöel Lonfat. Thanks also to William McMahon, John Deely, and Fr. Laurence Dewan, O.P., for sharing prepublication manuscripts of their papers. And I am especially grateful to Thomas Osborne for his very helpful comments on substantial portions of the manuscript.

Barbara Hanrahan of the University of Notre Dame Press shepherded the work to publication with grace, encouragement, and patience. Two anonymous reviewers gave the manuscript generous attention and detailed commentary, and the work benefited from Margo Shearman's expert copyediting. Margaret Gloster designed a lovely cover, integrating an image by a former student of mine, David Hancock, who kindly granted permission to reproduce his work.

Portions of this work, in earlier versions, appeared as independent articles. Much of what is covered in chapter 3 was published as "Analogy, Semantics, and Hermeneutics: The 'Concept vs. Judgment' Critique of Cajetan's *De Nominum Analogia*," in *Medieval Philosophy and Theology* 11 (2003): 241–60. Much of chapter 4 appeared in "Did Aquinas Answer Cajetan's Question? Aquinas's Semantic Rules for Analogy and the Interpretation of *De Nominum Analogia*," in *Proceedings of the American Catholic Philosophical Association* 77 (2003): 273–88. Parts of chapter 5 appeared in "Logic or Metaphysics in Cajetan's Theory of Analogy: Can Extrinsic Denomination Be a Semantic Property?" in *Proceedings of the Society for Medieval Logic and Metaphysics* 1 (2001): 45–69. And some portions of what became chapters 8 and 9 were included in "The Rest of Cajetan's Analogy Theory: *De Nominum Analogia* Chapters 4–11," in *International Philosophical Quarterly* 45 (2005): 341–56.

This research project has received more financial support from more institutions than it deserved. For grants in support of my doctoral studies I owe thanks to the University of Notre Dame, the Intercollegiate Studies Institute, the Marguerite Eyer Wilbur Foundation, and the Lynde and Harry Bradley Foundation. Special thanks are owed to the Russell Kirk Center for the privilege of a residential fellowship during 1999–2000. Subsequent work on the manuscript was supported by faculty development grants from Wheaton College (Illinois) and Mount St. Mary's University.

Lastly, my family. I can almost measure my progress on this project by the births of my four lovely children: Stephen Craig, born about halfway through the dissertation; Jeremy Augustine and Helen Mary, who entered the world at different stages of manuscript revision; and most recently, as I addressed final corrections, Benedict

John. Among other ways in which these four have blessed me, they have been inspirations to work on this book, and inspirations not to.

Naturally my greatest debt is to my wife, Paige, who has accompanied this project from the beginning and strengthened it with her faithful support and sacrifice.

Abbreviations

Works of Cajetan

CDEE *Commentaria in De Ente et Essentia.* 1495.
Edited by M. H. Laurent. Turin: Marietti, 1934.

CPA *Commentaria in Praedicamenta Aristotelis.* 1498.
Edited by M. H. Laurent. Rome: Angelicum, 1939.

CPI *Commentaria in Porphyrii Isagogen ad Praedicamenta
Aristotelis.* 1497.
Edited by I. Marega. Rome: Angelicum, 1934.

CST *Commentaria in Summam Theologiae St Thomae.* 1507–22.
Rome: Leonine Commission, 1906.

DCE *De Conceptu Entis.* 1509.
Edited by N. Zammit. Rome, 1934. Revised by H. Hering.
Rome: Angelicum, 1951.

DNA *De Nominum Analogia.* 1498.
Edited by N. Zammit. Rome, 1934. Revised by H. Hering.
Rome: Angelicum, 1951.

DCE, *DNA*, and *CDEE* are cited by section numbers as they appear
in the editions indicated (e.g., *DNA* §1). *CPA* and *CPI* are cited by

page numbers of the editions indicated (e.g., *CPA* 19). *CST* is cited by the part, article, and question of the text of Aquinas on which Cajetan comments, followed by a Roman numeral indicating the section of Cajetan's commentary as it appears in the Leonine edition (e.g., the second section of Cajetan's commentary on *Prima Pars*, question 13, article 5, is *CST* I.13.5, n. ii). All English translations of these texts are the author's.

Preface

Reinterpreting a Classic

*Now, the question "To what question did So-and-so intend this proposition
for an answer?" is an historical question, and therefore cannot be settled
except by historical methods. When So-and-so wrote in a distant past, it
is generally a very difficult one, because writers (at any rate good writers)
always write for their contemporaries, and in particular for those who are
"likely to be interested," which means those who are already asking the
question to which an answer is being offered; and consequently a writer very
seldom explains what the question is that he is trying to answer. Later on,
when he has become a "classic" and his contemporaries are all long dead, the
question has been forgotten; especially if the answer he gave was generally
acknowledged to be the right answer; for in that case people stopped asking
the question, and began asking the question that next arose.*

—R. G. Collingwood, *An Autobiography*

*Even disregarding all formal similarities that have nothing to do with the
generic concept, if a person transfers an expression from one thing to the
other, he has in mind something that is common to both of them; but this in
no way needs to be generic universality. Rather, he is following his widening*

experience, which looks for similarities, whether in the appearance of things or in their significance for us. The genius of verbal consciousness consists in being able to express these similarities. This is its fundamental metaphorical nature, and it is important to see that to regard the metaphorical use of a word as not its real sense is the prejudice of a theory of logic that is alien to language.

—H. G. Gadamer, *Truth and Method*

Thomas de Vio Cajetan was a young man, only twenty-nine years old, when he composed *De Nominum Analogia* late in the summer of 1498. He had earlier written about analogy in a commentary on Aquinas's *De Ente et Essentia* (1495) and had already commented on foundational logical works by Porphyry and Aristotle. Expounding Aristotle's *Categories*, Cajetan spoke briefly about analogy as a variety of equivocation, and then promised to address the topic in greater detail, God willing, in a separate "special treatise."[1] As it happens, it was later that same year that he found the time to fulfill his promise and write *De Nominum Analogia*.

Analogy was a central notion in the Thomistic tradition, and although Aquinas often discussed analogy, he never did so systematically and wrote no work dedicated to the subject. *De Nominum Analogia* seemed to fill a lacuna in the Thomistic oeuvre and quickly went on to become the most influential work on analogy not only in Thomistic circles, but in the broader Aristotelian tradition. Naturally Cajetan's teaching was not quite unanimously accepted, but even those few dissenters, such as Suarez, articulated their alternative positions using Cajetan's distinctive terminology. So even for its scattered critics, *De Nominum Analogia* at least set the terms of future debate; the rest, more sympathetic to *De Nominum Analogia*, considered its teaching decisive and definitive. John of St. Thomas (John Poinsot, 1589–1644), in his *Cursus Philosophicus Thomisticus*, treats analogy in the section on logic, where he faithfully transmits Cajetan's teaching. *De Nominum Analogia*, says John, handled the difficulties of analogy so subtly and thoroughly that there was nothing else to be considered on the matter.[2] Needless to say, scholars have been able to find more to say about analogy, but through the twentieth century no scholar dealing extensively with analogy has been able to ignore Cajetan's treatise. The influence of *De Nominum Analogia* leads us to believe that even if it had been Cajetan's only work, it would have made him famous.

Or would it? Even by the time he wrote *De Nominum Analogia*, Cajetan had achieved distinction and seemed destined for renown. Cajetan had been appointed to the Chair of Thomistic Metaphysics at the University of Padua in 1493, when he was not even twenty-five years old and before he had written his remarkable commentary on Aquinas's *De Ente et Essentia*. A year later, he debated the imposing humanist Pico della Mirandola; his performance earned him a promotion to master of sacred theology. If that were not enough, the subsequent achievements of its author certainly helped the reputation of *De Nominum Analogia*. Among over 150 works by Cajetan, mostly of philosophical, theological, and biblical commentary, there stands out a vast and meticulous commentary on Aquinas's *Summa Theologiae*—like most commentaries, much longer than the original, and deemed so important that it is reprinted with the original in the Leonine edition. (Written during the years 1507–20, this commentary often refers the reader back to *De Nominum Analogia* for further clarification.) And then there is Cajetan's prominence in his order, his church, and world affairs. Cajetan was appointed master general of the Dominican Order in 1508, and received the cardinal's hat in 1517; the next year, he was appointed papal legate to Germany, where he was charged to negotiate with a young Augustinian upstart named Martin Luther. In 1519 Cajetan was made bishop of his hometown in Italy, Gaeta (*Cajetanus* is a latinization of *Gaetano*).[3]

In short, posterity's judgment of the modest treatise *De Nominum Analogia* is difficult to separate from the fact that its author is remembered as an authoritative and influential Dominican, a master commentator, and a prominent representative of official Thomism. This reputation is no doubt one reason why Cajetan's *De Nominum Analogia* is usually treated as an attempt to comment on, or systematize, Aquinas's teaching on analogy.

Another reason that *De Nominum Analogia* has been so long treated as a (attempted) formalization of Aquinas's views is that its status as a classic makes it easy for interpreters to neglect inquiry into its intention. A text, as Collingwood reminds us, must be understood in relation to the question it aims to answer. One might think that the motivating question is hardest to discern in the case of little-known and obscure texts, where the historical evidence may be sparse. But in fact, as Collingwood points out, it is influential "classic" texts that are often most difficult to interpret, for if a text has achieved such status, it will have done so for two reasons: it will have been well-enough written to be tailored to an audience already asking the question, and so is unlikely to have dwelt on formulating the question; and its answer to that question will have been so effective that people stopped asking the question, "and began asking the question that next arose."

In the case of *De Nominum Analogia*, "the question that next arose" for the audience (Thomists) was naturally the question of how far its doctrine accorded with Aquinas's own teaching. This is the question that most scholars have treated as an interpretive starting point. But it is not the question that the text was meant to answer, and does not indicate anything about Cajetan's intent in writing on analogy. It is, however, a question that has elicited plenty of debate, allowing the prior question—*Cajetan's* question, the question that *De Nominum Analogia* was intended to answer—to be quietly forgotten. Even when the treatise was being canonized by John of St. Thomas for containing the unsurpassed and unsurpassable theory of analogy, we detect signs of the amnesia of posterity described by Collingwood. It is clear that John believed that *De Nominum Analogia* contains all the answers. But the answers to what questions?

— THIS STUDY SEEKS A REREADING OF *DE NOMINUM ANALOGIA* BY reconstructing the question(s) it seeks to answer, and then explaining and evaluating the answer(s) it provides.

The study's order is thus determined by neither purely historical nor purely theoretical considerations, but by the desire to initiate readers into the dialectal issues that occasioned it and were occasioned by it. The introduction thus serves a double purpose. Most obviously, and most useful to those who are new to Cajetan, it offers three discussions that lay the groundwork for an interpretation of Cajetan's text: an overview of the central theoretical issues involved in "analogy," a brief history of their treatment from Aristotle to Aquinas, and an outline of the central doctrines of *De Nominum Analogia*. But the introduction is not intended just for beginners. Those familiar with the variety of ancient, medieval, and modern discussions of analogy may appreciate the attempt to distill a coherent narrative; there is no such thing as "*the* history" of "*the* concept of analogy," but the introduction offers some clarifying distinctions and *a* history that is especially relevant to appreciating Cajetan's treatise. Even those familiar with *De Nominum Analogia* and its reception may find that the introduction raises new questions about its historical significance.

As for the main body of this study, part 1 as a whole serves to reconstruct, and show the importance of, the philosophical questions that Cajetan intended his treatise on analogy to answer. Chapter 1 recounts the history of interpretation of *De Nominum Analogia*, with concentration on twentieth-century debates, revealing that the diversity of positions can be understood as constituting an established "paradigm" that expects *De Nominum Analogia* to offer a generally "Thomistic" theory of analogy. The debates within this received paradigm of interpretation are shown to lead to a variety of anomalies, failing to account for certain features of *De Nominum Analogia*, and contradicting historical and textual evidence. The signs of crisis are reinforced by the historical work of a handful of scholars—Ashworth, Tavuzzi, and Riva—who help to show that Cajetan's treatise needs to be read as part of ongoing theoretical developments, and cannot be evaluated simply as an attempt to systematize Aquinas.

Therefore chapter 2 introduces an alternative, more historically sensitive interpretive paradigm that offers a better account of the particular questions Cajetan intended his treatise on analogy to answer. This chapter argues, first, that the treatise belongs to the part of philosophy medieval thinkers understood as *logic*, and can today be said to belong more specifically to *semantics*; and second, that the specific semantic questions the treatise aims to answer were those raised by Scotus's arguments against analogy. The evidence of the text and of its historical context indicates further that there were principally two semantic questions about analogy that Cajetan was trying to answer: How is a mean between equivocation and univocation possible? And, if analogy is a species of equivocation, how can analogical terms avoid causing the fallacy of equivocation?

Since these are questions that can be answered only by an analysis of the *semantics* of analogical signification, chapter 3 addresses the arguments leveled by several scholars to the effect that such a semantic analysis is inappropriate. One version of this critique has origins in Gilson's claim that attention to *concepts* is Scotistic rather than Thomistic; another argues more generally that semantic analysis necessarily reduces analogy to univocity. Replies to these criticisms require attention to Cajetan's understanding of a "concept," and to his sensitivity, in theory and in practice, to hermeneutic complexity.

Chapter 4 turns from the appropriateness to the urgency of Cajetan's semantic questions, arguing that Cajetan would not have been able to find explicit answers to his questions in the writings of Aquinas. The chapter reviews various claims made by Aquinas about analogy, arguing that none of them provides adequate semantic detail to address Cajetan's concerns. Finally, this chapter reconstructs the three views about the unity of analogical concepts alluded to and dismissed in the first paragraph of *De Nominum Analogia*: "disjunction," "order," and "unequal participation." None of these, it is shown, is sufficient to address the two semantic questions about analogy that Cajetan set out to answer.

The exposition of Cajetan's answers to these questions and the philosophical consideration of their success is the business of part 2. Drawing on several other of Cajetan's works—his commentaries on Porphyry's *Isagoge*, Aristotle's *Categories*, and Aquinas's *De Ente et Essentia* and *Summa Theologiae*—chapter 5 offers a sketch of the semantic principles that form the general framework within which Cajetan addresses analogy. Special attention is paid to the notion of *signification* and the related notions *conceptus* and *ratio*, and to *denomination* and Cajetan's distinction between *intrinsic* and *extrinsic* denomination.

Chapter 6 expounds the teachings of the first two chapters of *De Nominum Analogia*. It covers Cajetan's distinction between modes of analogy, discusses analogy of inequality and analogy of attribution, and compares the presentation in *De Nominum Analogia* to Cajetan's earlier treatments of analogy in his commentaries on Aquinas's *De Ente et Essentia* and Aristotle's *Categories*. The chapter responds to common criticisms of the notion of analogy of inequality and to the Suarezian objection to Cajetan's teaching that analogy of attribution never involves intrinsic denomination, and it argues that Cajetan has properly semantic reasons for dismissing inequality and attribution as less than proper forms of analogy.

De Nominum Analogia 3 defines analogy of proportionality and argues that it is the most proper form of analogy. Chapter 7 of this study explains Cajetan's arguments and articulates his notion of proportional unity, responding to common objections that proportional unity is *circular* and that it is *meaningless*, and explaining why analogy of proportionality cannot be reduced to univocation or equivocation.

Chapters 8 and 9 take up the analysis of proportionality in the oft-neglected final eight chapters of *De Nominum Analogia* (chaps. 4–11), which work out the implications of proportionally unified concepts through all three traditional areas of scholastic logic: simple apprehension, complex judgment, and discursive reasoning. Chapter 8 explains Cajetan's account of analogical concept formation and use, and takes up, among other things, the distinction between perfect and imperfect concepts; abstraction and "confusion"; predication and nonunivocal universality; definition, and the significations of relations. Chapter 9 treats analogy in discursive reasoning and the avoidance of fallacy.

— THE TERM 'ANALOGY' JUSTLY EVOKES SEVERAL INTERCONNECTED concerns, but the scope of the current study does not directly encompass analogy under some of the rubrics most commonly found in medieval and Thomistic literature. One is the metaphysics of being and its various categories, hinted at by Aristotle's famous dictum that "being is said in many ways," and later captured in a Latin phrase: *analogia entis* (the analogy of being). There is also the theological concern, about how human language and thought can stretch beyond the creaturely domain so that we can have and signify meaningful conceptions of God. And related to both of these is the traditional doctrine that such notions as truth and goodness are "convertible" with being, and therefore, transcending the highest genera, they are universal without themselves being generic or univocal. However much light the present study might incidentially shed on these topics—the analogy of being, divine naming, and the transcendentals—they are not and cannot be the primary concern here.

However, it is hoped that this historical and textual study of a treatise on the semantics of analogy will draw readers whose interest in analogy is rooted in these related metaphysical and theological topics. This is not only because Cajetan's treatise is the most influential treatise on analogy, whose teachings have already colored debates in these areas. Nor is it just because, as I argue, Cajetan's teachings have been almost universally misinterpreted. Rather it is because, once interpreted in light of their intended theoretical import, their continuing philosophical relevance can be appreciated. The foreseen audience for this study, then, is not just Thomist scholars—although much of part 1 aims to challenge some standard Thomistic prejudices. If the present interpretation is correct, the teaching of Cajetan, expounded in part 2, should be of interest not only to historians of medieval philosophy and to metaphysicians and theologians, but to contemporary philosophers of language, logic, epistemology, and science, as well as hermeneutics.

Communication and interpretation must attend to the rational flexibility of terms and concepts, and as Gadamer has reminded us, any decent logical theory must accommodate the "fundamental metaphorical nature" of "verbal consciousness." Cajetan's central concern is to show that the traditional Aristotelian semantic triangle can accommodate the extraordinary case of analogical language—or, rather, that the case of analogical language is not so extraordinary after all. As Cajetan saw, analogical signification is ubiquitous in human discourse, not just in metaphysics and theology, and the Aristotelian semantic framework, far from being "a theory of logic that is alien to language," provides rich resources for accounting for it.

Introduction

Some Theoretical and Historical Preliminaries

This introduction is intended to orient those readers who may not already be familiar with discussions of the history of analogy and the place of Cajetan's treatise within that history. It first presents a brief overview of some of the key concepts covered by the term 'analogy,' not in specific matters of theology or metaphysics, but in considerations of language, logic, and judgment about the world. It then gives an abbreviated history of thought about analogy before Cajetan, and outlines the central claims for which Cajetan's treatise has been known.

PRELIMINARY CONCEPTS: NONGENERIC LIKENESS AND ASSOCIATED MEANING

We must recognize at the beginning that it would be misleading to speak of "the" concept of analogy. What philosophers have come to treat under the aegis of "analogy" has no single stable meaning. Although an identifiable, coherent stream of philosophizing eventually emerges, it begins, historically and conceptually, from two distinct and quite separate tributaries.

The first is a matter of relationships between things. Consider two things that seem to be similar, although the respect in which they

— *1*

are similar is difficult to characterize or define. So, for instance, the items in the following pairs seem to be similar:

1. *The feathers of a bird* and *the scales of a reptile*
2. *Water for a fish* and *air for a mammal*
3. *The sole of a foot* and *the palm of a hand*

In each of these cases, the comparison is apparent, although perhaps difficult to characterize. Indeed, a definition of the basis of comparison may be somewhat awkward, vague, or even elusive. Awkward: feathers and scales are both kinds of flat, overlapping skin coverings. Vague: water and air are the appropriate oxygenating environments for fish and mammals, respectively. Elusive: the sole is the bottom of the foot, but the palm is not the bottom of a hand; we might call the palm the inside of the hand, but not the sole the inside of the foot.

But it is interesting that the relevant likeness is easily seen even if we don't have a readily available word or description for it. There is a functional similarity, not a precise equality: we do not say that the sole and the palm are the same, or that they have the same property, but that the sole is to the foot *as* the palm is to the hand. It is easier to describe these likenesses in terms of comparisons of relationships than in terms of some univocal features or common qualities equally realized in them. Feathers are *like* scales insofar as they each play a *similar* role for birds and reptiles respectively. Water is *like* air insofar as they each play a *similar* function in relation to different respective creatures. Let us call cases like these occasions of *nongeneric likeness.*

Now consider another phenomenon, this one not so much a matter of how things are related, but of how words are used. We often use the same word on different occasions, where the meaning implied by one use is close, but not identical, to the meaning implied by another use. For examples, consider the italicized words in the following pairs of statements:

4. Socrates is *wise*; Socrates' advice is *wise*
5. This is a *commercial* transaction; this is *commercial* real estate
6. I saw the moment of *impact*; the *impact* of the policy was increased productivity

At first one might not notice that the italicized words in each pair have different meanings. These are not cases where the words play different grammatical functions. ('Commercial' can be used as a noun, but it is an adjective in both statements above; 'impact' is sometimes employed as a verb, but it serves as a noun in both statements above.) And yet, on reflection, it is clear that a definition offered to account for one use might not fit the other use. Socrates and his advice are not "wise" in the same way: presumably Socrates *has* wisdom whereas his advice is either *evidence of* his wisdom or is *likely to produce* wisdom in one who follows it. The word 'commercial' as an adjective can describe what is an *instance* of, or an *instrument* of (or a *product* of, etc.), the activity of commerce. The noun 'impact' can designate either the *act of producing an effect*, or *the effect itself*. (Here I set aside what may be a further issue of trying to analyze any differences between a literal physical *impact*, when one body strikes another, and a more metaphorical *impact* when something other than a physical body—a policy or ideology—has consequences for something else.) In other words, we don't have strict synonymy here. On the other hand, we also don't have arbitrary equivocation, with unrelated meanings that just happen to be attached to the same verbal expression (as the case of 'bank,' which can mean the side of a river, or a financial institution). This kind of linguistic flexibility—with distinct but related senses of the same term—is fairly common. The dictionary is full of definitions that begin with such phrases as "of or pertaining to." Such a definition indicates that there are really several related meanings, meanings which do not make the word fully equivocal, and yet may be distinct enough to be spelled out with more precision, at least in principle. Let us call cases like these occasions of *associated meaning*.

Although conceptually distinct, occasions of nongeneric likeness and occasions of associated meaning *may* overlap: we may choose a common word to describe the likenesses between things. Noticing two things that are somehow similar (nongeneric likeness), we may use a word originally appropriate to one in connection with the other (associated meaning): "he *shoveled* food into his mouth"; "the sun *kissed* his face." This certainly describes what happens in instances of metaphor, whether in deliberately contrived poetic metaphors or in those established and conventional metaphors that are often not even recognized as metaphors in everyday speech.[1]

Nonetheless, associated meaning and nongeneric likeness remain theoretically distinct phenomena. One may have cases of associated meaning that are not based on nongeneric likeness (Socrates and his advice are both wise, but not because the advice is like Socrates in some way). And one may notice nongeneric likeness without having a common word available to signify the relevant associated meanings (like the sole of the foot and the palm of the hand—very few people would know, much less find a suitable nonpedantic occasion, to refer to them both as "volar surfaces").

A Very Brief History of Analogy from Aristotle to Aquinas

If we try to reconstruct a history of analogy as a general theme in ancient and medieval thought, we find that the distinction between these two phenomena—what I am calling associated meaning and nongeneric likeness—was noticed, even taken for granted, from the very beginning.[2] They were often treated separately and under different terminology—and each became connected with other terminology, sometimes diverging, sometimes intertwining, so that it is only very loosely that we can speak of *the* history of *the* notion of analogy.

In Aristotle's writings, the phenomena of associated meaning and nongeneric likeness remain distinct,[3] so much so that a study of his treatment of one need hardly touch on his treatment of the other.[4] For Aristotle, associated meaning was treated in the context of, and usually as a subclass of, homonymy or equivocation. His classic example is 'healthy,' which cannot be entirely synonymous when predicated of an animal, its complexion, and its urine. It is a kind of equivocation where the different meanings make reference to some one common or primary meaning. So the phenomenon of associated meaning is treated by Aristotle as a case of things being named, or of a word being said, with reference to one (πρὸς ἓν λέγεσθαι),[5] today commonly called "*pros hen* equivocation,"[6] or what some more recent philosophers have called signification with "focal meaning."[7]

We can see how, in the examples of associated meaning above, the definitions offered to explain each use of the term would be different, but related to a common meaning. The meaning of 'wise' as predicated of advice would, when fully articulated, make reference to the wisdom of a person called "wise." (Presumably "wise" advice is the kind of advice that would *come from* a wise person, or it advises one to *do the kind of thing that* a wise person would do.) Different senses of 'commercial' would all bear some relation to (or "make reference to") commercial activity. Different senses of 'impact' would relate or refer in different ways to the production of an effect.

The Greek word *analogia* was reserved, for Aristotle as well as other Greek thinkers, for the phenomenon of nongeneric likeness.[8] *Analogia* was originally a mathematical term for the comparison of ratios. It is captured in the familiar schema A:B::C:D (A is to B as C is to D). While originally describing quantitative comparisons,[9] the notion of *analogia* and its four-term schema was easily extended to areas of reflection that are not strictly mathematical.[10] Aristotle himself describes this schema in nonmathematical contexts (e.g., at *Topics* 108a), and examples of nongeneric likeness introduced above can readily be expressed in it:

7. Feathers:bird::scales:reptile
8. Water:fish::air:mammal
9. Sole:foot::palm:hand

Aristotle uses this first example himself (*Historia Animalium* 486b). Another Aristotelian example of what we recognize as like by *analogia* is the bone of an animal, the pounce (i.e., cuttle) of a squid, and the spine of a fish; in Greek these three organs did not share a name, "although these too possess common properties as if there were a single osseous nature" (*Posterior Analytics* 2.14 [98a20ff.]; cf. *On the Parts of Animals* 1.4 [644b11] and 2.6 [652a2–3]).

Aristotle's point here cannot be that *analogia* involves the same word being used in different ways, but that it involves things having similar relations to, or functions within, their respective contexts. Likewise, in the *Poetics*, *analogia* describes the relationships between things named metaphorically (1457b6ff.). *Analogia* is a kind of likeness or nongeneric commonality. Not surprisingly, then, it plays a significant role in Aristotle's biology and natural philosophy, where new things are analyzed by comparing them to similar things already known (like an organ in one creature that seems to have a function similar to that of a different organ in a different creature). Significantly, *analogia* appears in the *Metaphysics*, not when Aristotle says that 'being' is said in many ways, but when he classifies different kinds of unity; unity by *analogia* is listed after numerical, specific, and generic unity (*Metaphysics* 5.6, 1016b31–1017a3). Clearly for Aristotle, the phenomena of associated meaning and of nongeneric likeness should not be confused.

Even when Aristotle mentions both *analogia* and *pros hen* equivocation in the same context, it appears that his purpose is to contrast them: in the *Ethics* I.4 (1096b27–28) he asks how we should understand the relationship of the different senses of 'good,' and two of the choices are that the different senses are common *"pros hen"* (with reference to some one common or primary thing) or by *analogia* (not sharing a common genus), apparently assuming that these are alternatives. So for Aristotle, even if the relationship of *analogia* can be used to explain *one* of the ways in which a term may be said of many things, the issues of nongeneric likeness and of associated meaning remain distinct for him.

This is not the place to explore in detail all that Aristotle had to say about *analogia* and *pros hen* equivocation. Suffice it to say that, if for Aristotle they were consistently treated as distinct phenomena, the subsequent history of "the" notion of analogy brings them together in an increasing entanglement. Not that this entanglement implies confusion or error. As we have already noticed, there are possible instances of natural overlap between these two issues, and it is only to be expected that these conceptual possibilities are explored.

One essential part of this history is the tradition of Neoplatonic Aristotelian commentary. Here, especially in the context of commentaries on the *Categories*, commentators expanded on Aristotle's sparse remarks on equivocation to account for associated meaning or "deliberate equivocation." They furthermore often distinguished different varieties of such deliberate equivocation.[11] Consistent with what was implicit in Aristotle's comments in the *Ethics*, certain kinds of deliberate equivocation were supposed to take place because of some relation to something common or primary, and another kind of deliberate equivocation was according to Greek *analogia*. In other words, nongeneric likeness was used to differentiate some cases of associated meaning from others.

Another cause of the increasing entanglement of associated meaning and nongeneric likeness has to do with peculiarities of sources and translation. Here a pivotal figure, in this as in so many other instances of the Latin transmission of Greek ideas, is Boethius. Boethius helped to transmit the Neoplatonic commentary tradition, which came to treat *analogia* as something that describes a kind of equivocation. So, in his commentary on Aristotle's *Categories*, Boethius first distinguishes equivocation that is accidental or by chance (*a casu*) from equivocation that is deliberate or intentional (*a consilio*). He then lists several ways that the different meanings in deliberate equivocation can be related. Among them are equivocation by relation *to one* (*ad unum*, translating Greek *pros hen*), which is distinct from equivocation by "proportion" (where Latin *'proportio'* had the sense of Greek *analogia*).[12] Thereby Boethius transmits the Greek Neoplatonic tradition's distinction between deliberate equivocation by proportion and deliberate equivocation by focal reference.

In this respect Boethius is only passing on distinctions found in influential Greek commentators like Simplicius and Porphyry. But in another respect Boethius's treatment of analogy adds something to the tradition. Boethius was not always satisfied to translate *analogia* as *proportio*, and he sometimes used another term we credit him with coining. Note that Greek *analogia*, when it was not transliterated, was not precisely translated by Latin *proportio*, because *proportio* was also sometimes a translation, along with *ratio*, for Greek *logos*. So to recapture the special sense of a relation among relations, Boethius used the abstract of *proportio*, *proportionalitas* (proportionality), to characterize the technical mathematical sense of Greek *analogia*.[13]

It is worth noting that even in the strictly mathematical context of Boethius's *De Arithmetica*, *proportionalitas* exhibits some degree of flexibility. Most generally, it seems to express any kind of common relationship. Today we are in the habit of interpreting each side of a geometric proportionality as a function for calculating a quotient, and so we reduce the relationship between each function to equality. Thus 6:3::8:4 becomes $6/3 = 8/4 \, [= 2]$. For Boethius, however, *proportionality* is not an equation to be solved so much as an expression of a common relation. "Proportionality is a similar relationship of two or more ratios" (*De Arithmetica* 2.40). That is why it was useful for characterizing incommensurable relationships, which have no whole number or even rational number equivalent, and why often the proportionality scheme was used not so much to calculate a fourth term, given three others, as to exhibit a kind of relationship, given all four terms. (Alternatively, given the relationship, and two terms X and Z, the task may be to find the "proportional mean" between them—that is, the one number Y, such that X:Y::Y:Z.) But different kinds of relationships can be exhibited, and so different means between the same two numbers can be offered depending on the intended relationship or proportionality: so between 10 and 40, 25 is the arithmetic mean, 20 is the geometric mean, and 16 is the harmonic mean.[14] Nonetheless, for Boethius a geometric proportion is most properly called proportionality (*De Arithmetica* 2.44), and it seems to be the best model for nonquantitative proportionalities or analogies, such as *sole* is to *foot* as *palm* is to *hand*.

By coining a new term, *proportionalitas*, to translate Greek *analogia* (instead of simply transliterating it), Boethius only encouraged a subtle migration of the Latin term *analogia*, so that for most scholastics *analogia* comes to be used to describe not the phenomenon of nongeneric likeness, but the phenomenon of associated meaning, still commonly discussed in the context of homonyms or equivocals in *Categories* commentaries. Latin *analogia* thus becomes a mean between univocation and pure equivocation, a deliberate or intentional equivocation—thus for many later Latin authors it is effectively synonymous with what Aristotle called *pros hen* equivocation, not with what he called *analogia*.

Thanks to the ongoing influence of the commentary tradition, including especially Arabic sources, by the middle of the thirteenth century Latin *analogia* comes to be linked to other terms used to describe associated meaning: *convenientia* (or agreement), *ambiguitas, translatio* (transference of a name from one context to another), and *transsumptio* (another term for metaphor). Latin translations of Arabic Aristotelian commentators also introduce the notion of ordered or prioritized ambiguity, which Avicenna, for instance, understood as predication or signification *per prius et posterius*, loosely, "according to an order of priority and posteriority."[15] In all of these instances, the emphasis is on associated meanings of words rather than on proportional relationships between things. *Analogia* for early and high scholastic thinkers was primarily a linguistic phenomenon, deliberate equivocation, taken to be a mean between univocation and pure (arbitrary) equivocation, and thus thought to involve diverse but related meanings exhibiting some order of priority among themselves.

In tracing the history of reflection on associated meaning and nongeneric likeness, then, we see the convergence, or what I have called the entanglement, of these two threads. Whether, in general or in particular authors, this convergence or entanglement involves a strengthening resonance or a murky confusion is not the question here. Suffice it to say that the two threads become increasingly intertwined by the thirteenth century, when they joined other theological, logical, and metaphysical terminology (such as *participatio* and *imitatio*). Even so, the two issues remain logically distinguishable, so that in Bonaventure, for instance, it is still possible and quite illuminating to study his understanding of resemblance (including nongeneric likeness) separately from his theory of analogous naming (that is, associated meaning).[16]

Indeed, while Latin *analogia* comes to be almost synonymous with what Aristotle called *pros hen* equivocation, the Greek notion of *analogia*, or Boethian *proportionalitas*, as a fundamental insight about relationships between things, retains a wide significance across the disciplines. It is the basis of continuing reflections in mathematics, music, astronomy, architecture, and the physical sciences.[17] There was even a complicated board game, influential in medieval arts education, based on the notion of proportionality as taught in Boethius's *De Arithmetica*, with implicit links to the idea of virtue as a (proportional) mean.[18]

To be sure, for historians of philosophy nothing compares to the weight borne by this relationship in the fields of metaphysics and theology. In Aquinas especially, "analogy"—both as associated meaning and as nongeneric likeness—is a crucial concept for understanding the different senses of being, and the possibility of true predications of and knowledge about God.[19] Even here, however, the concern is not purely metaphysical or theological, but rather a nexus of metaphysical, epistemological, and semantic, logical or linguistic issues. It seems clear that Aquinas, like most other scholastics, used *analogia* primarily for cases of associated meaning, rather than for nongeneric likeness; but by the thirteenth century, as we have seen, many relations between these concerns have been explored and they are not always carefully distinguished. Thus one of the ongoing debates among scholars of Aquinas is whether analogy for him should be considered primarily a metaphysical question (of how things are related), an epistemological question (of how we know and judge things in relation to each other), or a logical question (of how different senses of terms are related to each other).[20]

This is not the place to try to enter into this disputed territory or summarize Aquinas's teaching about analogy. In the present context, nothing could do justice to the various primary texts and vast secondary literature on the subject. We will limit ourselves to noting that, in addition to the importance of analogy for Thomistic metaphysics and theology, there is another major reason that so much has been written and continues to be written about analogy in Aquinas: Aquinas himself never presented a systematic theory of analogy.

It has often been noted that there is no *ex professo* teaching on analogy in Aquinas's corpus. We would notice this just from reading his texts, where the mentions of analogy are occasional and *ad hoc*. There is no dedicated treatise or section of a treatise, no systematically elaborated doctrine of analogy, and the longest discussions of it are still tailored to address particular questions in theology. It seems that Aquinas never wrote comprehensively about analogy as a topic in its own right. Even passages that present apparently definitive classifications or explanations seem to be contradicted by other texts.[21] It is the absence of a clear theory or doctrine of analogy in Aquinas, as much as the obvious importance of analogy in his thought, that accounts for the extensive reflection on analogy by his later interpreters.

The Doctrine of Cajetan's *De Nominum Analogia*

The lack of an *ex professo* analogy doctrine in Aquinas also brings into stark relief the content of Cajetan's *De Nominum Analogia*. For when we turn to Cajetan's text we find something that, in style and format,

seems quite different from any writing of Aquinas: a dedicated treatise that articulates a systematic theoretical classification and explanation of analogy.

Cajetan's *De Nominum Analogia* is a treatise of eleven chapters.
It begins by invoking the significance of analogy in metaphysics, al-
luding to common confusions about analogy, and proposing to clarify
these confusions.

The text's main teaching of analogy, introduced in the first
chapter, is that it occurs in three forms or "modes" (*modi*, *DNA* §3).
Analogy of inequality, Cajetan says, occurs when things are called by
a common name and concept, but the concept is shared or participated in unequally (*DNA* §4). The example he gives is "body," which
is predicated equally (univocally) of all bodies, although there is an
order of superiority and inferiority among bodies (a plant is superior
to a stone, incorruptible bodies are superior to corruptible bodies).

The second mode of analogy Cajetan identifies is *analogy of attribution*, where the common name is used with different relations to
some one term (*DNA* §8). His first example here is the classic one of
"healthy," which, depending on whether it is predicated of an animal,
of urine, or of medicine, can signify what is *subject of*, or *sign of*, or
cause of health.

In the third mode of analogy, *analogy of proportionality*, Cajetan
says the different notions are related proportionally—that is, according to the scheme that Greeks called *analogia* and Boethius called *proportionalitas* (*DNA* §§23–24). The example here is *seeing* as predicated
of the eye and the intellect, because "just as understanding exhibits a
thing to the soul, so seeing [exhibits a thing] to an animated body."
The point is that something can be named in common with another
thing that is in a similar relationship. Cajetan says that sometimes
this takes the form of *metaphor*, when the transferred word does not
properly belong in the new context: for example, a field doesn't really
"smile," although its blooming might brighten it as a smile bright-
ens a face (*DNA* §25). Other times, analogy of proportionality is not
merely metaphoric, but is a case of *proper proportionality*, when the
name properly belongs not only in its original context but also in that
context to which it has been transferred (*DNA* §26): *vision* is really in
the body, and *understanding* is really in the intellect, so the intellect

can be said properly to *see*, by analogy with the sense in which the eye *sees*.

Cajetan's treatise goes on to describe different features of these modes of analogy, among which is that analogy of proper proportionality is distinguished from both metaphor and from analogy of attribution because it always signifies what is intrinsic: intellectual sight is really in the intellect, while a smile is not really in the field and health is not really in the urine (*DNA* §27). At least in part because it always thus involves "intrinsic denomination," as opposed to the extrinsic denomination that occurs in analogy of attribution (and metaphor), Cajetan insists that analogy of proper proportionality is the most true and proper form of analogy, and the most important for metaphysics (*DNA* §29). Presumably it is for this reason that the rest of Cajetan's treatise (chaps. 4–11, or §§31–125) examine further details of analogy of proportionality.

These, then, in superficial summary, are the signature teachings of Cajetan's analogy treatise: a threefold division of analogy, and a hierarchy ranking analogy of proportionality, with its essentially intrinsic denomination, as the most genuine form of analogy. As we will see in chapter 1, there are significant and sometimes contentious issues involved here that have drawn the attention of Cajetan's interpreters. The interpretation of Cajetan's analogy theory offered in the body of this study emerges from, and is presented within the context of, some of the established arguments of Cajetan's previous interpreters. But even without any prior awareness of recent hermeneutic controversies, the sketch of Cajetan's teaching offered here should raise several questions. What is the basis of Cajetan's threefold division? Is it meant to be exhaustive and exclusive? What theoretical work does Cajetan's classification do, what problems might his distinctions solve? Where does the theory fit into the framework of philosophy: Logic? Metaphysics? Epistemology?

More questions emerge in light of our preliminary theoretical distinctions. In the terminology introduced above, does Cajetan offer a theory of nongeneric likeness, or of associated meaning, or both? How might one be related to the other? It would seem, for instance, as if Cajetan is using nongeneric likeness ("proportionality") to distinguish one of several kinds of associated meaning (what he, following the Latin and not the Greek tradition, calls "analogy"). But then, does his project differ—and if so, how?—from the earlier medieval tradition of *Categories* commentary, which made *analogia* (proportionality) the basis of one of several kinds of associated meaning (equivocation *pros hen*)? And why does Cajetan insist on a hierarchical ranking of modes of analogy? What is the basis of his particular ranking? Why and in what sense is "analogy of proportionality" the most proper form of analogy? What problem might be solved by insisting on its preeminence? Can such a hierarchical ranking of kinds of analogy be found in the work of Aquinas? And in general, how does Cajetan's theory relate to Aquinas's thought about analogy, or to the wider history of reflection about analogy?

All of these questions arise naturally when Cajetan's main teachings on analogy are outlined within the context of the general theoretical and historical overview of "analogy" offered in this introduction. They are some of the questions that the rest of this study is intended to address.

Part 1
Cajetan's Question

Chapter One

Systematizing Aquinas?

A Paradigm in Crisis

Cajetan's theory of analogy has hardly been neglected by modern scholars. Its influence on all subsequent discussion of analogy has been widely felt and recognized, by both Cajetan's defenders and his critics. As we will see in this chapter, however, debates about Cajetan's theory of analogy have taken place within a framework of common assumptions—assumptions that, once made explicit, will allow us to suggest an alternative, more fruitful, interpretive approach.

CAJETAN'S RECENT INTERPRETERS

Central to contemporary concerns is the significance of Cajetan's classification and hierarchy of analogy: analogy of inequality, analogy of attribution, and analogy of proportionality (in order from least to most proper). For one group of scholars in the past century, the task has been to argue that Cajetan's threefold division and his preference of analogy of proportionality accord with Aquinas's own thought. Especially during the first half of the century, several scholars followed and defended Cajetan's theory of analogy as faithful to the teaching of Aquinas. To the extent that such scholars acknowledged novelty in Cajetan's presentation, this was explained as the development of a tradition, naturally growing out of a systematization of Aquinas's unsystematic remarks about analogy. Thus, according to M. T.-L. Penido, Cajetan set out to "restore the aristotelico-thomistic theory" of analogy.[1] Admitting that Thomas's texts are not obviously consonant, Penido admired Cajetan for synthesizing apparently inconsistent teachings.[2] Similarly, Aloys Goergen defended the harmony between Thomas and Cajetan. He argued that Cajetan developed, expounded, and systematized Aquinas's views. The title of Goergen's thesis summarizes the concern that occupied him and most other interpreters of Cajetan at this time: Cardinal Cajetan's teaching on analogy *and its relation to Thomas Aquinas*.[3]

The case made by Penido and Goergen depended especially on two texts in Aquinas. In his commentary on the first book of *Sentences*, d. 19, q. 5, a. 2, ad 1, Aquinas says that "there are three ways in which something can be said according to analogy," and he goes on to distinguish between things that are analogous (1) "according to intention only, and not according to being"; (2) "according to being and not according to intention"; and (3) "according to intention and according to being."[4] Cajetan indicates (at *DNA* §§6, 19, and 30) that his own threefold distinction parallels this threefold distinction in Aquinas's *I Sent*. 19.5.2 ad 1.

In another text—question 2, article 11 of the disputed questions *De Veritate*—Aquinas distinguishes between analogy according to an agreement of *proportion* and analogy according to an agreement of *proportionality*. In this text, Aquinas favors the agreement of proportionality as the most useful mode of analogy for theology. Cajetan cites this passage (at *DNA* §77) in support of the primacy of what he calls analogy of proportionality.

For Penido and Goergen, Cajetan's theory of analogy seemed to grow out of an assimilation of *I Sent*. 19.5.2 ad 1 and *DV* 2.11. It was natural for these interpreters to depend on these two passages in Aquinas to justify the Thomistic authenticity of the threefold division itself, and the priority of analogy of proportionality.

Other scholars endorsed Cajetan's teaching, especially the classification and hierarchy of modes of analogy, but without trying to demonstrate that this was also Aquinas's own teaching. Without much argument for its consonance with Aquinas, Garrigou-Lagrange,[5] Maritain,[6] Phelan,[7] Simon,[8] and others promoted Cajetan's classification and hierarchy of modes of analogy. Likewise, the extensive discussions of analogy by Anderson[9] follow much of Cajetan's teaching, articulating and defending the details of the theory without examining the textual or historical relations between Cajetan and Aquinas.

It was thus consistent with this early twentieth-century consensus that *De Nominum Analogia*'s only previous English translators, Bushinski and Koren, presented the work as "the unsurpassed systematization of the Aristotelian-Thomistic theory of analogy" by "a faithful interpreter of St. Thomas" who "points out the self-consistency of St. Thomas."[10]

But when Bushinski and Koren published these words in 1953, the tide of opinion was beginning to turn. Despite—or rather largely because of—the longstanding influence and status of Cajetan's theory of analogy, a new wave of scholarship emerged that tried to separate Cajetan's teachings from the teachings of Aquinas. By the middle of the twentieth century, as the search for the "aristotelico-thomistic" tradition gave way to the search for the historical teaching of Aquinas, Cajetan's theory of analogy was immediately called into question as another of the accretions of tradition which had obscured from view the authentic Aquinas.

In criticizing Cajetan as a commentator of Aquinas, many scholars focused on Cajetan's use of the two key texts of Aquinas already mentioned (*DV* 2.11 and *I Sent.* 19.5.2 ad 1). Ramirez, who three decades earlier had contributed to the tendency to consider Cajetan as synthesizing "the aristotelico-thomistic doctrine" of analogy,[11] was among the first to call into question the equation of Thomas's threefold distinction at *I Sent.* 19.5.2 ad 1 with Cajetan's three modes of analogy.[12] According to Ramirez, the tradition that bases a division of analogy on the *Sentences* passage "lacks a solid foundation."[13]

Several other scholars argued that *DV* 2.11 and *I Sent.* 19.5.2 ad 1 were not consistent; and indeed, upon examination of the relevant texts, it became increasingly common to argue that Aquinas's occasional statements about analogy indicated changes in his views. In his detailed collation and analysis of Aquinas's various statements about analogy, Klubertanz found that Aquinas abandoned his preference for proportionality after 1256–57, changing his mind after *DV* 2.11.[14] Montagnes came to similar conclusions.[15] Descoqs, following some older objections by Suarez (further discussed below), made even stronger claims, saying that analogy of proportionality could not apply in the crucial case of the analogy between God and creatures.[16]

Such findings were consistent with the arguments of Hampus Lyttkens, one of the earliest and most influential opponents of Cajetan's theory. Lyttkens criticized the "Thomistic" tradition that privileged proportionality, arguing that in Aquinas proportionality plays a subordinate role.[17] In this Lyttkens, Klubertanz, and Montagnes have been followed by many others, including Ashworth,[18] Mahoney,[19] Marion,[20] and Masiello,[21] who all agree that Cajetan reverses a Thomistic priority of attribution over proportionality.[22]

Scholars also disagreed about Cajetan's characterization of attribution and proportionality. Cajetan says that analogy of attribution always involves the extrinsic denomination of analogates, and analogy of proportionality always involves intrinsic denomination; thus Cajetan pairs analogy of proportionality with the analogy *"secundum intentionem et secundum esse"* of Thomas's *I Sent*. 19.5.2 ad 1. But according to Ramirez, for instance, Aquinas's analogy *"secundum intentionem et secundum esse"* should not be identified with what Cajetan calls analogy of proportionality, because it can encompass an intrinsic case of analogy of attribution.[23] Ramirez's criticism on this point has a long pedigree. The most famous early Cajetan critic, insisting on cases of intrinsic attribution, was Suarez,[24] who has been followed more recently by Descoqs.[25]

Another question that concerned several critics of Cajetan was the relative emphasis on logic or metaphysics in Cajetan and Aquinas. On the one hand, Klubertanz charged that Cajetan had emphasized metaphysics, while he should have emphasized logic.[26] Similarly, McInerny argued that Cajetan entirely misinterpreted *I Sent*. 19.5.2 ad 1, and that the division of analogy found in *De Nominum Analogia* was based on metaphysical considerations that are irrelevant to the kind of properly logical consideration of analogy appropriate for Aquinas.[27]

On the other hand, some scholars have criticized Cajetan for emphasizing logic too much, especially for focusing on semantic formalities. Many, following Gilson, have disapprovingly cited Cajetan's focus on *concepts* as evidence that he was too influenced by Scotus, and that he has ignored the role of *judgment* in a genuine Thomistic understanding of analogy.[28] Probably the most developed criticism of

Cajetan on this basis is that of David Burrell, whose work rounds out the list of major scholarly criticisms of Cajetan's analogy theory from the early 1950s through the early 1970s.[29]

In all of these criticisms, the standard of evaluating Cajetan's text has been clear, and has been the same as the standard used by such defenders as Penido and Goergen: fidelity to Aquinas. Battista Mondin is quite explicit about his criteria for judging *De Nominum Analogia*. Cajetan, according to Mondin, was writing as an "interpreter" of Aquinas, and *De Nominum Analogia*, at least in intention, "systematically explains the whole Thomistic theory of analogy."[30] Mondin speaks of "Cajetan's interpretation of Aquinas's doctrine of analogy,"[31] and says, "We do not have the least doubt that Cajetan intended to give a systematic and faithful presentation of Aquinas's doctrine of analogy."[32] According to Mondin, this intention is entirely reasonable, but it is not realized. "It is not Cajetan's intentions but his results that are unsatisfactory."[33]

Montagnes also makes it clear that he regards the main standard for evaluating *De Nominum Analogia* to be its conformity to Aquinas's own teaching.[34] He outlines three possible positions on the question. Some hold that "the accord of master and student is incontestable"; others hold that Thomas has no explicit theory of analogy, but that Cajetan's theory does not accurately describe Thomas's practice. Montagnes takes the third position, arguing "that there is an explicit theory in Thomas which is different from Cajetan."[35]

Recently John F. Wippel has approvingly cited Lyttkens, Montagnes, Klubertanz, and McInerny as having demonstrated that Cajetan's theory is not Thomistic.[36] Indeed, over the last several decades it is increasingly remarked that the analogy studies of the last century separated Aquinas from his "commentators," Cajetan chief among them.[37] David Burrell writes of Lyttkens, McInerny, Klubertanz, and Mondin that their studies "differ from the bulk of Thomist commentary in their careful attention to Aquinas' actual usage. The case against Cajetan is documented from it."[38] Paul G. Kuntz, summarizing the recent scholarship on analogy, especially that of McInerny and Burrell, remarks that "the history of analogy has . . . been freed from Cajetan's dead hand, as has the logic of St. Thomas' analogy."[39] A prominent theologian can now refer casually, as if to a familiar phenomenon and established historical event, to "the endless difficulties raised by the formulation after the fact of a 'Thomistic doctrine of analogy.'"[40]

THE RECEIVED PARADIGM

Because, as so often noted, there is no *ex professo* teaching on analogy in Aquinas, it is natural that a treatise on analogy by a major commentator should come to be treated as an interpretation of Aquinas, and evaluated as such. Recent attempts to understand better what Aquinas himself thought, which have led to many criticisms of Cajetan, have done nothing to displace this hermeneutic assumption. In fact, they have reinforced it. Indeed, in general, despite the genuine opposition between defenders and critics of *De Nominum Analogia* during the last century, there has been a startling number of shared assumptions.

The recent history of interpretations of Cajetan's analogy theory can in fact be depicted as constituting a unified research program in the sense that Thomas Kuhn described, in which genuine disagreements, and genuine advances in inquiry, take place against the background of a set of shared assumptions. Some of these shared assumptions have already been pointed out, but it is worth enumerating the common elements of the received paradigm of interpreting *De Nominum Analogia*:

1. *Cajetan was attempting to interpret or systematize,*[41] *or even comment on and summarize,*[42] *Aquinas's views on analogy.* This assumption seems supported by an easy inference: Cajetan knew that Aquinas had not written systematically on the subject of analogy, and Cajetan therefore knew that in his own systematic work he was going further than Aquinas; since Cajetan was a Thomist, his aim in writing his treatise on analogy must have been to impose order and coherence on Aquinas's own scattered remarks on analogy.

2. *The most important teaching of* De Nominum Analogia *is its threefold division of analogy.* What is most commonly remembered about Cajetan's theory of analogy is the threefold distinction between kinds

or modes of analogy. Cajetan himself emphasizes this distinction from the beginning, and his first three chapters address each mode in turn. Most scholars have implicitly or explicitly maintained that this threefold division is the central and distinctive feature of Cajetan's theory of analogy. Indeed, reviews of Cajetan's theory tend to focus on the first three chapters of *De Nominum Analogia*, in which each of these three modes is described in turn.[43]

3. *Cajetan based his threefold classification on Aquinas's* I *Sent. 19.5.2 ad 1.*[44] As we noted already, Cajetan refers to this passage and its language in *De Nominum Analogia*, claiming that each of his three kinds of analogy pairs up with a different member of Aquinas's distinction. It has been concluded that this passage in Aquinas is the basis—both the inspiration and the justification—of Cajetan's threefold division. Indeed, Cajetan's defenders claim this in support of Cajetan's fidelity to Aquinas, while Cajetan's critics accept that Cajetan was inspired by *I Sent.* 19.5.2 ad 1 and point to evidence that Cajetan misinterpreted, or misapplied, Aquinas's distinction.

4. *Cajetan based his preference for analogy of proportionality on Aquinas's* DV *2.11.*[45] Again, Cajetan refers to this passage as textual support for the priority of analogy of proportionality over analogy of attribution. Scholars have therefore treated *DV* 2.11 as the inspiration for Cajetan's ranking, and critics have faulted Cajetan for misinterpreting the text or failing to appreciate how it differs from other texts in Aquinas.

5. *Cajetan distinguishes analogy of attribution and analogy of proportionality in terms of metaphysical differences in the things named by analogical terms.* Cajetan says that analogy of attribution always involves "extrinsic denomination," and that analogy of proportionality always involves "intrinsic denomination."[46] Although phrased in logical or semantic terminology, this has been seen as an ingenious (or, alternatively, as a fallacious) way of connecting his discussion of analogy to metaphysical concerns, namely, whether or not the *ratio* or form signified by a term *really inheres* in the thing it names. Accordingly, Cajetan's interpreters have also tended to conclude that:

6. *Cajetan prefers analogy of proportionality because of its metaphysical characteristics.*[47] Cajetan's clear preference for analogy of proportionality as the most "proper and true" mode of analogy is taken to be based on his position that analogy of proportionality always involves intrinsic denomination. In other words, scholars find that Cajetan prefers proportionality precisely because in this mode the analogous property or "form" really inheres in each of the things named by that term.[48]

TEXTUAL ANOMALIES

The necessity of approaching Cajetan afresh can best be brought out by pointing to certain observations that are not obviously or automatically accounted for in the received paradigm just outlined in the six points above. We may start by pointing out a slight tension between Cajetan's supposed dependence on Aquinas (points 1, 3, and 4 above) and the supposed originality in his threefold division, implied in point 2. But one may make other and more significant observations. These can be catalogued in such a way that they correspond roughly to the points of the received paradigm with which they are in tension (although sometimes these individual observations pose a difficulty for the established paradigm in more than one way):

1.* *Cajetan's treatise is not presented as an interpretation, systematization, or summary of Aquinas's views on analogy.* Cajetan certainly knew how to write commentaries, and this is not one. And even as a text presenting his own thought, it does not give indication of being primarily intended as an interpretation or systematization of Aquinas. Aquinas is mentioned, as are others—chiefly Aristotle and Averroës. In all cases, Cajetan appears to be showing (in a rather Thomistic way) how what other people said is consistent with, or can somehow be accounted for in, his own theory. But the undeniable impression one gets from Cajetan's text is that he is presenting his *own* teaching. Indeed, at least one scholar has tried to account for this fact in the old paradigm by *criticizing* Cajetan for giving his *own views*: thus Robert Meagher complains that "Cajetan's own independent thought and writing intrudes itself between exegete and text."[49]

2.* *Cajetan had already presented the threefold division three years earlier in his commentary on Aquinas's* De Ente et Essentia. In that commentary, Cajetan speaks first of the sense in which univocal terms
can be said *"per prius et posterius"* (§18). He then speaks of two more
genuine kinds of analogy, one in which something is said "according
to a determinate relation of one to another" (*secundum determinatam
habitudinem unius ad alterum*) and another in which something is said
"according to proportionality" (*secundum proportionalitatem*, §21). It
is clear from Cajetan's discussion that he is talking about what in *De
Nominum Analogia* he calls respectively analogy of inequality, analogy
of attribution, and analogy of proportionality.[50] But if Cajetan had
articulated this threefold distinction in 1495, can it really be the main
theoretical contribution of his separate treatise on analogy in 1498?

3.* *Cajetan does not mention the passage from Aquinas's* Sentences *commentary until after presenting his divisions in* De Nominum Analogia,
and he does not mention Aquinas's text at all in his commentary on De
Ente et Essentia. Cajetan cites Aristotle and Averroes in support of
his division, not just Aquinas. But more importantly, he gives arguments, philosophical reasons, for classifying analogy as he does. In the
De Ente et Essentia commentary, Cajetan offers his threefold division
of analogy without mentioning Aquinas's *Sentences* text at all. And
in *De Nominum Analogia*, Cajetan does not cite the *Sentences* text as
the "basis" of his classification, but rather notes, after the fact, that his
classification is consistent with the *Sentences* text. Of course, it is hard
to prove the negative position that Cajetan did *not* base his division on
the *Sentences* text; but the evidence available just does not support the
widespread contention that Aquinas's texts are the *basis* of Cajetan's
division. Given that a number of Cajetan's predecessors cited *I Sent.*
19.5.2 ad 1 in their own discussions of analogy, it is just as reasonable
to conclude that Cajetan was trying to accommodate a text that tradition had already deemed important.[51]

4.* *Cajetan offers independent reasons for preferring analogy of proportionality, and Aquinas's DV 2.11 seems to bear little weight here.* Cajetan
offers extensive argument for why analogy of proportionality is the
most proper form of analogy, and in addition to his purely theoretical reasons, he gives historical and etymological support (in Greek

etymology and the authority of Aristotle and Averroës). Indeed, his reference to *DV* 2.11 comes relatively late in his treatise (§77), well after he has established the priority of proportionality, and later than one would expect if it were in fact its "basis."[52]

5.* *Cajetan does not define the two genuine modes of analogy in terms of extrinsic or intrinsic denomination.* Cajetan gives carefully formulated definitions of each of his three modes of analogy. These definitions parallel the definitions of univocation and equivocation in Aristotle's *Categories*; they do not include a mention of extrinsic and intrinsic denomination, which are mentioned only as characteristics or conditions (*conditiones*) that *follow from* these definitions. (More is said about this below in chap. 6.)

6.* *Cajetan is clear that he intends to analyze analogy as a logician, not as a metaphysician.* The first and most obvious piece of evidence supporting this claim is the title of Cajetan's treatise: *De* Nominum *Analogia*, "On the Analogy of *Names*." But there is more, and in fact the evidence for Cajetan's logical, as opposed to metaphysical, intention is overwhelming. Nonetheless, because this is still a somewhat controversial claim, contradicted by several interpreters of Cajetan, more will be said in its defense later in this chapter and in chapter 2.

— How should this set of observations affect the interpretation of *De Nominum Analogia*? One strategy is accommodation: treating these six points as problems to be solved within the received paradigm of interpretation—that is (to continue applying Kuhn's language), one may treat these as "puzzles" to be handled by the "normal science" of the established research program.

In general, to the extent that any of these observations have been acknowledged, this has been the dominant strategy, especially among Cajetan's recent critics, who take these observations as evidence that Cajetan's theory of analogy is inconsistent, incoherent, and flawed. Indeed, critics have faulted Cajetan not only for articulating his *own views* about analogy, but also for trying to separate logical from metaphysical concerns. Commentators have also faulted

Cajetan's treatment of analogy for, among other things, focusing on "concepts";[53] being too selective in choosing passages from Aquinas; and attending to differences between Latin and Greek meanings of terms, especially following Aristotle's usage rather than Aquinas's on the meaning of the term *"analogia."*[54]

All such criticisms stem from a desire to accommodate this second list of observations within the received paradigm of interpretation represented by the first list of assumptions—desperate attempts, as it were, to preserve that paradigm, in the light of phenomena that do not fit well with it. But there is another possible interpretive response. These observations can be understood, not as mere *puzzles* to be solved within the received paradigm, but as genuine *anomalies*, signaling the crisis of an exhausted paradigm, and pointing to the need for a new paradigm in interpreting Cajetan's teachings on analogy.

The received paradigm, consisting of both defenders and critics of Cajetan, grew up around a shared assumption about what question it was that Cajetan hoped his treatise would answer. Until recently, readers of Cajetan's treatise on analogy have all assumed that it was meant to answer some such question as: *What is a Thomistic theory of analogy?* Or *What is Aquinas's own teaching on analogy?* Or *How can order be imposed on Aquinas's scattered remarks about analogy?*

The first of these is too general a question to prompt the kind of treatise Cajetan wrote. The second question is more specific, but implies that Cajetan was writing a commentary or gloss, which is not suggested by the form or tone of his work. Though Cajetan does mention Thomas's works, they are cited as corroborating *Cajetan's* teaching, not as clues to *Aquinas's* teaching. Cajetan's manner of citing Aquinas thus also does not suggest the third question.

Some authors have assumed that the question Cajetan's text answers is: *What is the genuine metaphysical analogy?*[55] The textual evidence that this was Cajetan's own question is thin. Cajetan does emphasize that analogy is important for an understanding of metaphysics, and that metaphysics is one of the most important (though certainly not the only) areas where analogy is applied.[56] For many interpreters, Cajetan's discussion of extrinsic and intrinsic denomination is a discussion of the metaphysical implications of the different modes of analogy.[57] But Cajetan does not say that he is searching for the true metaphysical analogy. (The very phrase "metaphysical analogy," which some scholars have used,[58] is anachronistic—it does not appear in *De Nominum Analogia*.)

Many recent criticisms of Cajetan can actually be understood as following from the observation that *De Nominum Analogia* does *not* answer these questions. That Cajetan has imported his own interests; that Cajetan articulates his position in later scholastic terminology that differs from the terminology of Aquinas; that Cajetan's theory of analogy cannot really be derived from Aquinas's texts; that Cajetan only very selectively refers to texts from Aquinas—all of these have been taken as evidence of Cajetan's failure. But rather than conclude that Cajetan has given bad answers to such questions as "What are Aquinas's views on analogy," we might instead consider that Cajetan was trying to answer entirely different questions.

Some Lessons of Recent Historical Scholarship

That Cajetan was asking his own questions about analogy is suggested by the recent work of a handful of scholars who together have helped to recover the historical and philosophical context of Cajetan's treatise. The most important of these scholars are E. J. Ashworth, Michael Tavuzzi, and Franco Riva.

Ashworth has argued that "Cajetan needs to be read in the light of his more immediate predecessors, rather than as a man wrestling in solitude with the works of Aquinas."[59] She notes that Cajetan's treatise begins by rejecting three alternative views about the nature of the unity of the analogical concept. This raises a number of questions about what Cajetan is talking about, and to whom he is responding, and yet, Ashworth says, "So far as I can tell, the extensive literature on both Aquinas and Cajetan offers no satisfactory answers to these questions."[60] Addressing these questions herself, Ashworth considers a handful of authors—especially Peter Aureol (d. 1322), Hervaeus Natalis (d. 1323), and John of Jandun (d. 1328)—whose views were considered by some of Cajetan's immediate predecessors, especially Johannes Capreolus (d. 1444), Dominic of Flanders (d. 1479), and Paulus Soncinas (d. 1495). Because these authors all considered analogy, Ashworth claims, Cajetan should not be understood or evaluated just in light of the writings of Aquinas; instead, she finds that Cajetan "had his own philosophical agenda, which in many ways owed more to fourteenth-century developments than it did to Aquinas himself."[61]

The fourteenth-century developments that Ashworth has in mind are especially those having to do with philosophical logic, and the emergence after Aquinas of even more specialized vocabulary for the semantic properties of terms. She classes many of these as having "ontological facets," especially concerning the character of common natures.[62] But even more relevant to the problem of analogy are other questions:

> On the epistemological side, there is the problem of concepts and how they are to be described. Can one concept have an indeterminate content, or must it be determinate? How does a concept acquire its unity? From an object or nature or from something else? Can the mind form united concepts in the absence of one nature? What is the arithmetic of concepts? Can two concepts appear to be as one, as Henry of Ghent held? Can several concepts be united without losing their distinctness? Is there a distinction between a concept as an act of mind, and the content of that concept, what it is of or about? If so, how is this distinction to be described; and what status does the content of the concept have? Can it be identified with a common nature?

Ashworth concludes, "A good deal of the difficulty attached to the discussions of analogy in the fourteenth and fifteenth centuries is closely related to the fact that often several of these questions are asked at once, without being carefully distinguished."[63]

Tavuzzi agrees that "Cajetan was not writing in a vacuum," and that Cajetan "was not presenting simply a systematic exposition" of Aquinas "without recourse to any intermediary."[64] Instead, *De Nominum Analogia* must be understood within the context of "Renaissance Thomism."[65] Tavuzzi cites the work of Riva[66] (and even Montagnes)[67] in support of the suggestion that "Cajetan stood in a tradition with its roots in the late middle ages."[68]

Like Ashworth, Tavuzzi argues that there are particular philosophical issues that developed after Aquinas which are relevant to
the context of Cajetan's theory of analogy. These are "issues dealing
with the epistemological background of logic . . . those of the nature
of being of reason (*ens rationis*), of the nature of first and second intentions and of the nature of truth." According to Tavuzzi,

> When it came to the matter of [these] crucial issues of philosophical
> logic . . . the Thomists of the Renaissance found that more often
> than not St. Thomas had simply not treated explicitly or even ade-
> quately the problems in question—if for no other reason than that
> they were problems which had emerged, or at least gained their
> greatest intensity and precise identification and definition, in the
> years following St. Thomas' death.[69]

Tavuzzi is speaking here of general issues in philosophical logic, but
the same is true of specific questions regarding analogy—that often
the question addressed emerged in the years following St. Thomas.
The most basic evidence for this is that "several of Cajetan's contemporaries dealt explicitly with the theme of analogy."[70] It appears that
one of Cajetan's predecessors in the chair of Thomistic metaphysics
at Padua, Francesco Securo da Nardò (d. 1489), was known for being
a follower of Thomas Anglicus's theory of analogy. More striking, we
know that one Vencenzo Merlini da Venezia (d. 1502), who was re-
gent master during Cajetan's student years at the *studium generale* of
Sant'Agostino in Padua (1491–93), composed a work (now lost) on
analogy, also called *De Nominum Analogia*.[71]

Tavuzzi himself has presented a compendium of texts discussing
analogy from a variety of Renaissance Thomists. Among the most
significant from our perspective are those by Dominic of Flanders
and Soncinas. Cajetan could have known Dominic's work, and may
have actually been taught by Soncinas.[72] Dominic and Soncinas both
made divisions of analogy, the latter making use of Aquinas's distinctions at *DV* 2.11 and *I Sent.* 19.5.2 ad 1.[73]

These conclusions of Ashworth and Tavuzzi are confirmed by
the more comprehensive historical investigation of Franco Riva.[74]
Riva's thorough study of Cajetan explodes the opposed but symmetrical "myths of originality and continuity" that had character-

ized most reactions to Cajetan, even through the twentieth century.[75] Instead, as Riva shows, Cajetan's theory is neither wholly original, nor wholly continuous with its predecessors; Cajetan was rooted in classical sources, and in post-Thomistic developments, and yet within that tradition he makes specific interpretive choices, often with polemic intent, against not only Scotists but also the "attributionistic school" of Thomists who had already attempted to classify and analyze analogy.[76]

With the work of Ashworth and Tavuzzi, Riva helps to bring to our attention another common assumption of the received paradigm which must be rejected. Cajetan's interpreters have often presented *De Nominum Analogia* as if it was the first to formalize distinctions between modes of analogy. According to both defenders and critics, a strict classification of varieties of analogy, which was so important for Cajetan, had never been crucial to discussions of analogy in the "Aristotelian-Thomistic" tradition. Yet it can no longer be ignored that other Dominicans, including some of Cajetan's teachers, had tried to work out distinctions between modes of analogy. Indeed, as Ashworth has helped remind us, the tradition of distinguishing modes of analogy goes back through Aristotle's commentators to Aristotle himself.[77] Moreover, Scotus, in his arguments against analogy, even criticizes a threefold division of analogy.[78] It is clear that Cajetan's theory of analogy must be understood in light of a tradition of late scholastic reflection on analogy; and that, regarding those aspects of his theory that have seemed most original (his emphasis on concepts, and his classification of different kinds of analogy), he was taking cues from predecessors, working in and responding to a tradition that developed through the fourteenth and fifteenth centuries.

TOWARD A NEW INTERPRETIVE PARADIGM

The historical work of Ashworth, Tavuzzi, and Riva points toward a new paradigm of interpreting Cajetan's treatise on analogy. Their findings provide many of the observations listed above as "anomalies" of the old paradigm, and they reconstruct the historical context of Cajetan's treatise. Yet to some extent Ashworth and Tavuzzi remain within the old paradigm. Although they see that Cajetan's text needs to be evaluated in the context of a tradition of reflection on analogy, they still can be found evaluating *De Nominum Analogia* in terms of its relation to Aquinas,[79] and both Ashworth and Tavuzzi are in the end critics of Cajetan insofar as they find other thinkers among his contemporaries whose views seem closer to Aquinas's own. Treating *De Nominum Analogia* as a classic, they still do not directly investigate what question it was trying to answer; instead of recovering this forgotten question, they are still asking "the next question that arose."

Riva more successfully steps outside of the received paradigm. Yet Riva's work has not had wide influence in Anglophone circles, and in any case his historical study does not completely succeed in distilling Cajetan's particular philosophical concern.[80] So although this historical work has been important—showing that others were concerned with analogy at this time, and that Cajetan was not working in a philosophical vacuum—we must turn directly to the task of reconstructing the particular question or questions that *De Nominum Analogia* was intended to answer.

Chapter Two

Reconstructing Cajetan's Question

The Semantic Intent of De Nominum Analogia

What is *De Nominum Analogia* about? A scholastic commentator would raise this question in terms of several more specific ones. A proper prologue, according to longstanding medieval convention, communicates not only the title (*titulus*) of the work, the name of the author (*nomen auctoris*), and the order of its parts (*ordo libri*), but also the intention of the author (*intentio auctoris*), the subject of the book (*materia libri*), the part of philosophy to which it belongs (*cui parti philosophiae supponatur*), the method of its procedure (*modus agendi*), and its usefulness or significance (*utilitas*).[1] Our less precise question of what a work is "about" depends mainly on the questions of the *part of philosophy*, the *intent*, and the *subject*. This chapter addresses these three questions about *De Nominum Analogia*.

Framed in terms of Collingwood's dictum—that a text must be understood as an answer to a question—the aim here is to discern as precisely as possible Cajetan's question. What particular problem or problems was Cajetan trying to address in writing *De Nominum Analogia*? First, we will try to discern the general *kind* of philosophical question Cajetan was asking; then try to discern specifically *what* that question or those questions were. Together, this twofold inquiry supports and gives detail to the position taken in the rest of this study, that the subject of *De Nominum Analogia* is *the semantics of analogy*.

CUI PARTI PHILOSOPHIAE, OR, WHAT KIND OF QUESTION WAS CAJETAN ASKING?

Although analogy is often treated in the context of metaphysics and theology, every indication is that *De Nominum Analogia* is to be understood as belonging to the field of logic. There are several obvious reasons to believe that in composing *De Nominum Analogia*, Cajetan was deliberately treating analogy from the point of view of a logician:

1. According to the title of the work, Cajetan is not treating analogy, but the analogy *of names*. Even when he is concerned with reality outside the soul, Cajetan seems to do so in the context of the logical analysis of names in terms of the traditional semantic triangle of word, concept, and thing. As Cajetan explains in his fourth chapter, "In names are found three things—namely [1] the *word*, [2] the *concept in the soul*, and [3] the *thing outside [the soul]* or the *objective concept*" (*DNA* §31). To deal with names is to deal with those items that names as such (as opposed to names as vocal utterances or ink marks, for example) necessarily involve; but dealing with these items in their relation to names as such is the business of logic. As Cajetan explains in his commentary on Aristotle's *Categories*, the first part of logic, "simple apprehension," is concerned with words, concepts, and things; indeed, Cajetan argues that this part of logic can be properly considered as concerned with things, that is—"*things*, not [considered] absolutely but as *conceived* [i.e., by concepts] simply, and of consequent necessity, as *signified* [i.e., by words]."[2]

2. In the first paragraph of *DNA* Cajetan explains the importance of the work by claiming that it is required for a correct understanding of metaphysics and other sciences: "Knowledge of this [subject] is so necessary that without it, it is not possible that anyone reason about metaphysics, and many errors in other sciences proceed from ignorance of it." While this suggests a close connection to metaphysics, it is not a claim that the relevant knowledge of analogy is itself metaphysical knowledge. To the contrary, we can infer that insofar as Cajetan considers an understanding of analogy to be *prior* to

metaphysics, he does not consider it to be a *part* of metaphysics; and insofar as it bears on other sciences, it pertains to reasoning itself, and so to the art of reasoning about reasoning: logic, the "art of arts" or "science of sciences."

3. In the first paragraph of *DNA*, Cajetan also explains the importance of his work by claiming that it solves problems introduced by three misguided attempts to explain the unity of the analogical concept. Throughout the work it is clear that Cajetan is concerned to describe the nature of the *unity* that characterizes *concepts* signified by analogous *terms*, and this would have been a concern that scholastic philosophers treated under the auspices of logic.

4. Cajetan regards analogy as a mean between univocation and equivocation, and says that the nature of the mean is to be made clear by reference to the extremes.[3] That analogy is a mean between univocation and equivocation became a commonplace among Greek and early medieval commentators when addressing the first chapter of Aristotle's *Categories*. In the commentary tradition, the example of equivocation—"animal" predicated of a man and of a picture of a man—invited consideration of nonarbitrary equivocation, which might include analogy.[4] Univocation and equivocation are defined by Aristotle in the beginning of the *Categories*, which medieval philosophers understood to be a work on the first operation of the intellect, simple apprehension, and so the beginning of the logical *Organon*. It is worth noting that in his *Categories* commentary of 1498, after a brief discussion of equivocation, Cajetan expresses a desire to write a separate treatise on analogy—later that same year he would fulfill this promise by writing *De Nominum Analogia*.[5]

5. Cajetan distinguishes three kinds or "modes" of analogy, and in doing so gives definitions of each of the three modes. These definitions precisely parallel the Aristotelian definitions of univocation and equivocation in the *Categories*. From the Latin version on which Cajetan commented, here are Aristotle's definitions (literally translated into English, emphases added):

They are called *equivocals* whose *name* alone is *common*, while the essential *concepts*[6] according to that name are *different*. (Aequivoca dicuntur quorum solum nomen commune est, secundem nomen vero substantiae ratio diversa.)[7]

They are called *univocals* whose *name* is *common*, and the essential *concept* according to that name is *the same*. (Univoca dicuntur quorum nomen commune est, et secundum nomen eadem ratio substantiae.)[8]

Note the parallelism in the definitions Cajetan gives for his three modes of analogy (again, literally translated):

They are called *analogues according to inequality* whose *name* is *common*, and the *concept* according to that name is *wholly the same, but unequally participated*. (Analoga secundum inaequalitatem vocantur, quorum nomen est commune, et ratio secundum illud nomen est omnino eadem, inaequaliter tamen participata. §4)

They are *analogues according to attribution* whose *name* is *common*, while the *concept* according to that name is *the same with respect to a terminus, but different with respect to relations to that terminus*. (Analoga autem secundum attributionem sunt, quorum nomen commune est, ratio autem secundum illud nomen est eadem secundum terminum, et diversa secundum habitudines ad illum. §8)

They are called *analogues according to proportionality* whose *name* is *common*, and the *concept* according to that name is *proportionally the same*. ([A]naloga secundum proportionalitatem dici, quorum nomen est commune, et ratio secundum illud nomen est proportionaliter eadem. §23)

This parallelism of the *Categories* and *De Nominum Analogia* definitions indicates a clear intention to place the analysis of analogy in the same context as established logical analysis of equivocation and univocation.[9]

6. After the first chapter's brief exposition of the first mode of analogy, analogy of inequality, Cajetan dismisses it on the grounds that, from the point of view of the logician, it is not a case of analogy but a case of univocity. "Analogues of this mode the logician calls univocals" (*DNA* §5). "Thus it is not necessary to determine how unity, abstraction, predication, comparing, demonstration and others of the sort are found in analogues of this mode; for according to truth they are univocals, and the rules of univocals serve for them" (*DNA* §7). Analogy of inequality only counts as a kind of analogy at all from the point of view of metaphysics, and Cajetan passes over it once he explains why this is the case. We deduce from this that in *De Nominum Analogia* Cajetan wants to treat only what counts as analogy from the point of view of the logician. (For more on analogy of inequality, see chap. 6 below.)

Taken singularly, each of these observations provides a strong reason to categorize *De Nominum Analogia* generally as a work of logic. Taken collectively they make the case entirely secure. Commentators in fact tend to agree that Cajetan's *De Nominum Analogia* is an attempt to treat analogy from the point of view of logic.[10] Cajetan's concern is not relations between things but relations between significations of words; in the terminology of our introduction, what is at stake is the phenomenon of associated meaning, which in scholastic philosophy was a matter of logic (as opposed, say, to metaphysics or theology).

Indeed, most interpreters have noticed the treatise's logical perspective, and apparent exceptions only prove the rule. Robert Meagher, for instance, has written that "Cajetan missed altogether" that "the analogy of names is a logical rather than metaphysical question." It was "the cardinal presupposition of Cajetan," he continues, that "the analogy of names is a metaphysical doctrine."[11] This interpretation, for which Meagher cites no basis in Cajetan's text, is apparently derived from an exaggeration of the position of Ralph McInerny, who argues that Cajetan allowed metaphysical considerations to intrude on his analysis of analogy.[12] But McInerny's argument—that Cajetan confused metaphysical and logical distinctions and so did not present a properly logical treatment—still assumes that Cajetan in fact intended, but only failed to execute, a logical analysis of analogy.[13]

Edward Bushinski also mistakenly attributes a metaphysical, rather than logical, intention to Cajetan's treatise. Cajetan was motivated to write about analogy, says Bushinski, because he had discerned a "neglect of the nature of analogy."

> True, the name itself of this treatise may give the impression that [Cajetan] considers analogy primarily as a logical subject. However, as he tells us in Chapter Four, the term *names* is not to be taken as synonymous with words, i.e. as grammatico-logical elements, but comprises not only the external word and the concept in the mind, but also the reality outside the mind.[14]

Bushinski infers a "metaphysical" intent from Cajetan's mention of extramental reality. But simply talking about the reality outside the mind is not sufficient to move us from logic to metaphysics. As already mentioned, Cajetan conceives of the first part of logic as treating things "not absolutely, but as conceived simply, and, by consequent necessity, as signified." Indeed, as argued in point (1) above, the passage to which Bushinski refers as evidence of Cajetan's "metaphysical" intention actually strengthens the case for Cajetan's "logical" or *semantic* intention: the concept in the mind and the reality outside the mind are two corners of the classic semantic triangle of *word-concept-thing*.

Why "semantic"? As noted, Cajetan begins the fourth chapter of his treatise with the observation that "in names are found three things—namely the *word*, the *concept in the soul*, and the *thing* [*res*] *outside* [the soul], or the *objective concept*" (*DNA* §31). Cajetan considered these to be objects of logic; Bushinski notes that they are not merely "grammatico-logical elements," but they are nonetheless *semantic* elements. Although strictly speaking anachronistic, I call Cajetan's concern "semantic" rather than merely logical, insofar as the modern field of semantics is concerned with signs in their relations to those of which they are signs, and so with relations between language, thought, and reality. We have seen that this is exactly what Cajetan said was the concern of the logicians, and these are the basic terms of inquiry in *De Nominum Analogia*.[15]

INTENTIO AUCTORIS — CAJETAN'S QUESTION

The fundamental semantic question about analogy that arises within the framework of Aristotelian logic is how it is possible to have a mean between univocation and equivocation. To see how this question arises, and why it is difficult to answer, note that classical assumptions about the philosophy of language allow us to understand univocation and equivocation as involving relations between two semantic functions. Thus, according to the traditional definitions, given above from Aristotle's *Categories*, things are called equivocals whose name is common, and the concept or *ratio* according to that name is diverse; while things are called univocals whose name is common, and the *ratio* according to that name is the same (*Categories* 1). Following these definitions of univocation and equivocation, Cajetan in his commentary on *De Ente et Essentia* offers the following definition of analogy:

> They are univocals whose name is common, and the *ratio* according to that name is absolutely the same. They are pure equivocals whose name is common and the *ratio* according to that name is absolutely diverse. They are analogates whose name is common, and the *ratio* according to that name is somehow the same, and somehow different, or the same in some respect, and different in some respect. . . . Whence the analogue is the medium between the pure equivocal and the pure univocal, as between the simply the same and the simply diverse falls the mean, the same in some respect and diverse in some respect.[16]

This characterization of analogy as a mean, and hence as involving concepts "somehow the same and somehow different," is in fact entirely traditional, and uncontroversial within the Aristotelian tradition. However, consider the puzzle that arises should we try further to specify how exactly analogy is a mean between univocation and equivocation. The definitions of univocation and equivocation can be easily illustrated by showing the relationships between pairs of semantic triangles, representing relationships between word, concept, and thing:

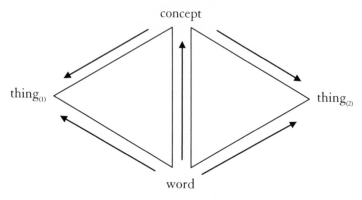

Figure 1. Univocation

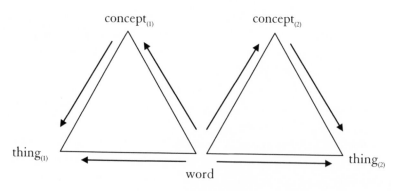

Figure 2. Equivocation

These are the two "extremes" of which analogy is the mean. But how could one complete a similar picture of the semantic triangles for analogy?

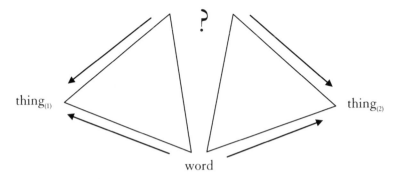

Figure 3. Analogy

The diagram for univocation gives us one concept and one arrow from word to concept (fig. 1), and the diagram for equivocation gives us two concepts and two arrows from word to concept (fig. 2). What could complete the diagram for analogical signification (fig. 3)? How is it possible that there be a mean between *one* concept and *many* concepts? *One* and *many* are not the kind of extremes that, at least in familiar arithmetic, are assumed to admit a mean. This is why one of the many questions that analogy raises is that concerning what E. J. Ashworth has called "the arithmetic of concepts."[17]

Nonetheless, this is the puzzle of analogy, at least if analogy is to be considered a mean between univocation and equivocation. Long before Cajetan, the traditional strategy for solving this puzzle had been to admit that in a sense, no mean is possible, that analogy is really a species of equivocation. What makes analogy still a mean between univocation and equivocation, then, is that in "pure" equivocation, the equivocated things are signified by means of unrelated concepts and only accidentally related by a common term, but in analogy the equivocated things are intentionally related, so apprehended by the intellect by related concepts. Thus the medieval distinction, traced back through Boethius, between *aequivocatio a casu* (or in Pseudo-Augustine *fortuitate*) and *aequivocatio a consilio* (or in Pseudo-Augustine *voluntate*).[18] Before Cajetan, most divisions of analogy were based on distinctions between different ways that a case of equivocation could have two concepts that were deliberately related, and so were in a sense more "unified" than in pure (*a casu*) equivocation.

But this leads to a further question: if analogy is really a form of equivocation, how does it avoid the fallacy of equivocation? That it must do so is obvious if metaphysics and theology are to be genuine sciences. If they are sciences they must use valid inferences, and yet in these sciences especially there are key terms used in these inferences which are not univocal but analogical. Aquinas, aware of this, gives the following example: Whatever is in potentiality is reduced to act by something actual; all things are brought into being by God; therefore, God is actual (*De potentia* 7.7, *corpus*). Cajetan offers as an example: Every simple perfection is in God; wisdom is a simple perfection; therefore wisdom is in God (*DNA* §105). Bochenski, recognizing the need for valid syllogisms depending on analogical terms, gives as an example: Every being is good; God is a being; therefore God is good.[19] In each of these syllogisms, the inference depends on terms ('bringing something into act,' 'being actual,' 'perfection,' 'wisdom,' 'being,' 'good') whose meanings are first learned from created things. The validity of the syllogisms depends on these meanings also being stretched to apply to God—for each of these thinkers, God can only be analogically named. So within the Aristotelian tradition, these syllogisms are valid, but their mediating terms are not univocal.

It had long been recognized that (at least some) nonunivocal terms needed to avoid the fallacy of equivocation, but Aristotle and Aquinas are typical in acknowledging this need without explaining it.[20] Within this tradition, it was simply taken for granted that this was possible. The crucial figure who forced closer attention and deeper consideration to this matter was John Duns Scotus. The semantic puzzle of analogy was intensified by the arguments of Scotus and his followers against the Thomistic notion of analogy.[21]

While Scotus's arguments specifically address the analogy of *being*,[22] much of his objection is not so much metaphysical as logical; Scotus challenges the very possibility of any sort of analogical signification.[23] In the minds of Thomists, Scotus's arguments did not so much refute the Thomistic notion of analogy as intensify the puzzle of its semantic conditions.

At the heart of the matter is Scotus's understanding of univocity:

> I call a concept univocal which is so unified that its unity suffices to cause contradiction when affirmed and denied of the same thing: and so it suffices for the middle term of a syllogism, as the extremes united by a middle term which is so unified are to be united together without the fallacy of equivocation.[24]

In other words, only univocity preserves the soundness of scientific reasoning; equivocation causes the fallacy of equivocation—and this would appear to be true whether the equivocation is by chance or by design. Thomists wanted to insist that they could have a science of being. But if this is the case, and this science is to avoid the fallacy of equivocation, there must be one concept of being, not many concepts.[25] But then it looks as if "being" is univocal. As Scotus summarizes his rigorous and unrelenting position elsewhere, "Where there is one and the same concept, there is univocation."[26] According to Ashworth, "John Duns Scotus' arguments about the univocity of being seem to have persuaded logicians that it makes sense to postulate just one concept of being, even if one goes on to reject the claim that '*ens*' is a univocal term."[27]

In short, Scotus discerned a tension between analogy, understood as a species of equivocation, and the notion that metaphysics was a science. In his mind, the tension was irreconcilable, and he was willing to reject analogy, insisting on the univocity of "being," in order to preserve the status of science for metaphysics. Other responses are available. One could opt to preserve a place for analogy, and reject the notion of metaphysics as a science. Alternatively, one could preserve analogy, and yet refuse to analyze it in terms of the traditional semantic assumptions that seem to make it inevitable that analogy would cause the fallacy of equivocation. (This seems to be the route eventually taken by James Ross[28] and by Burrell.[29] Reasons for and against this strategy will be taken up in the next chapter.) However, *if* one wants to maintain traditional semantics *and* preserve analogy, one cannot ignore Scotus's challenge. One must characterize the unity of the analogical concept.

Cajetan's *De Nominum Analogia* is fruitfully read as an answer to this challenge.[30] Scotus raises the question of how many *rationes* or concepts are involved in analogy, and of what kind of unity they have. The general strategy of Thomists after Scotus was still to describe analogy as a kind of equivocation, but to explain how it is possible that some kinds of equivocation avoid the fallacy of equivocation. This is a challenge to which (as argued below in chap. 4) a solution is not found in the writings of Aquinas. Before Cajetan's *De Nominum Analogia*, other Thomists, such as Dominic of Flanders and Paulus Soncinas, had included in their discussions of different kinds of analogy considerations of which kinds do and do not cause the fallacy of equivocation;[31] and Thomas Sutton addressed arguments that analogy would cause the fallacy of equivocation.[32]

It is noteworthy that in his commentary on the *De Ente et Essentia*, Cajetan confronts other Scotistic arguments for the univocity of being, but he avoids explaining precisely how analogy avoids the fallacy of equivocation. He responds to the question by asserting that that some nonunivocal terms still have a unity—the unity of proportion—which *for Aristotle* sufficed to avoid the fallacy of equivocation in scientific reasoning.[33] But the limitation of this appeal to authority may explain why Cajetan felt the need to supplement his extensive treatment of analogy in the commentary on *De Ente et Essentia* with further logical analysis in a separate treatise on analogy.[34]

In that separate treatise, a concern to characterize properly the unity of the analogical concept is apparent from the first paragraph, and a specific problem Cajetan wants to solve by the end is: How can analogy avoid the fallacy of equivocation?[35] Indeed, Cajetan pays attention to the unity of the analogical concept in order to explain how such a concept can have enough unity to avoid fallacy, but yet not so much unity to make it univocal. While Scotus had defined a univocal concept as one that is unified enough to avoid a fallacy of equivocation, Cajetan followed the Aristotelian description of univocity from the beginning of the *Categories* (which makes no reference to validity or fallacy of argument), without assuming that *only* univocity preserves the validity of syllogisms. He thus set out to determine what kind of unity could characterize the analogical concept such that it could mediate valid syllogisms.

MATERIA LIBRI—WHAT IS DE NOMINUM ANALOGIA ABOUT?

As far as Cajetan and some of his fellow Thomists were concerned, Scotus's criticisms of analogy were not so much metaphysical as logical or semantic. Scotus called into question the possibility of valid reasoning with nonunivocal terms, and Thomists, given their semantic assumptions about the role of concepts in signification, were challenged to specify precisely how or in what sense analogical signification involved a concept "one" or "the same" enough to sustain valid inferences. That is why, in *De Nominum Analogia*, Cajetan sets out to characterize the unity of the analogical concept,[36] and why I call the subject of his treatise "the semantics of analogy."

Reading *De Nominum Analogia* as an answer to Scotus's semantic challenge has significant advantages over previous treatments of Cajetan's analogy theory. First, it accounts for what we have called the "anomalies" of the old "paradigm" of interpretation. Reading Cajetan's analogy treatise as a commentary on, summary of, or synthesis of Aquinas's own teaching on analogy led to too many difficulties, such as the conclusion that Cajetan was both a willful innovator intentionally departing from his master and a clumsy interpreter who couldn't get Aquinas right. Now we see that Cajetan had a very specific theoretical problem to address. Appreciating his intention to address this problem, we can thus also account for those distinctive features of Cajetan's theory that the old paradigm had tried to account for—namely, the threefold division of modes of analogy, and the privileging of analogy of proportionality. The threefold division is a threefold answer to the question of how it is possible to have a mean between univocation and equivocation; and Cajetan gives preference to analogy of proportionality because, he argues, it, and not analogy of attribution, is sufficiently unified to avoid the fallacy of equivocation.[37]

— THIS RECONSTRUCTION OF THE SUBJECT AND INTENT OF *De Nominum Analogia* can best be evaluated and validated in light of a more thorough exposition of the text, articulated within the framework of Cajetan's general semantic principles. Such an exposition occupies part 2 of this study. But first, the remaining two chapters of part 1 defend respectively the theoretical appropriateness, and then the historical urgency, of Cajetan's attention to the semantics of analogy.

Chapter Three

Analogy, Semantics, and the "Concept vs. Judgment" Critique

A Semantic Analysis of Analogy?

Some critics of Cajetan who have discerned his general semantic intent have charged that Cajetan's theory had to fail because of this very intent. If these critics are correct, Cajetan's theory of analogy is historically significant for exposing weaknesses latent in medieval semantic assumptions. According to the critics, the Aristotelian assumptions that words signify by means of discrete "concepts," and that the meaning of propositions depends on the significations of its component terms, cannot do justice to the complexity, variety, and flexibility of actual human discourse; in *De Nominum Analogia* they see the elegant structure of classical semantics collapsing under the pressure of analogical language.

Objections

Ashworth and Ross on the Limits of Classical Semantics

Cajetan, along with other medieval thinkers, analyzed analogy in accordance with two roughly Aristotelian semantic assumptions: (1) that the meaning of a proposition depends on the meaning of its component terms, and (2) that the meaning of a term is a nature signified (and understood) by means of a "concept." On these assumptions, a term is univocal in different sentential contexts if, in the different contexts, the same term signifies the same nature by means of the same intellectual act of conception (as 'animal' signifies the sensitive nature when predicated of different animals, as in the sentences "A horse is an animal" and "A bird is an animal"); and a term is equivocal in different sentential contexts if, in the different contexts, the same term signifies different natures by means of different intellectual conceptions (as 'bat' must signify a different nature—indeed one natural and one artificial—when it is predicated of the flying mammal and of what a baseball player swings at a ball). Analogy, as a mean between univocation and equivocation, must involve the same term in different contexts signifying a nature (or natures) partly one and partly many, by means of concepts (or a concept) in some sense the same and in some sense different.

This raises interesting questions. How can there be a mean between one nature and many? How can the concept, by virtue of which that nature (or those natures) is signified and understood, be somehow the same and somehow different? Obviously context will be valuable for determining *whether* particular uses of a term are exhibiting univocity, equivocity, and/or analogy; but even within the context of individual occasions of utterance, *what* univocity, equivocity, and analogy are is primarily a matter of the semantics of terms. It is on this level that determining how there can be a mean between one and two natures, or between similar and different acts of conception, seems to be necessary for a general theory of the nature of analogical signification. Indeed, the general theoretical semantic questions raised about analogy as a mean between univocity and equivocity can be addressed completely independently of, and indeed would be unaffected by, attention to the actual context of particular utterances of analogous terms.

This accounts for the phenomenon noted by E. J. Ashworth, namely that "medieval logicians . . . discussed analogy and equivocation as if they were properties of single terms, as if neither sentential context nor speaker use and intention were at issue."[1] Since analogical signification manifests itself only in the context of different propositions, it does not seem as if an analysis of isolated terms can entirely explain the fact that human language exhibits the flexibility that it does. According to Ashworth, however, this indicates a weakness of medieval semantic assumptions, which made it difficult to analyze analogy in any other way. Paying more attention to "contextual clues," Ashworth writes, "would have required a completely different approach to language than was found in thirteenth and fourteenth century logic texts."[2]

In another article, Ashworth writes that medieval logicians inherited and passed on "a theory of language that tends to take words as units, endowed both with their signification and their *modi significandi* before they enter sentences and independently of speaker intention on any given occasion." She continues:

> One might think that equivocal and analogical terms are precisely those whose functioning is best explained through context and use, but . . . there was a tendency to speak as if equivocal and analogical terms formed special classes that could be identified in advance of use. To the extent that Aquinas's doctrine of analogy is embedded in such a general theory, one may fear that it will share the theory's defects.[3]

Elsewhere, Ashworth makes similar observations that potentially "cast doubt on the viability of the whole enterprise" of medieval discussions of analogy:

> The theory of analogy as presented by medieval philosophers is . . . gravely affected by the belief that each word is endowed with its signification, including its grammatical features or consignification, as a unity. Such an assumption is not easy to reconcile with the thought that language is flexible, and that one and the same word can have different shades of meaning.[4]

Later, Ashworth is willing to put the matter in even stronger terms. Writing about some fourteenth-century logicians, she summarizes one significant "result" of her findings:

The burden of analogy cannot be carried by single words or single concepts. A term cannot be used to express priority and posteriority and attribution, and yet these notions are expressed in language. The obvious solution is to give up the attempt to categorize terms as equivocal, univocal, or analogical, and to look instead at how they behave in different contexts and in relation to different sentential structures. Unfortunately, this solution seems to have been incompatible with medieval approaches to language.[5]

Ashworth voices this criticism—that medieval semantic assumptions limited medieval philosophers from properly handling the phenomenon of analogy—somewhat more tentatively than James F. Ross, whose book *Portraying Analogy*[6] she occasionally cites. Ross's book begins with severe criticism of "classical" approaches to analogy, including Cajetan's. Says Ross:

The key assumptions and metaphors of the classical story about analogy were exhausted, as far as fruitful theoretical elaboration is concerned, by the time Cajetan produced *De Nominum Analogia* in 1498, the last systematic explanation of analogy of meaning since the middle ages.[7]

What Ross here calls the "key assumptions . . . of the classical story" constitute the basic framework of traditional Aristotelian logic. Thus Ross says that "the classical theory [of analogy] suffers from limitations of scope and perspective," and furthermore that it is "based on false premises." Among the allegedly false premises are two we have noted and which we could call, respectively, the conceptualist and the compositionalist assumptions: "that word meanings are ideas- (concepts-, thoughts-) in-the-mind-signified-by-conventional-sounds" and "that sentence meaning is the molecular sum (syncategorematically computed) of the atomic meanings of the component words."[8]

Ross does little in *Portraying Analogy* to explain the suspect "classical" premises, to show that they are indeed "classical," or to formulate any particular criticisms of them.[9] But his charges are shared implicitly and explicitly by others, and on the face of it, the two premises criticized by Ross do seem to be assumptions made by Cajetan in *De Nominum Analogia*. Cajetan's explicit project is to describe the character of the *unity* of the *concepts* signified by analogous terms, in order to explain both the nature of true *predication* and the possibility of *valid inferences* that contain such terms. If the Aristotelian compositionalist and conceptualist semantic assumptions underlying this project are false, that is *ipso facto* an indictment of Cajetan's theory of analogy.

Gilson's "Concept vs. Judgment" Criticism

This is also an indictment of anyone else who would theorize about analogy within the framework of Aristotelian semantic assumptions. As such, this criticism could implicate Aquinas as easily as Cajetan (as is already acknowledged in one of the above quotations from Ashworth). This is why some partisans of Aquinas have taken comfort in the fact that Aquinas never ventured an explicit semantic analysis of analogical signification on the order of Cajetan's. That Aquinas's writings on analogy are restricted to limited remarks on the occasions of particular philosophical difficulties, and that these remarks never suggest anything like a systematic formal analysis, is taken by some to be evidence of Aquinas's greater sensitivity to the analogy phenomenon. Even if, as Ashworth suggests, Thomas may have shared the basic semantic assumptions of the medieval logical tradition, he never attempted their rigorous application to explain analogical signification.

In this connection, we must examine another common criticism of Cajetan: that his theory of analogy is unduly preoccupied with "concepts" as opposed to "judgment." The claim made by Thomistic scholar Armand Maurer is typical:

> It is not generally realized that St. Thomas' doctrine of analogy is above all a doctrine of the *judgment* of analogy, and not of the analogy of *concept*—at least if we mean by "concept" the expression of an act of simple apprehension.[10]

Elsewhere Maurer elaborates on this point, making it a specific criticism of Cajetan and relating it to a charge of inappropriate Scotistic influence on Cajetan's doctrine:

> Cajetan's treatise *On the Analogy of Names* is an attempt to put into order the Thomistic notion of analogy. Whereas in St. Thomas' writings analogy is used with great suppleness and flexibility as a means of approaching God, who is unknown in his essence, Cajetan proposes a rigid classification of the types of analogy that excludes all but the analogy of proper (or non-metaphorical) proportionality as the true metaphysical analogy. Throughout his treatment of analogy he tends to leave out of consideration the central notion of *esse* and to conceive of analogy in terms of concepts rather than judgment. In both regards he resembles the Scotists against whom he argued.[11]

Maurer is not alone in his evaluation of Cajetan's strategy. Patrick Sherry has criticized Cajetan's decision "to devote a disproportionate amount of time explaining how there can be a single analogical concept." Anticipating the strategy of Ross, he concludes:

> We can avoid such contortions, I think, if we make a radical break with the tendency to view concepts as psychological entities and instead approach the matter by examining the truth conditions of judgments [which involve analogy].[12]

This recurrent contrast of the role of *concepts* with the role of *judgment* in analogy can be traced back to Étienne Gilson. According to Gilson:

> The Thomist doctrine of analogy is above all a doctrine of the *judgment* of analogy. It is in fact thanks to judgment of proportion that, without a change of nature, one can make of the concept a usage sometimes equivocal, sometimes analogical, sometimes univocal. . . . The analogy of which Duns Scotus thinks is much more an analogy of *concept*. For, under the plan of the concept and of representation, analogy is practically confused with likeness. It is no

longer a matter of knowing whether two terms play an analogous role in a judgment of proportion, but whether the concept designated by one term is or is not the same as the concept designated by the other.[13]

Gilson's interpretation of Thomistic analogy, and its implicit criticism of Cajetan's concern to characterize the analogical *concept*, has had wide influence.[14] David Burrell has perhaps given it the most extensive elaboration. According to Burrell:

> Whoever understands that analogy is to be explicated "on the level of judgment" and not of concepts, Gilson contends, has also grasped the real divergence between Aquinas and Scotus. . . . Judgment is indispensable precisely because responsible analogous usage requires that we assess the way in which a term is being used in relation to its primary analogate.[15]

In Burrell's presentation, there is a clear connection between the charge that a concern with concepts is more Scotistic than Thomistic, and the charge that analogy is not fruitfully subjected to traditional semantic analysis. In his first book about analogy—with which his later writings about analogy have remained essentially consistent—Burrell explains that he wants to get away from "attempts . . . to collate the ways we use analogical expression into one theoretical mold."[16] In a section on the "limits of formal analysis," Burrell considers some recent attempts to "salvage" Cajetan's "formal analysis":[17]

> Formal attempts to explain analogous usage seem self-defeating. They shunt from the formally correct but too narrowly stipulative to a more adequate but formally less acceptable scheme. The very recurrence of this pattern is revealing. Analogy, it seems, is closely linked to a purposive use of language. One of the serviceable features of analogous terms is their adaptability to diverse contexts. Yet the language we use to express our judgment about entire frameworks, and their adequacy to the more comprehensive purposes of inquiry, is also markedly analogical. Hence a formal characterization seems impossible in principle since formal logic

constructs languages and tests their consistency but does not appraise them with respect to extralogical purposes.[18]

In the words of one commentator, Burrell wants, "in lieu of a *theory* about analogy, [to] establish his own thesis that paying close grammatical attention to the way analogous terms are actually *used* will demonstrate the freedom, fluidity, responsibility, and judgment actually involved in such usage."[19]

Burrell notes that he thinks Ross's *Portraying Analogy* actually cooperates with the work of Gilson and Lonergan and other scholars by whose efforts "Aquinas is justly liberated from a Thomistic rendition of 'abstraction' often more beholden to Scotus."[20] Burrell elaborates: "Lonergan's account of concept-formation in *Verbum: Word and Idea in Aquinas*, for example, independently corroborated by Peter Geach, could offer the necessary bridge linking Aquinas' efforts with Ross' semantic sophistication."[21]

Thus Burrell can separate Aquinas from the "Thomist" tradition that has been engaged in the problematic pursuit of a semantic analysis of analogy. For Burrell, it is Thomists such as Cajetan, but not Thomas Aquinas himself, who attempted to analyze analogical signification in terms of relations of *concepts*. In so doing, the "Thomist" tradition inadvertently succumbed to Scotistic influence,[22] necessarily resulting in philosophical confusion.[23]

Burrell finds confirmation for this criticism of Cajetan in the treatment of analogy by Yves Simon. In his article "On Order in Analogical Sets," Simon speaks of analogical terms as terms that signify "analogical sets," sets in which there is some kind of "order."[24] Simon then considers in what sense a common meaning can be "abstracted" from the analogical set. Because there is an "irreducible plurality" in analogy, analogical unity resists abstraction in the proper sense. The strict impossibility of abstracting a common analogate is not always recognized, says Simon. Analogates are "partly different," but they are also "partly similar," and so given this similarity it is tempting to assume that "in spite of it all, the meanings do have a common feature, albeit a very thin one, which survives the differences and makes it possible for a term, whose unity is but one of analogy, to play the role of a syllogistic term."[25] But for Simon it is naive to assume that "some common feature will be disclosed" and abstracted from diverse analogates.[26]

Of course diverse analogates have analogical unity, but, Simon says, this "unity is traced to an operation of the mind,"[27] an operation that is only a kind of partial abstraction. Says Simon, "Besides unqualified abstraction, which pertains to the univocal alone, there is such a thing as an analogical abstraction, although, in this expression, the adjective weakens the signification of the noun."[28] Simon calls this "an abstraction *by way of confusion*. . . . an incomplete, weak, partial abstraction" (emphasis Simon's).[29] Reiterating this sense of abstraction "by way of confusion," Simon says, "Analogical abstraction proceeds by 'fusing together' the members of a set. But such 'fusing together' involves assertions and negations that define priorities and posteriorities."[30]

In Simon's analysis, Burrell finds a confirmation of the Gilsonian theme that analogy is a matter of judgment rather than concepts, and that analogy will thus resist semantic analysis. As Burrell puts it, Simon is saying that "the 'analogical concept' . . . is a half-way house," that "the 'analogous concept' points beyond itself to a series of judgments."[31] For, according to Burrell, the analogical "abstraction" described by Simon "is in the order of judgment, not of apprehension."[32] According to Burrell, Cajetan's search for the unity of the analogical concept is thus inherently flawed. Rather than speak of formal analysis of analogical concepts, according to Burrell, we must approach analogy by attention to the different ways that analogical terms are used.[33]

Summary

Some of the above commentators could be criticized for failing to keep separate the general issue of analogical signification on the one hand, and such specific issues as divine naming and "the metaphysical analogy of being" on the other hand.[34] But such confusions do not undermine the genuine objections that, although diverse, can be amalgamated into the following general criticism of Cajetan: "Signifying analogically" is not a property of terms independent of their use in particular sentences; to recognize analogical signification requires judgment. Thus analogical signification cannot be considered apart from the particular linguistic circumstances in which it arises. A proper philosophical treatment of the phenomenon of analogical signification will thus not consider words independently of their context, independently of actual usage. This, however, is not Cajetan's strategy; his *De Nominum Analogia* is not about judgment and context, but about relations of concepts. Cajetan's attempt to characterize the analogical "concept" is evidence that he is concerned with abstracting the semantic properties of terms from the context of actual predications and inferences. That this strategy results in a strict classification of kinds of analogy, rather than a flexible and sensitive understanding of the varieties of analogous usage, is further evidence of its inadequacy.

REPLIES TO OBJECTIONS

To frame a response to this criticism, the rest of this chapter will address three things: in particular, (1) Cajetan's understanding of a "concept"; more generally, (2) the theoretical question of the compatibility of insights about the importance of interpretation, context, and judgment with a semantic analysis of terms; and lastly, (3) Cajetan's own practice of treating cases of analogical signification and his sensitivity to context and judgment.

Cajetan's Notion of the "Concept"

As we have seen, Cajetan's critics often charge that his concern with "concepts" is Scotistic, rather than Thomistic. Now on one level it must be granted that Cajetan's concern with concepts is the result of Scotus's influence. Scotus and his followers had argued that analogy was impossible, and some of their arguments were based on the premise that a concept that could preserve the validity of a syllogism must be univocal. Thomists were thus pressed to respond to this premise, and one common tactic was to discuss the notion of a concept and in what sense it had to be "unified" in order to preserve the validity of a syllogism.

But is Cajetan's understanding of "concepts" un-Thomistic, or otherwise at odds with a Thomistic understanding of analogy? Fortunately Cajetan's writings make very clear what he takes a "concept" to be. In the most basic sense, the *conceptus* is just *that which mediates thinking and signifying.* The concept is an interior quality that is the terminus of an act of simple apprehension, the "intention" by virtue of which some object is understood, and by virtue of which a word is said to signify a thing. Cajetan spells this out in his commentary on *De Ente et Essentia*: "A thing is understood at the time when we form its concept. . . . [T]he formation of a concept is the making of the external thing actually known."[35] Furthermore, in his commentary on the *Summa Theologiae*, Cajetan writes: "Words only signify things by the mediation of intellectual conception; therefore signification is caused by conception."[36] In short, a word signifies a thing by the mediation of a concept, and a concept is just what causes a thing to be understood.[37]

Cajetan's position about the "*conceptus*" here is the general medieval one that to form a concept is to establish an understanding. Given the common notion of signification as the establishment of understanding,[38] it is not at all controversial to assert that signification takes place by the mediation of a concept.[39] And so it should not be at all controversial that the logical consideration of simple apprehension manifests itself as consideration of "concepts," and that terms that signify analogically would be analyzed with respect to the concepts by virtue of which they so signify.[40]

Now obviously such an understanding of "concepts" *is not inconsistent* with the observation that signifying analogically is a property of terms only in the context of particular propositions, representing particular acts of judgment. Such is the nature of what medieval thinkers, including Aquinas, called the first and second acts of intellection—that is, *simple apprehension* and *composing and dividing* (or *judgment*).[41] Indeed, Gilson, who most fully articulated the supposed contrast between *concept* and *judgment* in analogy, not only affirms

that the "concept" should be understood in the sense Cajetan did,[42] he
recognizes that the formation of such concepts is consistent with, indeed part of, forming judgments.[43] In the long passage quoted earlier,
Gilson makes it sound as if "whether the concept designated by one
term is or is not the same as the concept designated by the other" is a
question raised by Scotus but not by Thomas; but clearly if one makes
a Thomistic "judgment of proportion" that allows one to "make of
the concept a usage . . . [which is] analogical," the "Scotistic" question
can arise. For instance, judging that there is a proportion between
the relation of the eye to its object and the relation of the intellect to
its object, we agree to predicate "sight" of both the eye and the intellect. But then we can ask: Is the same concept signified by the predicate when we say "the eye sees" as is signified by the same predicate
when we say that "the intellect sees"? To be sure, the question about
the identity or nonidentity of *concepts* does not need to be answered
before we are able to form the former *judgment* of proportion; but
the question about concepts is compatible with, in fact raised by, the
judgment. The question becomes especially pressing when we are
confronted with Scotistic arguments that call into question the logical possibility of making such judgments.

In fact, understood in their context, Gilson's remarks about the
difference between Aquinas's emphasis on judgment and Scotus's emphasis on concepts should never have become the basis for an objection
to a semantic analysis of analogy. First, it must be remembered that
in the relevant passage, Gilson is not concerned with analogy as such,
but with "the analogy of being" (*analogie de l'être*) and Scotus's objections to it; Gilson intends to explain how Aquinas and Scotus differ in
understanding the central metaphysical notion, being. Second, in explaining this difference, Gilson several times emphasizes that Aquinas and Scotus are not so much *disagreeing* as they are *talking past* each
other.[44] And third, as the source of their different approaches to *being*,
Gilson identifies their different views of what concepts are, how they
are formed, and how they signify; he nowhere denies, nor could he,
that for Aquinas judgments of proportion are made with concepts.
Indeed, in the long passage quoted above, Gilson said, "It is in fact
thanks to judgment of proportion that, without a change of nature,

one can make of the *concept* a usage sometimes equivocal, sometimes analogical, sometimes univocal" (emphasis added). Such an observation simply cannot be the basis for the conclusion that it is against the spirit of Aquinas for a logician to consider the concepts that result from such a judgment of proportion—that is, those concepts by virtue of which analogous terms signify.

The consistency of attending to both concept and judgment is further borne out by Yves Simon's reflections, which Burrell had taken as implicitly critical of Cajetan. Simon closely follows Cajetan's theory,[45] and his remarks on analogy demonstrate that even within the framework of Cajetan's semantic analysis and an attention to concepts, one can be sensitive to the role of judgment in analogy.

Indeed, the core of Simon's paper "On Order in Analogical Sets" can be considered an elaboration of Cajetan's discussion of abstraction in the fifth chapter of *De Nominum Analogia* (§§41–58, *Qualis sit abstractio analogi ab analogatis*).[46] There, Cajetan clarifies the sense of "abstraction" that applies to analogy of proper proportionality,[47] and his conclusions become the central points of Simon's reflection. A more extended discussion of what Cajetan says in that chapter cannot be articulated here (see chap. 8 below), but we will briefly note that we can find in Cajetan precisely those points made by Simon and highlighted by Burrell: since analogical unity is irreducible (*DNA* §49), from diverse analogates there cannot be abstraction, properly speaking (§§44, 56; cf. §§33–34), but there is a qualified sense of abstraction (§56) which actually involves a kind of "confusion" (§57);[48] thus analogical unity always "retains distinction" (§49), which is why we must be vigilant lest we ignore the distinctions and treat an analogical term as univocal (§§53–54, 57).

This confirms that Cajetan's project is not to try to reduce analogy to something else, but to characterize as specifically as possible the semantics of analogical terms. That Cajetan's semantic characterizations vindicate what Simon calls the irreducibility of proportional unity, and the impossibility of a common element's being purely abstracted, speaks to both the strength and the limits of semantic analysis; it certainly does not falsify the phenomenon of analogy, nor is it an abuse of semantic analysis.[49] Indeed, these insights only help to distill the further semantic question that concerned Cajetan, one that Simon leaves unanswered (though acknowledged):[50] How does proportional unity suffice to unify syllogistic inferences?

Context, Judgment, and the History of Medieval Logic

There is nothing about a semantic analysis of terms as such which is incompatible with a sensitivity to the role that a sentence or inference plays in giving context to terms. As a matter of fact, historians of logic have long noted that it is precisely the context of particular inferences, especially problematic or questionable inferences (*sophismata*), which helped to foster the medieval development of sophisticated treatments of the logical properties of propositions and terms. L. M. de Rijk has shown that the analysis of fallacy was a primary motive in the development of terminist logic.[51] And in his *Introduction to Medieval Logic*, Alexander Broadie explains:

> It was not uncommon for medieval logicians to begin their logic textbooks, at least those of their textbooks containing comprehensive accounts of logic, by considering terms first, and then reaching their study of inferences by way of an analysis of propositions. . . . But the fact that certain logicians adopted this order of exposition should not be taken to signify that they would have rejected the notion that terms, or at least some terms, should be expounded by reference to the role they play in valid inferences. On the contrary, their practice shows that they accepted this point.[52]

As we have seen, the very issue of the unity of the analogical concept arises out of a concern to account for certain kinds of inferences: in the face of Scotus's arguments that nonunivocal terms subject potential syllogisms to the fallacy of equivocation, Thomists felt obliged to explain how a nonunivocal term could preserve the validity of a syllogism. In this sense, the discussion of the semantics of analogical terms, by Cajetan and others, grows out of a concern to account for certain kinds of arguments; acts of simple apprehension are discussed because of their role in predications and inferences—that is, because of their role in judgments. The discussion of the semantics of analogical terms, then, like much of medieval logic, can be seen as arising from possible *sophisms* and the intention to avoid them. Understood in this way, the discussion of analogous terms is of a piece with the rest of the project of the *logica moderna* as understood by De Rijk, and described by Norman Kretzmann:

> Perhaps the *logica moderna* was aimed originally at nothing more than providing *ad hoc* rules of inference to cover problematic locutions in ordinary discourse, but, although it retained that aim throughout its three-hundred year history, its principal aim soon became the development of a reasonably general account of the different ways in which words are used to stand for things and to operate on other words.[53]

Cajetan's Hermeneutic Sophistication

A semantics of terms is not only theoretically compatible with a concern for judgment and context, it is in fact compatible in Cajetan's own philosophical work. Though one would not know it from the above criticisms, *De Nominum Analogia* deals not only with concepts but also with inferences in the often-neglected later chapters: the tenth chapter is about how it is possible to reason using analogous terms (*Qualiter de analogo sit scientia*); and the eleventh chapter offers warnings about understanding and using analogous terms (*De cautelis necessariis circa analogorum nominum intellectum et usum*).

Indeed, this final chapter ends with a passage that explicitly speaks to the concern that analogy is always a matter of context. Cajetan here anticipates some possible confusions about analogous usage. After considering them individually, he concludes with a general warning:

> Whence if someone does not wish to err, *he ought habitually to consider the occasion of the speech*, and recall that he will apply the conditions of the extremes to the mean; for then it will be easy to explain everything soundly, and to follow the truth. . . . [emphasis added][54]

In other words, Cajetan explicitly reminds his readers that the proper sense of a term depends on the particular occasion of its use; when interpreting a term in an argument, one must be aware of the purpose of the argument. Far from recommending that the sense of the argument be determined from a prior analysis of its terms, Cajetan is reminding his readers that the only way to avoid mistakes in interpreting terms is to keep in mind the larger dialectical context in which those terms play a role.

Such a point is rather obvious, and hardly incompatible with a discussion of the semantics of terms, even analogous terms. Indeed, even if Cajetan had not included this explicit acknowledgment of the importance of context in his treatise on analogy, his own practice would have implicitly affirmed his recognition of it. Cajetan wrote many commentaries, and even by 1498, when he composed *De Nominum Analogia*, he had written commentaries on Porphyry's *Isagoge*, on Aquinas's *De Ente et Essentia*, and on several of Aristotle's logical works. In each of these his interpretation of terms is consistently sensitive to the context of the arguments in which they are used. Even later, when he was writing his commentary on Aquinas's *Summa Theologiae*, Cajetan still often referred readers to his analysis of analogous terms in *De Nominum Analogia*; and yet in that commentary, Cajetan's remarks on each article almost invariably begin with a discussion of how the terms of the article must be understood in dialectical context—that is, in a manner consistent with the author's intended arguments.[55] Clearly Cajetan's concern with concepts did not preclude attention to context and judgment. Indeed, it would be more correct to say that it is precisely Cajetan's concern with acts of judgment and with the inferential context of propositions which led him to analyze concepts.

HERMENEUTICS AND SEMANTICS

In sum, the criticisms leveled against a semantic analysis of analogy, and against Cajetan's discussion of analogical concepts, do point to important truths about the limits of a semantic analysis of terms, but they fail to condemn Cajetan's approach to analogy. Context *is* important to analogy, because analogical signification does not take place outside of particular judgments expressed in propositions, which themselves usually must be understood in larger dialectical contexts such as inferences. But Cajetan does not ignore this. His attention to the signification of terms, and to the concepts that mediate such signification, does not imply that context and judgment are irrelevant; indeed it is partly motivated by the recognition that particularly important dialectical contexts, such as the arguments of metaphysicians, need to be better understood, and even defended.

So the historical lesson is, first, that Cajetan's concern with the "concept" is not exclusively Scotistic or otherwise un-Thomistic. Moreover, far from polluting Cajetan's theory, Scotus's influence clarifies the propriety, and precipitates the necessity, of a semantic analysis of analogy. Interpreters of *De Nominum Analogia* need to remember that Cajetan's concern with concepts is motivated by an attempt to develop a semantic analysis of analogy which will do justice to certain inferential contexts. In particular, Cajetan wanted to account for the possibility of syllogisms mediated by analogical terms, syllogisms, common in metaphysics and theology, which depend on a judgment of nonunivocal similarity.

There is also a larger philosophical lesson here about the theoretical alternatives available to philosophical semantics. The criticisms considered here all assume that semantic principles that are *conceptualist* and *compositionalist* are also necessarily *reductionist*. As we have seen, however, it is possible to analyze propositions as if their meanings depended on their component terms, yet without insisting that the propositions' meanings are *pre*determined by *fixed* meanings that their terms have *independently* of sentential and inferential context. Cajetan, at least, worked with a semantic framework that was conceptualist and compositionalist but also *organicist*. That is (to draw an analogy), for Cajetan a proposition is related to its component terms much as an organism is related to its organs. The function of the whole depends on the functions of the parts, but the functions of the parts are also determined by, and in some sense depend on, the function of the whole. To speak more precisely, the general principle of *semantic* dependence of wholes on parts—compositionality—does not itself establish the semantic values of the parts. The semantic values of the parts must be determined by interpretation, with attention to context; and there is nothing about semantic compositionality that rules out—indeed we have seen that for Cajetan it presupposes—the *hermeneutic* dependence of parts on wholes.

Chapter Four

Some Insufficient Semantic Rules for Analogy

Semantic Rules Before Cajetan

Cajetan's interest in a semantic analysis of analogy was not only theoretically interesting and appropriate, but urgent. Cajetan's teaching on analogy must be understood as an attempt to respond to a particular challenge, issued most famously by Scotus, that analogy, understood as a mean between univocation and equivocation, is semantically impossible, and that nonunivocal terms cannot be used in reasoning because they would precipitate the fallacy of equivocation. It was this Scotist challenge that led Cajetan, and several of his predecessors, to try to characterize the nature of the unity of the concept signified by the analogous term, a unity that must not be the same as the unity exhibited in univocation, and yet like univocation must differ enough from equivocation not to cause the fallacy of equivocation.[1] The need for such a semantic analysis of analogy can be highlighted by pointing out that, before Cajetan, standard semantic analyses of analogy were insufficient to meet the Scotist challenge.

In Aquinas and in other authors it is possible to find characterizations or "rules" for the semantic function of analogical terms. This chapter will first review some semantic rules that have a basis in the writings of Aquinas. It will then consider three proposed rules that Cajetan himself explicitly identifies and rejects at the outset of *De Nominum Analogia*. None of these rules adequately addresses the possibility of nonunivocal terms mediating valid inferences without causing the fallacy of equivocation.

Thomas's Semantic Specifications of Analogical Unity

Though Aquinas was not explicitly concerned with the question of the unity of the analogical concept, or the other attendant semantic questions that would come to occupy Thomists in the fourteenth and fifteenth centuries,[2] he did articulate some apparent semantic rules that touch on this concern. Moreover, he was interested to establish that analogical terms do not cause the fallacy of equivocation. In his discussions of analogy Aquinas is always aware, at least implicitly, that some cases of analogical signification—especially the central cases of metaphysics and theology—must exhibit enough unity to allow valid inferences.[3] Indeed, it would be difficult to ignore this requirement, since this is part of the reason analogy is understood as a mean between univocation and equivocation: analogical signification is not so completely unified to count as univocation, and yet it has sufficient unity to distinguish it from pure equivocation. This is why so many Thomistic and other commentators have emphasized that analogy provides orthodox theology a safe path between the Scylla of anthropomorphism and the Charybdis of agnosticism; God must be "other" enough that words said of creatures are not univocally said of Him, and yet, if we are to avoid agnosticism, our language must apply to God somehow, so that we can legitimately reason from creatures to God.

But despite the essential requirement of (at least some) analogical terms that they do not cause the fallacy of equivocation like pure equivocals, and despite this requirement's central role in orthodox theology, in only a handful of passages does Aquinas explicitly address the issue of analogical terms in valid reasoning. In only two texts does Aquinas explicitly acknowledge the need for analogy to have sufficient unity to avoid the fallacy of equivocation. In *Summa Theologiae* Ia, q. 13, a. 5, he says that what is said of God and creatures cannot be predicated equivocally, because if it were, nothing could be known or demonstrated about God, because attempts to reason about him would commit the fallacy of equivocation.[4] In *De Potentia Dei* bk. 3, q. 7, a. 7, he elaborates on the same point, saying that if words said of both God and creatures are purely equivocal, then proofs about God would be sophisms; he even gives an example of a good theological syllogism that would be a sophism if analogical terms caused the fallacy of equivocation.[5]

A handful of other texts, while not explicitly mentioning the fallacy of equivocation, directly acknowledge that analogy must sustain valid inferences. In *Summa Contra Gentiles* bk. 1, ch. 33, speaking of the possibility of gaining knowledge of God from creatures, Aquinas says that pure equivocation would not suffice for us to gain knowledge about God from our knowledge of creation; equivocal terms "break the continuity of argument."[6] In the disputed questions *De Veritate* q. 2, a. 11, Aquinas again addresses the same difficulty in confronting the question of whether knowledge (*scientia*) is predicated equivocally or univocally of God and creatures.[7] And in his commentary on Aristotle's *Metaphysics* bk. 4, lectio 3, Aquinas insists that 'one' and other central terms of metaphysics are, while not univocal, nonetheless unified enough to sustain a single science because of "reference to one."[8] Similarly, in his commentary on the *Sentences* (prol., q. 1, a. 2, obj. 2), Aquinas considers the objection that theology is not a science because God and creatures do not share a genus; he responds that it is enough that God and creatures have analogical community.[9]

While all of these passages acknowledge the possibility, indeed the necessity, of nonunivocal terms mediating valid inferences, none of them addresses the semantic puzzle this presents. Aquinas only asserts *that* analogy exhibits sufficient unity to sustain valid reasoning, without explaining *how* this is possible. An opportune occasion for explanation would have been his commentary on Aristotle's brief mention of analogical middle terms in the *Posterior Analytics*, and yet there too Aquinas's remarks are very limited.[10] And in no other text does Aquinas explicitly set out to explain how different analogical uses of a term can be sufficiently unified to avoid the fallacy of equivocation.[11]

Nonetheless, neither this lack, nor the often-noted fact that Aquinas never presented a systematic, *ex professo* treatment of analogy, prevents us from looking in Aquinas's writings for some further specificity about the semantics of analogy. What is needed is some account of the unity of the mediating concept(s) involved in analogy, an account that provides some specificity to the more general semantic characterization that the analogous concept(s) must be "partly the same and partly different."[12] What kind of sameness, and what kind of difference? Further semantic detail, in the form of specific answers to these questions, is needed,[13] and some more specific characterization is available in Aquinas. In several places, and in several different formulations, Aquinas offers what appear to be general and categorical descriptions of analogical signification which give some of the necessary further semantic detail. It is not surprising that some of these formulations have been taken as universal "rules" for analogy by Aquinas's readers, although Klubertanz, in collecting the relevant texts, has decisively shown that "not every discussion that appears to be a general description applicable to all analogies is such in actual fact . . . even when the description is couched in categorical language and no qualifications at all are explicitly made."[14] For present purposes, it does not matter whether the proposed "rules" are in fact applicable to all analogies. Indeed, the semantic detail we are looking for need not be a feature of all analogical terms, as not every instance of an analogy needs to exhibit sufficient unity to support inferences between the different analogical senses of a term. But, whether the rules considered here are applicable to all analogies or not, we will see that none of them succeeds in explaining how an analogical term could avoid causing the fallacy of equivocation.

We can find in Aquinas three main characterizations of analogy that could be treated as semantic rules for analogy. They are the following: (1) analogy involves a term that signifies *per prius et posterius*; (2) in analogy the *ratio* of one analogate is posited in the definitions of the others; and (3) in analogy there is a "proper *ratio*" that is found only in one analogate—*ratio propria non invenitur nisi in uno*. After considering these, we will consider one more proposed rule that has a basis in Aquinas, that (4) in analogy, there is a common *res significata* (thing signified) and diverse *modi significandi* (ways of signifying).

1. Analogy involves a term that signifies per prius et posterius

The first Thomistic proposal to consider as a semantic rule of analogy is that an analogical term signifies *per prius et posterius*. The phrase *"per prius et posterius"* (according to priority and posteriority) is one of the most common descriptions of analogical signification in Aquinas.[15] Considered on its own, the phrase seems to offer some of the semantic detail that is required to explain how analogy can be a mean between univocation and equivocation. Apparently in analogy, different analogical senses are related according to an order of priority. This alone, however, does not address the issue of how the different senses display enough unity to sustain inferences from one sense to another.

Even if the order of priority is further specified, however, we still do not have the right kind of semantic detail to respond to the Scotist challenge. E. J. Ashworth has shown that Aquinas spelled out the notion of signification *per prius et posterius* in terms of the order of reality, the order of knowledge, and the order of the imposition of terms.[16] While distinguishing these different orders allows us to understand how analogical terms can be learned, and how there are different senses of priority that are especially important to keep in mind in discussions of religious language, they do not allow us to understand why an analogical term is sufficiently unified to sustain valid inferences.

In most of its occurrences, it is clear that the characterization of analogy in terms of *"per prius et posterius"* is meant primarily to distinguish analogy from univocation.[17] Aquinas will often introduce the phrase by noting first that univocal things are named equally, and then noting that, in contrast, things named analogically are not named equally but exhibit an ordering *per prius et posterius*.[18] Yet the kind of characterization we are presently looking for would not emphasize how analogy differs from univocation, but how it differs from pure equivocation. Specifically, it would emphasize how analogy so differs that it does not cause the fallacy of equivocation. Signifying *"per prius et posterius"* does answer this question partially, for the multiple significations of purely equivocal terms are not so ordered, but under this rule analogy is still just a special case of equivocation, exhibiting, like equivocation, multiple significations. Thus, as McInerny has put it, "The analogous name is a name of multiple signification, but the multiplicity has a unity of order, *secundum prius et posterius*."[19] While this does distinguish analogy from pure equivocation, it does not do so in a way that would exempt analogy from the fallacy of equivocation. If signifying *per prius et posterius* is for Aquinas a rule of all analogical signification,[20] it is not the kind of rule that addresses with sufficient detail the semantic unity of analogical signification.[21]

2. In analogy the ratio *of one analogate is posited in the definitions of the others*

At first glance, the rule that "the *ratio* of one analogate appears in the definitions of the others" appears more promising as a semantic rule that distinguishes analogy from pure equivocation. The primary textual basis of the rule is *Summa Theologiae* Ia, q. 13, a. 6, where Aquinas says, "In all names which are said analogously of many, it is necessary that all are said with respect to one; and therefore it is necessary that that one is posited in the definition of them all."[22] Silvestro Mazzolini (1456–1527) regarded this passage as offering "the decisive rule" of Thomistic analogy[23] and more famously Francis of Ferrara (aka Francesco Silvestri da Ferrara, 1474–1528) also regarded this passage as determinative.[24] Authors continue to refer to it as giving Aquinas's "rule" for analogy,[25] although, as a rule for all analogies, it is controversial; Aquinas himself denies the universality of the rule in *De Veritate* q. 2, a. 11, ad 6. Klubertanz finds the rule rejected as often as accepted.[26] In any case, it is worth considering whether it provides a semantic characterization adequate to the present concern.

We can see from the quoted passage that the "one in the definition of the others" rule is connected to, and apparently derived from, the requirement that analogical signification involves a *relation* or *reference to one*. In this sense, it fits with other well-known descriptions of analogy, from Aristotle's *pros hen* equivocation[27] to Owen's "focal meaning."[28] Analogy is a special kind of equivocation, where diverse significates are united by a single, "focal" significate to which all other significates are related. This "relation to one," or *pros hen* equivoca-tion, thus entails that the *ratio* of the "one" in question appears in the definition of the others, for they are understood under the analogical term only because of a relation to that *ratio*.

We know that this "relation to one" is, in Aquinas's mind, impor-tant for analogy.[29] Moreover, we know that it is important for unify-ing terms under a single science, for in the passage from Aquinas's *Metaphysics* commentary discussed above, it is "relation to one" that is supposed to make it possible for things not univocally named to be the subject of a single science. However, though Aquinas says *that* this does unify a science, it is not clear *why* it does. And upon inspection, the rule seems to apply best to the cases that are least relevant to our present semantic concern. This is why Ross, for instance, takes "one in the definition of the others" as a rule for only one kind of analogy, analogy of attribution.[30] Ross's classification of kinds of analogies is more indebted to Cajetan than to Thomas, but even Thomas saw that the rule works better for some cases of analogy than others. For instance, the rule seems to apply well to the classic example of an ana-logical term, 'healthy,' but it does not seem to apply as well to other analogical terms, for example 'wisdom.' The health of the animal ap-pears in the definition of 'healthy' predicated of urine and food, be-cause urine and food have a relation to (respectively *sign of* and *cause of*) the animal's health. The animal's health is obviously the one to which all the senses of 'healthy' are related. But such an analysis does not obviously work for 'wise.' Human wisdom need not be defined in terms of a relation to divine wisdom, nor need divine wisdom be defined in terms of a relation to human wisdom.[31] But, to stick with these examples, it is the term 'wise,' and not 'healthy,' for which we need sufficient unity to avoid the fallacy of equivocation.

The rule does appear to hold for at least some terms of metaphys-ics. For example, the term 'being' is said analogously of substance and accident, and 'being' as predicated of an accident implies a reference to and is defined in terms of the being of substance. (This is not the case for 'being' as said of creatures and God.)[32] However, the rule still doesn't help us to see how such a term could sustain valid inferences free of the fallacy of equivocation. To say that the *ratio* of one appears in the definition of the others is, then, a rule insufficient to meet the Scotist semantic challenge.

3. In analogy there is a "proper ratio" that is found only in one analogate (ratio propria non invenitur nisi in uno)

Another proposed rule for analogy is that it always involves a proper *ratio*, which is found in only one of the analogates—*ratio propria non invenitur nisi in uno*. One source of textual support for this rule is *Summa Theologiae* Ia, q. 16, a. 6: "When something is said analogically of many, it is found according to its proper *ratio* in only one of them, from which the others are denominated."[33] The rule is very similar to the previous one; whereas the second rule discussed above described how the definitions of primary and secondary analogates are related, the present rule emphasizes that secondary analogates lack a proper *ratio*, which is found in the primary analogate. We may assume that the two rules entail each other—secondary analogates would be defined in terms of the primary analogate precisely because their definitions must make reference to that *ratio* that is found only in the primary analogate. At least, like the previous rule, this one seems to work best for 'healthy' and other terms that exhibit the kind of analogy that has come to be called analogy of attribution; it is not clear how the rule relates to 'truth,' say, as it is found in both created intellects and the divine intellect—indeed, this is not even clear in *ST* Ia.16.6 where Thomas invokes the rule.

In any case, what is important to note for our purposes is that this rule could not address the challenge with which Cajetan was concerned. It emphasizes the *difference* between analogates, saying that the *proper ratio* is found only in one. What we need to address Scotus's challenge is a rule that explains how the different analogates, or the different *rationes* by which those analogates are signified, are sufficiently *unified* to avoid the fallacy of equivocation. The current rule, *ratio propria non invenitur nisi in uno*, offers nothing in response to this, and in this sense is even less helpful than the previous rule, which told us that the different *rationes* would at least be unified inasmuch as the *ratio* of one would appear in all the rest.

— TAKEN INDIVIDUALLY, THEN, NONE OF THE THREE THOMISTIC rules for analogy considered above is sufficient to address the particular semantic challenge with which Cajetan was concerned. But before dismissing them, it is worth considering whether taken collectively they provide detail that no individual rule provides. It is not difficult to consider them together. It is easy to see how (2) can be a clarification, or specification, of (1); indeed, this is already apparent in Aquinas, who says that "the prior is included in the definition of the posterior."[34] And we have already seen that (3) is an implication of (2). McInerny's interpretation of Thomistic analogy provides a good example of how (2) and (3) together can be taken as specifications of (1). According to McInerny,

> The analogous name signifies a plurality of *rationes* which are related *per prius et posterius*; that is, one *ratio* is primary and presupposed by the others, this being revealed by the fact that the first *ratio* enters into the others. These secondary *rationes* signify diverse *proportions* or *analogies* to the first; they are said *per respectum ad unum*.[35]

And again:

> Things are named analogously when they share a name that receives several accounts and one of them is controlling or primary, a sign of which is that it enters into the other accounts. The rule expressing this is that the proper meaning of the term, its *ratio*, is found in only one of the analogates and the others are named with reference to, by proportion or relation to, it.[36]

In these and other passages,[37] it is clear that rule (1) can be clarified by rule (2), which in turn implies rule (3): a term signifies *per prius et posterius* in the sense that one *ratio* is primary and appears in the definitions of all the others, and this primary *ratio* is necessarily found properly only in the primary analogate.

But considering these three rules together does not add to the semantic detail that they provide when considered separately. The account of analogical signification that they provide may be true, but it is still not sufficient to explain how it is possible that an analogical term could support valid inferences from one of its analogous senses to another. Analogy is still a kind of equivocation, albeit an equivocation in which the different significates are related, but the characterization of that relation—that the *ratio* of one is included in the others—is not sufficient to make this kind of equivocation exempt from the fallacy of reasoning that is named for equivocation.

4. In analogy there is one res significata and diverse modi significandi

Lastly, let us consider a fourth rule for which several interpreters claim to find support in Aquinas. According to McInerny, for instance, the above rules can be further specified in terms of the logical distinction between *res significata* and *modus significandi*. In particular, says McInerny, the *ratio propria* of a term must be understood as not just *what* it signifies, but this together with *how* it signifies. That is, the *ratio propria* includes not just the *res significata*, but also the *modus significandi*.[38] Thus, according to McInerny, an analogical term is a term that has one *res significata* and multiple *modi significandi*.[39]

As a proposed Thomistic rule for analogy, this is controversial. Although McInerny treats this as Aquinas's express doctrine,[40] there is very little textual support for it as a general rule of analogy. Aquinas often appeals to the variation of *modi significandi* to explain how some terms can be common to God and creatures, but outside of discussions of religious language it is not clear that Aquinas ever describes analogical signification as involving one *res significata* and diverse *modi significandi*. One of McInerny's best texts is from Aquinas's commentary on the *Sentences*,[41] though, as Ashworth has pointed out, the text speaks not of *modi significandi* but of *modi praedicandi*.[42] While other texts do explicitly mention *modi significandi*,[43] according to Ashworth the distinction between *res significata* and *modus significandi* is "central to Aquinas's theory of religious language," but "it is in no way central to his theory of analogy (insofar as he has a general theory)";[44] for Aquinas, Ashworth says, "*modi significandi* have no role in analogy as such."[45]

Whether or not Aquinas meant it as a general analysis of all ana-logical terms, it is still worth considering the rule that an analogical term has one *res significata* but diverse *modi significandi*. The interpre-tation has been widely held by scholars other than McInerny,[46] and even if it was not Aquinas's view, Ashworth has pointed out that the rule could be attributed to another medieval figure, Peter of Spain.[47] Furthermore, even supposing the rule is not a general one for all ana-logical terms but pertains only to religious language, it is still worth considering, for theological reasoning is an important example of the kind of reasoning involving analogical terms that a semantic analysis of analogy intends to safeguard. Words like 'good' and 'wise' said of both God and creatures are much better examples than, for instance, the stock example of 'healthy,' if what we are looking for is an ac-count of the unity of the analogical concept that can overcome the Scotist challenge to the semantic possibility of a nonunivocal term immune from the fallacy of equivocation.

However, a first indication that multiple modes of signifying a common significate is not a satisfactory semantic rule is that its pri-mary recent defender takes it to apply to the word 'healthy.' Accord-ing to McInerny, the analogical term 'healthy' can be understood as having a single *res significata* (the health that is manifested by a healthy living thing, say, the proportion of its humors or the harmony of its life functions), and the term is made analogical by its several *modi significandi*—that is, the several ways that health is signified.[48] McIn-erny does not carry out such an analysis, but apparently the various analogous senses of the predicate "(is) healthy" exhibited by the sen-tences "Socrates is healthy," "This food is healthy," and "This urine is healthy," would be achieved by using the common *res significata*, the health of the animal, to complete the various respective *modi signifi-candi*: "has . . . ," "is a cause of . . . ," and "is a sign of . . ."[49]

Whether or not this analysis of 'healthy' is *ad mentem Thomae*, it clearly shows that understanding analogical terms in this man-ner does not help us secure the validity of syllogisms that depend on analogical terms. For again, 'healthy' is not the kind of analogical term for which we are seeking a semantic rule. The different senses of 'healthy' are logically speaking equivocal in precisely the way that should cause a fallacy of equivocation if these different senses are interchanged in an inference. For example, in the syllogism 'Whatever is on your plate is healthy, and whatever is healthy is alive; therefore, whatever is on your plate is alive,' the premises, insofar as they are plausibly true, contain the term 'healthy' in different analogical senses, and this is precisely the reason why the conclusion does not follow from these premises. Yet if these different senses can be analyzed in terms of a common *res significata* and diverse *modi significandi*, then the proposed rule that analogy involves a common *res significata* and diverse *modi significandi* does not help us explain why some analogical terms can be used in syllogisms without causing the fallacy of equivocation.

— ON THE BASIS OF THESE CONSIDERATIONS, IT IS SAFE TO conclude that Aquinas does not offer a rule for the semantic unity of analogy sufficient to meet the Scotist semantic challenge.[50] The claim is not that Aquinas does not have the intellectual resources to address the question, but simply that his proffered rules for analogy do not address the question. Of this we should not be surprised, because, as Ashworth has shown, the question of the unity of the analogical concept was considered by Thomists in the contexts of philosophical developments after Aquinas.[51] This further explains why Cajetan's treatment of analogy differs from Aquinas's, to the extent that it does, and why Cajetan's departure from Aquinas would in fact seem to him rather necessary or urgent: Cajetan was trying to answer particular semantic questions to which he did not find, and could not find, answers in the writings of Aquinas.

INDISJUNCTION, ORDER, AND UNEQUAL PARTICIPATION

There are three more semantic accounts for analogy worth considering, these ones mentioned explicitly and rejected by Cajetan in *De Nominum Analogia*. When Cajetan names three mistaken theories about the unity of the analogical concept, they are not recognizable as formulations of Aquinas himself. They rather seem to be derived from later Thomists. This further confirms our position that Cajetan's treatise must be read in light of the context of fourteenth- and fifteenth-century philosophical developments, rather than as a simple commentary on or interpretation of the writings of Aquinas.

Indeed, Cajetan does not respond directly or primarily to the semantic rules expressed by Aquinas and already discussed. Nonetheless, it must be admitted that these rules are treated indirectly and by implication in *De Nominum Analogia* and in other writings by Cajetan. In general, Cajetan seems to find them not so much wrong as inadequate. It is clear, for instance, that Cajetan regards signifying *per prius et posterius* as too general a description of analogy,[52] and he regards the rule "the *ratio* of one is posited in the definition of the others" as a proper feature of only one kind of analogy, namely analogy of attribution.[53] Cajetan also rejects the rule "*ratio propria non invenitur nisi in uno*," saying that it is not universally true of all cases of analogy.[54]

But these are not the rules that Cajetan sets out to attack in *De Nominum Analogia*. In the very first paragraph of the treatise, Cajetan attributes the need for his treatment of analogy both to its inherent philosophical importance, and to peculiar confusions regarding analogy exhibited by his contemporaries. In particular, he names three theories about the unity of analogy, lamenting that analogy is wrongly said to be constituted by "[1] unity of (in)disjunction, or [2] of order, or [3] of a precise concept unequally participated."[55] Cajetan is apparently motivated to correct the errors inherent in each of these three proposals, and to offer an alternative.

Despite their obvious significance for the motivation of *De Nominum Analogia*, these three rejected accounts of analogical unity have rarely been discussed by interpreters of Cajetan's theory of analogy. One notable exception is Ashworth, who gives the best historical and philosophical background.[56] Ashworth shows that the question of the unity of the analogical concept grew up in the context of late scholastic developments of logical and epistemological terminology, especially the distinction between "objective" and "formal" concepts. As Ashworth shows, it was widely agreed that an analogical term could and did involve one formal concept; that is, one intellectual intention can mediate the understanding of several analogously related things. Thus the question of the number and unity of the analogical concept was a question about the objective concept—the intelligible content that is grasped by the formal concept.[57] As Ashworth presents it, this question of the unity of the objective concept was related to the question of whether the objective concept that covers all the analogates is distinct from the proper *rationes* or objective concepts of the analogates taken singly. Thus the three theories that Cajetan rejects can be understood as three options that present themselves concerning these questions of unity and distinctness. As Ashworth describes it with reference to the particular case of the analogous term 'being':

> If one holds that the analogical *ratio* expressed by the word 'being' is a single *ratio* which is unequally participated in by God and creatures, substance and accidents, then it will be distinct from the proper *rationes* which apply to God, creatures, substance and accidents taken singly. On the other hand, if the analogical *ratio* derives its unity from an ordering of proper *rationes*, either as a group or as a disjunction, it is difficult to see how it can be genuinely distinct from these proper *rationes*.[58]

So either an analogical term signifies a single *ratio* (objective concept), which is distinct from the proper *rationes* of the analogates and is unequally participated in by those analogates, or an analogical term signifies a complex of multiple proper *rationes* that are either ordered—that is, by attribution to something—or united in a disjunction.[59]

To understand better these three alternatives and the historical context in which Cajetan rejects them, it helps to connect the three views, insofar as possible, with that thinker or those thinkers who proposed them. It seems that the "unequal participation" theory of analogy was the most widespread, and is easiest to attribute to particular thinkers.[60] Capreolus (d. 1444) argued that the objective concept of *being* was a single *ratio* diversely participated in by its analogates.[61] Capreolus cited the authority of Aquinas, *In Sent.* 19.5.2.1, and was followed in this by Soncinas (d. 1495).[62] Soncinas said that 'being' was the type of analogical term that had "one *ratio* in act, but unequally participated."[63] Johannes Versor (John Versorius, d. 1485) mentions the view but rejects it.[64] Dominic of Flanders (d. 1479) says that in one mode of analogy, exemplified by 'healthy,' different things are "the same according to one *ratio* diversely participated"; but it is not clear that Dominic believes this to be the case with 'being.'[65] In fact, the view that analogy involves unequal participation in a single *ratio* was not entertained just by Cajetan's immediate predecessors; Ashworth argues that it can be traced at least as far back as Simplicius's commentary on Aristotle's *Categories*.[66]

Of the other two views—unity of order and unity of (in)disjunction—only one of them can easily be located historically. As described already, both views involve the denial that there is one *ratio* involved in analogy, insisting that there is a group of *rationes*. If, following Ashworth, we understand unity of order to be the order that attends a group of *rationes* attributed to a single one, this appears to be the view espoused by John of Jandun (d. 1328) and by Henry of Ghent.[67] It also seems to be the view of Versorius, who says that the "unity of analogy" consists in a word's being said "first and principally of one and of others insofar as each one of them has a relation to that first."[68]

The other possibility, that the multiple *rationes* are not ordered by attribution but are unified in a disjunction, seems to have been occasionally considered, but it is not clear who advocated it. Pinchard[69] and Ashworth[70] find it expressed by Soncinas, but he more often and explicitly advocated the "unequal participation" view. Dominic of Flanders considers whether "being signifies a disjunct concept," only to deny it.[71] Dominic and others attributed the view to Hervaeus Natalis (d. 1323), who does discuss the view but apparently did not espouse it.[72] Stephen Brown finds the view in Gerard of Bologna, an early critic of Scotus,[73] and finds the view criticized in Peter Aureol (d. 1322).[74]

It remains for us to examine why each of these three proposed rules for the unity of the analogical concept fail to overcome the Scotistic challenge to the semantic possibility of analogy. Cajetan apparently expects that they are plainly seen as mistaken only in light of the alternative, true theory of analogy that he claims to expound in *De Nominum Analogia*, and he does not criticize them except in light of that theory.[75] Yet even before presenting Cajetan's alternative theory, we can consider these three proposals on their own terms and see if they can meet the semantic challenge that Cajetan had before him, to find a mean between univocation and equivocation, and in particular a nonunivocal term that could be used in inferences without precipitating the fallacy of equivocation.

At least two of the proposals obviously fail in light of our previous considerations. The proposal that analogy involves "unity of order," or that analogy is unified by an "ordered concept," can be assimilated to the rule already considered that diverse senses of an analogical term signify *per prius et posterius*—that is, according to an order of priority. We have seen that this description of analogy remains too general to address the specific semantic concerns that occupied Cajetan.

The other proposal that is easy to dismiss is that analogy involves unity of disjunction. In other words, diverse concepts are unified by positing another concept in which they are conceived collectively, as members of a disjunct set. This hardly appears to be an attractive theory of analogy in the first place, and seems to rely on a merely *ad hoc* principle of unification. The diverse analogates still appear only equivocally related, and this rule provides no sense of how their unity into one concept is sufficient to avoid the fallacy of equivocation just like pure equivocation.[76]

When we turn to the third proposal, that analogy involves a single concept or *ratio* that is unequally participated in, it is more difficult to evaluate whether or not it meets the Scotistic challenge. As a semantic rule for analogy, it avoids the difficulty of the other two proposals Cajetan mentions and rejects, because it does not posit diverse *rationes* that are somehow united; instead, it posits a single *ratio*, in which the various analogates participate in diverse ways. Because it involves one *ratio*, it appears that it can avoid the fallacy of equivocation.

But we would need to know in further detail what it means for analogates to unequally participate in a *ratio* before we could deem this an adequate characterization of analogy. On the one hand, if unequally participating in a *ratio* makes things different enough to be only analogically, and not generically, related, then we would still need some account of how this unequal participation would not occasion the fallacy of equivocation. On the other hand, if "unequal participation" involves a single *ratio* (a single precise concept), uniting things alike in conception although different in reality (like "animal" as predicated of higher and lower animals), then it is really a special form of univocation (as Cajetan himself describes for what he calls "analogy of inequality"). In either case, we do not have a satisfactory answer to the Scotistic challenge to describe nonunivocal signification sufficiently unified to preserve valid inferences.

THE CHALLENGE

Our analysis of this last "unequal participation" proposal, and of the other rules considered in this chapter, leads us to acknowledge a question that may have haunted some readers from the beginning: Is this attempt to find a semantic mean between univocation and equivocation an impossible balancing act? Would any rule fail? It certainly seems as if the conceptual space for a nonunivocal, nonequivocal term shrinks to the infinitesimal once we insist on a rigorous semantic analysis. It appears that as soon as we prevent a term's being prone to the fallacy of equivocation, we make it univocal, and as soon as we distinguish it from the univocal, we make it equivocal. Of course, before trying to give it a systematic formulation, it seemed that there was space for such a mean, and in particular that there was logical space for nonunivocal terms that did not cause the fallacy of equivocation. But this space proves elusive once we try to define it with a rigorous semantic analysis. So is a rigorous semantic analysis asking too much?

As we have seen from the previous chapter, some scholars have apparently thought so. But whether or not it is asking too much, we must remember in reading *De Nominum Analogia* that Cajetan didn't think that it was asking too much. Not only was he aware of this balancing act, but he even thought he pulled it off. On the basis of the above reflections we may be tempted to think, even before considering Cajetan's attempt, that it could not succeed, and that if it even appears to succeed it could only do so by some kind of magician's trick.

But before we dismiss his attempted balancing act as *a priori* impossible, we owe it to ourselves to try to understand how Cajetan thinks he can pull it off, to see, as it were, what kind of trick he might have up his sleeve, and to decide whether the trick is a trickster's deception or in fact what it claims to be: a clever solution to a challenging puzzle. This will be the business of part 2. Before turning to Cajetan's own theory, starting in chapter 6, we must first make sure that we understand the semantic principles that form the conceptual framework within which Cajetan's theory is proposed. Thus part 2 begins with a chapter offering an overview of Cajetan's semantic principles.

Part 2

Cajetan's Answer

Chapter Five

Cajetan's Semantic Principles

INTRODUCTION

In response to objections to a semantic analysis of analogy, we began to examine Cajetan's semantic principles in chapter 3. There I clarified that for Cajetan the *concept* was simply that which mediated thought; a concept is simply the intellectual intention by virtue of which someone understands something. Thus, we saw, the *concept* played a role in the general notion of signification. For signification is the function of a word that makes someone aware not of the word but of whatever is signified by the word. A word that signifies is a word that makes something known. That is to say, in the common medieval formulation traced back to Boethius, signification is the establishment of an understanding.

This initial and partial clarification of Cajetan's notion of the "concept" needs to be put in the context of a more ordered, if still sketchy, presentation of Cajetan's semantic principles. The present chapter contains such a sketch, preparing the way for a consideration of Cajetan's teaching on analogy by providing the philosophical context in which he offered that theory.

Cajetan nowhere systematically articulates what we would call a theory of semantics, but his semantic principles can be reconstructed from a variety of his works. His commentaries on two logical works—Porphyry's *Isagoge* and Aristotle's *Categories*—are obvious sources.[1] Much can be learned of Cajetan's semantic principles also from his commentary on Thomas Aquinas's *De Ente et Essentia*. All three of these works were completed within the few years before Cajetan wrote *De Nominum Analogia*. We can also learn about Cajetan's semantic principles from his commentary on Aquinas's *Summa Theologiae*, a work written several years later. These are the sources that inform the following outline of Cajetan's semantic principles.

Among the topics we will consider along the way is the relation between Cajetan's semantic principles and metaphysics. So, for instance, this chapter addresses the ontological commitment of Cajetan's logical "realism." It also addresses a more particular issue, which will prove more directly relevant to the later discussion of analogy: the question of whether claims about terms denominating *intrinsically* or *extrinsically* are metaphysical claims, or more properly logical or semantic ones.

SIGNIFICATION

Cajetan's notion of signification can be introduced by turning to his description of the subject matter of Aristotle's *Categories*. Briefly, Cajetan explains that while the metaphysician considers things as they are, the logician considers things as they are understood and signified. As Cajetan describes it, in the part of logic that regulates the most basic intellectual act, simple apprehension,

> incomplex things are not united and distinguished with the conditions that they have in the nature of things, but as they are received by the intellect, that is, as they stand under the simple apprehension of the intellect, that is, as objects of simple apprehension of the intellect, and things so received are nothing other than things said by interior words, or (which is the same) things conceived by simple concepts; and things of this sort are nothing other than things signified by incomplex words (since words are signs of concepts and concepts [are signs] of things).[2]

This passage is illuminating in several ways. At the end, as an aside, Cajetan introduces what has come to be called the "semantic triangle":

word, concept, and thing. The discussion leading up to this helps us to understand how the three terms of this semantic triangle are related. The concept is equated with an "interior word," which is just that which makes simple apprehension possible, in other words, that by which the intellect is made aware of something in some way. So in saying that "words are signs of concepts and concepts are signs of things," we see that Cajetan means that a word signifies immediately an intellectual intention or "concept" that necessarily mediates understanding, and ultimately signifies what is understood by the mediation of that concept, that which the concept makes one understand.

So a word immediately signifies a concept and ultimately signifies some "thing." The things signified and understood are not concrete individuals, but what Cajetan will speak of as their "forms" or "natures."[3] It is important to note that in a strictly semantic context, such terms are not to be taken in their full, metaphysical, sense, but in an extended sense to cover whatever can be understood or signified *as if after the manner of a form*. Cajetan will say that the "nature" is simply "that which is signified by the definition," to be contrasted with the "supposit" or referent of the term, which has that nature.[4] Again, in such contexts, "by the name 'form' we understand anything by which something is said to be such and such, whether it is really an accident, or substance, or matter, or form."[5] So the difference between a "nature" or "form" in its strict, metaphysical sense, and its broader logical or semantic sense, is that in the former sense it is some real quiddity of a thing, while in the latter case it is whatever a word can signify. Cajetan explains this difference at some length:

Note that just as the *what of the thing* [*quid rei*] is the quiddity of the thing, so the *what of the name* [*quid nominis*] is the quiddity of the name. However, the name, since it is essentially a sign of those passions which are objectively in the soul according to *Perihermenias* 1, does not have another quiddity except this, that it is the sign of something understood or thought: a sign, however, as such, is relative to what is signified. Whence to know the *what of the name* is nothing other than to know to what such a name has a relation as sign to signified. Such knowledge, however, can be acquired through accidents of that signified thing, through common characteristics, through essential characteristics, through nods, and whatever other ways, as by asking a Greek the *what of the name* "*anthropos*," if by a finger he indicated a man, then we perceive the *what of the name*; and similarly of others. But in asking the *what of the thing*, it would be necessary to assign that which belongs to the thing signified in the first mode of adequate perseity. And this is the essential difference between the *what of the name* and the *what of the thing*, namely that the *what of the name* is the relation of the name to the signified, while the *what of the thing* is the essence of the thing related or signified. And from this difference there follow all others which are usually said, such as that the *what of the name* may be of complex non-beings, by accidental, common, or extraneous characteristics; while the *what of the thing* is of an incomplex being known properly and essentially. For the relation of the word can terminate in what is not a being in the nature of things, and in what is complex, and can be declared through accidents, and suchlike; while the essence of the thing is not had except through the essential properties of incomplex entities.[6]

In light of contemporary philosophical concerns, and familiar criticisms of scholastic logic, two things are worth emphasizing. First, by speaking of a "concept" Cajetan is not introducing some controversial psychological or epistemological entity, but simply giving a name to a necessary element of the activities of thought and speech. Wittgensteinian and other criticisms of "concepts" in philosophy of mind and philosophy of language notwithstanding, Cajetan's "concepts," understood in the sense that he intended them as the intellectual acts that mediate conception and signification, are just not the kind of things whose existence could be contested. Someone who denied that there were such concepts, or that he had any such concepts, would be denying that he understood anything, or that he uttered significant speech.[7]

Similarly, the claim that what words signify are "forms" or "natures" should be seen as more universally acceptable than it otherwise might. For as we have seen, reference to "forms" or "natures" in the context of logic is reference not to metaphysical forms *in rerum natura* but to whatever can be understood by simple acts of apprehension,

or signified by simple terms. That these are *not* forms in the metaphysician's sense is perhaps most easily seen from the fact that we can
think about and refer to nonexistent things, to privations, to beings
of reason, none of which would, on a standard Aristotelian hylomorphist account, be construed as real forms or real natures.[8] Indeed, it is
worth pointing out that in principle such "forms" or "natures" need
not even imply an Aristotelian hylomorphist metaphysics or philosophy of nature[9] (though of course both are present in Cajetan). Furthermore, we see in this clarification the material for an answer to the
famous nominalist charge that realists multiplied entities for every
significant term.[10]

Cajetan and other semantic "realists" did not distinguish logical
from metaphysical "forms" or "natures" merely as an *ad hoc* strategy
of ontological reduction; the distinction quite naturally follows from
the nature of logic and the observation with which we began this discussion, that the business of logic is to consider things not as they are
in reality but as they are understood and signified by the mediation
of human concepts.

It is necessary, however, to clarify further Cajetan's use of the
term 'concept.' Cajetan adopted the later scholastic distinction between the "formal concept" (*conceptus formalis*, also sometimes the
conceptus mentis or *conceptus mentalis*, "mental concept") and the "objective concept."[11] As Cajetan explains the distinction:

Note that there are two sorts of concepts: formal and objective. The
formal concept is some likeness that the possible intellect forms in
itself, and which is objectively representative of the thing understood; this by the philosophers is called the intention or the concept,
by the theologians the word. The objective concept is the thing represented by the formal concept, terminating the act of understanding; for example, the formal concept of a lion is that image which
the possible intellect forms of leonine quiddity, when it wants to
understand it; but the objective concept of the same is the leonine
nature itself, represented and understood. Nor should it be thought
when it is said that a name signifies a concept that it signifies only
one of these; for the name "lion" signifies both, albeit in different
ways; it is the sign of the formal concept as of the means, or *that by*

which [it signifies], and it is the sign of the objective concept as of the end, or *that which* [it signifies].[12]

So what Cajetan here calls the "formal concept" is what was introduced above as simply the concept, that which mediates thought and signification. What Cajetan here calls the "objective concept" sounds like what has already been introduced as the object of such a mediating intention, the "nature" that is understood or signified. This is why, in other contexts, Cajetan will assimilate the "objective concept" to the "*res*" or "*res extra anima*" of the semantic triangle.[13] Indeed, it is fair to think of the objective concept and the signified nature as the same thing, with this qualification: considered as the *nature*, it is the object of understanding and signification *considered just in itself*, while considered as the *objective concept*, it is this object considered as terminating an act of thought or signification—that is, *considered as an object of conception*. So the objective concept, even though it is in some sense what is "outside" of the soul (*res extra anima*), is also "in" the soul—not in it as in a subject, as the formal concept is in the soul, but in the soul as the object of the intellect's attention.[14]

Another and related term that plays a role in Cajetan's understanding of signification is "*ratio*." The word is notoriously difficult to translate. Among the main English renderings that have been employed are "content,"[15] "analysis,"[16] and "formality."[17] In clarifying the use of "*ratio*" in a passage from Aristotle's *Categories* (a passage that will prove relevant to our discussion of analogy), Cajetan says that the *ratio* is the definition, when there is a definition, and otherwise it is what is "directly signified by the name." In either case, Cajetan suggests translating "*ratio*" as "*conceptus*." It would seem from this context that by this suggestion Cajetan does not intend the *formal concept* or mediating intellectual intention, but what this formal concept represents to the intellect as terminating its act—that is, the *objective concept*.[18] However, in another context, Cajetan will clarify that "*ratio*" can be taken in either way, as indicating the definition, or as indicating the formal concept.[19]

It should not be surprising, then, that the *ratio* can be said both to be in things and to be in the intellect. Indeed, the *ratio* appears to be even more versatile than the objective concept, which as we have just seen is in the intellect objectively, and outside of the intellect as what is understood. The *ratio* can be considered (1) as in a thing, as its own individual intelligible structure, prior to and independent of our thought and signification; (2) in itself, as just the intelligible structure that it is, which may be intellectually abstracted from things and serve as an object of signification; (3) as that intelligible structure, considered insofar as it is actually conceived and signified by means of an intellectual intention (the objective concept); and (4) as that very intellectual intention or "mental word" by which that intelligible structure is understood, the quality inhering in the intellect which mediates thought and signification (the formal concept).

PREDICATION

It is in the second of these four ways of understanding the *ratio* that we can say that the *ratio* is predicated of something. Indeed, this is why, when there is a definition (*id quo explicatur nominis significatum*), it can replace the *ratio* without changing the sense of the predication. Cajetan subscribes to what has been called "the inherence theory" of predication, according to which to predicate a common term of something is to signify the inherence of the significate of the predicate in that thing.[20] So a predication is true if and only if the significate of the predicate actually inheres in that of which it is predicated. Here, we must distinguish between what is predicated, and what verifies the predication. The significate of the predicate is what is predicated, and its actuality in the subject is what verifies the predication. Put another way, what is predicated is the nature, absolutely considered—that is, the nature considered in itself without any of the conditions that accompany it as it exists in a particular thing. That is why, when I say, "Socrates is a man," I predicate of Socrates only what is included in the significate of "man," namely humanity.[21] But what verifies the predication is the actual humanity in Socrates—that is, *Socrates' humanity*, the individuated nature by virtue of which Socrates is a real living human being.[22]

In the example just given there happens to be a neat correspondence between the *ratio* of humanity, which is predicated, and the real nature *humanity*, which verifies the predication. This will not always be the case, because what it is for the significate to be actual or to exist will be different with different kinds of significates. For instance, when the *ratio* is a privation, the actuality of that *ratio* will be the absence of the corresponding positive form. The typical example is "blindness," which is actualized when someone lacks the real form, sight. Indeed, in this case, this is just what blindness is—the absence of sight—which would presumably be spelled out in the definition of the *ratio* of blindness. But privations are not the only complicating cases, and in general we can say that what it is for a significate or *ratio* to be actual in something will vary with the kind of significate or *ratio* that it is.

Indeed, although we can say in general that for Cajetan a predication is true if and only if the significate of the predicate *is* (or *exists* or *is actual*) in its subject, there will prove to be different senses of "being" (or "existing," or "being actual") which are appropriate for different kinds of significates.[23] A fuller account of these different senses, and how they are systematically related, would be needed for any really thorough explanation of Cajetan's semantic principles.[24] For our purposes, the essential point is only that different kinds of predicates will have different verification conditions—that is, different senses in which the significates of the predicates can be actual.[25]

DENOMINATION

The notion of denomination will be of particular importance for understanding certain claims Cajetan makes about the properties of different modes of analogy. Considered generally, denomination seems to be closely allied to predication; a term denominates those things for which it can supposit—that is, those things of which it is truly predicable. In the typical construction, a thing is denominated by a term *from* something. That *from* which something is denominated is the denominating *form* (again, a form in the semantic, rather than metaphysical, sense). In many cases, this denominating form may just be the form signified by the denominating term, as a white thing is denominated "white" on account of its whiteness. Thus, in the discussion at the beginning of the *Categories*, Aristotle's "paronyms" (*paronuma*, 1a12) was translated as "denominatives" (*denominativa*), and in commenting on the passage Cajetan describes a strict sense of denomination in which the denominating form is just that which the denominating term signifies.[26]

But this strict sense of denomination is not the most commonly employed. There are clearly other senses in which the denominating form is not simply the significate of the term but a part of its significate or some other connotation or consignificate. It seems that it was usually thought that the denominating form would have some connection to the etymology of a term. Thus denomination is closely allied with *imposition*—the denominating form could, in principle, be understood as that from which a term is imposed. However, it appears that where that from which a term is imposed to signify is *merely* an etymology unconnected with the terms current signification, it was not considered the denominating form.[27] So it seems to be that the denominating form needs to be somehow consignified by the term, in such a way that it would appear as a part of its *ratio*—that is, it would be included as part of the definition of that thing insofar as it is denominated by that term. For instance, something that is not itself a living, healthy creature can be called "healthy" insofar as it helps *produce* or gives *evidence of* a living healthy creature, so that a meal or a urine sample may not actually possess the relevant denominating form (*health* or *healthiness*) which is nevertheless that on account of which they are called "healthy." This observation, then, raises the question that will be addressed in terms of whether, on given occasions, denomination is "intrinsic" or "extrinsic."

EXTRINSIC VS. INTRINSIC DENOMINATION

Though it becomes commonly invoked by later scholastic philosophers, the technical distinction between intrinsic and extrinsic denomination has murky origins.[28] Though there are passages in Aquinas that seem to describe and employ the distinction,[29] it does not appear to be referred to as such in a technical way.[30] The distinction is formulated in the *Summa Totius Logicae*, long spuriously attributed to Aquinas,[31] as follows:

Now something can be predicated denominatively, or can denominate that thing, in two ways. In one way such predication or denomination is made from something which is intrinsic to that of which such predication or denomination is made, which namely perfects that thing either by identity or inherence. . . . In the second way denomination is made from the extrinsic, namely from that which is not formally in the denominated thing, but is some extrinsic absolute, from which the denomination is made.[32]

It is completely in accord with this that John Doyle has offered the following description of extrinsic denomination: "Extrinsic denomination [is] a designation of something not from anything inherent in itself, but from some disposition, coordination, or relationship which it has toward something else."[33] Doyle's description serves to explicate the obvious sense of the terms, that in extrinsic denomination something is *named from* something that is extrinsic to it, something that, by implication, is intrinsic to, or "inheres in," something else. Indeed, Doyle's mention of a "disposition, coordination, or relationship . . . toward something else" recalls a discussion in the *Summa Totius Logicae* in which the denominating form is described as the foundation to which the denominated thing is related:

> It must be known that extrinsic denomination requires some essential relation between the extrinsic denominating [form] and what is denominated from it . . . and therefore it is necessary that that from which such denomination is made is the essential foundation of this relation.[34]

Cajetan seems to think that this description does not entirely capture all cases of extrinsic denomination. Sometimes extrinsic denomination requires that the denominating form be an extrinsic foundation of a relation; other times it needs only to be a relation itself, which is extrinsic. Defining both of these in contrast with intrinsic denomination, Cajetan says:

> Denomination is twofold, sometimes intrinsic, and sometimes extrinsic. It is called intrinsic denomination when the denominating form is in that which is denominated, as white, quantity, etc.; while denomination is extrinsic when the denominating form is not in

the denominated thing, as location, measure, and the like. . . . But there are two ways in which it occurs that something is said to be such from something extrinsic. In one way, so that the *ratio* of the denomination is that relation to something extrinsic, as urine is called "healthy" only by its relation as sign to health. In the other way, so that the *ratio* of the denomination is not the relation of similitude, or whatever else, but the form which is the foundation of the relation of similitude to something extrinsic: as air is said to be "bright" [*lucidus*] from the brightness of the sun [*luce solari*].[35]

So something can be denominated extrinsically either by an extrinsic relation, or an extrinsic foundation of a relation.

This might suggest that talk of extrinsic and intrinsic denomination is just a sophisticated way of describing *metaphysical* states of affairs, rather than of making a *logical* claim about the semantic function of terms. Indeed, when medieval authors said that a term denominates intrinsically or extrinsically, it is clear that they often meant to be making a metaphysical claim. Some of the typical examples of terms that were said to denominate extrinsically—in addition to the ones mentioned, common examples include "is seen" (*videtur*), or "is understood" (*intelligitur, cognoscitur*)—are often so described in contexts that make it clear that the main point is metaphysical: that when an object becomes such, it is not because of some real change in it, but because something else has changed.[36] In such cases, it is safe to say that to speak of intrinsic or extrinsic denomination, while on the surface it pertained to terms, was in fact intended as a device to describe properties of things.[37]

It is interesting, however, that the metaphysical claim was couched in semantic language. The claim seems to be the following:

A term P denominates some thing x extrinsically iff for the form signified by P to be actual in x is for some other form F, consignified by P, to be actual in something other than x.

According to this definition, determining whether a predicate denominates extrinsically would indeed require metaphysical consideration of what it is for a significate to be actual. But could it ever follow from the *semantics* of a term that for the significate to be actual in some thing is for some form to be actual in something *else?*

Apparently this was considered to be so in the case of the category of *relatives*, where reference to something else is built into the *ratio* of a relation.[38] As Aquinas put it, "Amongst those which are called relatives, something is denominated not only from that which is in it, but also from that which is extrinsic to it."[39] Indeed, both of Cajetan's alternative occasions of extrinsic denomination described above (air called "bright" and urine "healthy") require that there be a relation between the thing being denominated and something extrinsic to it on account of which it is denominated. While this may still look like a metaphysical claim, even if it is one that seems bound up with the semantics of terms, we must remember that in speaking of the categories, the medieval tradition took it that we were speaking not of things as they are in themselves, but of things as they are signified by our terms.[40]

One way to see that "denominating extrinsically" can be regarded as a semantic property of a term is to imagine a case where the semantic claim and the corresponding metaphysical claim, which usually coincide, would diverge, for example a case in which we want to make the *semantic* claim that a term denominates a thing extrinsically, but the corresponding *metaphysical* claim—that the thing denominated does not actually possess the denominating form—would be *false*. We can contrive such a case by altering the classic example of extrinsic denomination, when something is denominated as "seen" (*videtur*). Suppose that what is seen is the very object that is doing the seeing. For example, when I look at myself in the mirror, we could say that my eye sees itself, and so my eye is seen by itself.[41] From the metaphysical point of view, "seen" here does not seem to denominate the eye extrinsically; the sight by virtue of which the eye is seen inheres in it, because, *ex hypothesi*, it is that very eye that is seeing.

But from the point of view of semantics, it is completely accidental that that which is denominated as "seen" because of its relation to sight happens to be the very thing in which the sight inheres. But then we are justified in saying that, from the point of view of the semantics, the eye is denominated as "seen" not intrinsically but extrinsically. To be more precise, we could say that, *insofar as it is seen*, the actuality of the object of sight (viz., the eye) is distinct from the actuality of the sight, indeed, that the sight is *logically* extrinsic to the thing seen, even if in this case it happens not to be *metaphysically* extrinsic.

This is not just a clever theoretical exercise. There are good textual grounds for making this distinction between a metaphysical and a semantic reading of claims about intrinsic or extrinsic denomination. Indeed, the very distinction I am exploiting, between considering the denomination relation from the metaphysical point of view and considering it from the semantic point of view, is expressed in Cajetan's distinction between taking a relation *materially* or *formally*:

> The term "to something [*ad aliquid*]" or "relative" can be taken in two ways, namely: *materially*, for that thing which is relative or is denominated *to something* [*ad aliquid*]; and *formally* for that relation or thing *as it has* [*ut habet*] the relation. For example, "lord" can be taken for that man, who is denominated lord; and it can be taken for [that man] *insofar as he has* lordship [*in quantum dominium habet*].[42]

Consistent with Cajetan's precision, then, we could clarify the definition of extrinsic denomination given above to make explicit that it is to be taken "formally" and not "materially"—that is, as making a semantic as opposed to a metaphysical claim:

> A term P denominates some thing x extrinsically iff for the form signified by P to be actual in x is for some other form F, consignified by P, to be actual in something other than x *insofar as x is P*.

On this definition, even though in our example of the eye seeing itself, for *being seen* to be actual in the eye is for that very eye to have an act of sight *inherent* in or intrinsic to it, we can still say that the denomination of that eye as "being seen" is *extrinsic*, because for the eye to be seen, insofar as it is seen, is not for that act of sight as such to be in that eye; because, of course, sight is in that eye only insofar as the eye *sees*, and it is only by accident, from the semantic point of view, that in this case the eye that *sees* is the same eye that *is seen*.

In sum, then, claims about a term denominating extrinsically (or intrinsically) can be understood as having semantic, as opposed to metaphysical, weight; that is to say, talk of extrinsic or intrinsic denomination can be a matter of the semantic properties of terms, rather than a matter of the metaphysical characteristics of the things denominated by the terms. That is why this discussion is properly included in a sketch of Cajetan's semantic principles; but it is especially appropriate as a preparation for a reading of Cajetan's *De Nominum Analogia*, for, as we will see in the next chapter, it helps us understand some of the most controversial claims that Cajetan makes there, namely that analogy of attribution always involves extrinsic denomination, and analogy of proportionality always involves intrinsic denomination.

— LET THIS SUFFICE, THEN, AS A GENERAL PREPARATION FOR THE philosophical context of Cajetan's *De Nominum Analogia*. It needs repeating that this is not a complete outline of Cajetan's semantic framework. Other topics common to medieval semantics (e.g., supposition, *modi significandi*, ampliation, the different semantic properties of abstract and concrete terms) have been omitted here, and a thorough reconstruction of Cajetan's semantic principles would include discussion of these and other issues. But what has been discussed will allow us to appreciate Cajetan's strategy for characterizing the unity of the analogical concept, and to understand the central and often controversial claims that Cajetan makes about analogy in general and about the different particular forms it can take.

Chapter Six

The Semantics of Analogy

Inequality and Attribution

This is the first of four chapters that directly explicate Cajetan's teaching on analogy in *De Nominum Analogia*. It will consider his definitions of analogy at the beginning of that treatise, and his relatively brief discussions of analogy of inequality and analogy of attribution. It is relevant to begin, however, with a consideration of two earlier works, Cajetan's commentaries on Aquinas's *De Ente et Essentia* (1495) and on Aristotle's *Categories* (1498). The prior writings prove valuable because they show us how Cajetan was developing an analysis of the semantics of analogy before he wrote the *De Nominum Analogia*, thus helping to clarify precisely what is, and what is not, novel in his more dedicated and systematic treatment. Specifically, it confirms that Cajetan's *De Nominum Analogia* was intended to answer particular questions about the semantics of analogy: characterizing the unity of the analogical concept, and explaining how, at least in some cases, such a nonunivocal unity may suffice to preserve the validity of demonstrative syllogisms.

THE *CATEGORIES* AND *DE ENTE ET ESSENTIA* COMMENTARIES

Cajetan briefly touched on analogy in his commentary on Aristotle's *Categories*, in the context of the discussion of equivocal terms. Aristotle's definition had said that equivocals have a common name but were different with respect to the concept. Cajetan clarifies the sense of "diversity" or "difference":

> The word "diverse" is not taken for simple diversity, but is commonly accepted as it comprehends under itself diversity *simply*, and *in some respect* [*secundum quid*], total or partial, so that they are called equivocals both whose concept [*ratio*] according to that common name is entirely diverse, and whose concept [*ratio*] according to that common name is in some way diverse.[1]

By interpreting Aristotle as intending this more general sense of diversity or difference, Cajetan can say that Aristotle means implicitly to include analogy in his definition of equivocation. Thus Cajetan continues:

> And because of this, do not say that here are defined only pure equivocals, which are also called *equivocals by chance* [*aequivoca a casu*], but that here are defined equivocals in general, as comprehending analogues, which are *equivocals by choice* [*aequivoca a consilio*], and pure equivocals; and pure equivocals have concepts [*rationes substantiae*] *entirely* diverse, while analogues [have concepts] diverse *in some way* [*aliquo modo*].[2]

Cajetan offers two pieces of evidence that it is Aristotle's intention to include analogues among equivocals. One is that Aristotle's examples of equivocals—a man, and a picture of a man, which can both be called "animal"—count as an instance of equivocals by choice. The other is the intention of the work, which is to define things as they are united under transcendental words, which are not purely equivocal but analogical.[3]

Cajetan suggests that there is more to say on the subject of analogy:

> But about *how many ways analogy varies*, and *how*, since now we speak in summary, we pass over in silence; I aim to make a special treatise about this, if it please God.[4]

Here is the promise that was fulfilled, later that same year, in the treatise *De Nominum Analogia*.

However, even before that treatise, Cajetan had spoken to the question of "how many ways analogy varies," in his commentary on the *De Ente et Essentia* of Aquinas.[5] There, following the definitions of equivocation and univocation from Aristotle's *Categories*, Cajetan had already given a rough definition of analogy:

> They are univocals whose name is common, and the concept [*ratio*] according to that name is absolutely the same. They are pure equivocals whose name is common and the concept [*ratio*] according to that name is absolutely diverse. They are analogates whose name is common, and the concept [*ratio*] according to that name is somehow the same, and somehow different [*aliquo modo eadem, et aliquo modo diversa*], or the same in some respect, and different in some respect [*secundum quid eadem, et secundum quid diversa*].[6]

As a general characterization of analogy, this much was, in fact, entirely conventional. But within the framework of this characterization Cajetan began to sketch different ways in which analogy can occur, as different ways in which we can say that a concept or concepts are *unum secundum quid* and *diversa secundum quid*. Indeed, within this framework Cajetan must address the question, pressed by Scotus, of how analogy, considered as a kind of equivocation (*aequivocatio a consilio*), can avoid the fallacy of equivocation. As we will see, Cajetan shows himself already attuned to this question in his *De Ente et Essentia* commentary.

Because Cajetan, in this part of the commentary, is considering analogy as involving a *ratio* that is "somehow the same, and somehow different, or the same in some respect, and different in some respect," he does not here discuss what he will later call analogy of inequality, since this "mode" of analogy is really a form of univocation, having a *ratio* entirely the same. But Cajetan had mentioned analogy of inequality earlier in the commentary, when he introduced the notion of predication *per prius et posterius*. Cajetan wrote:

There are two ways in which something can be predicated *per prius et posterius*. By one way, according to the being [*secundum esse*] of that predicate. By another way, according to the proper concept [*secundum propriam rationem*] of it. That is said to be predicated analogically according to being [*secundum esse*] which has a more perfect being [*esse*] in one than in another; and thus every genus is predicated *per prius et posterius* of its species, so that it necessarily has a more perfect being [*esse*] in one species than in another.[7]

For the predication *per prius et posterius* of genus terms, what he will later call analogy of inequality, Cajetan cites the authority of Averroës. Yet he immediately dismisses the consideration of terms *secundum esse* as irrelevant to his present concerns, for in this sense even Scotus would agree that "being" is said analogically of substance and accident, because Scotus can say that though "being" is a genus term the species of substance is more perfectly being than the species of accident. The argument between the Thomists and the Scotists, according to Cajetan, is whether "being" said of substance and accident is said *per prius et posterius* in the other way—that is, *secundum propriam rationem*.

It was in order to answer this question that Cajetan described analogy as a mean between univocation and equivocation, in the words cited above. Cajetan continues by distinguishing two different ways in which this mean between univocation and equivocation can occur:

Note that there are two kinds of analogates: some according to a determinate relation of one to another, and some according to proportionality. For example: substance and accident are analogates in the first way under the term "being"; but God and creature are analogates in the second way, for the distance between God and creature is infinite [and therefore there can be no determinate relation between them]. These differ in several ways: since analogates of the first sort are so disposed that the secondary, insofar as it is named by the analogue, is defined in terms of the first—as *accident*, insofar as it is a *being*, is defined in terms of *substance*. But this is not the case with analogates of the second sort; for *creature*, insofar as it is a *being*, is not defined in terms of *God*.[8]

Sometimes analogates have a determinate relation to each other, sometimes they are related by proportionality. In terminology, this much of Cajetan's presentation seems to be nothing more than a reconstruction of what Aquinas says about the difference between proportion and proportionality in *De Veritate* q. 2, a. 11. (Cajetan does not cite that text here, but he does cite it a few paragraphs later when applying this twofold distinction to a particular theological conclusion.) Cajetan goes further, however, translating this discussion into the terms of the semantic problem of specifying how there is a mean between univocation and equivocation—how, that is, the concept (or concepts) can be the same in some respect and different in some respect:

> Whence analogates of the first sort have a common name, and the *ratio* according to that name is in some way the same and in some way different, in this sense: *that the analogue is said simply, that is without addition of anything, of the first, and of the others it is only said with some relation to the first, which falls in their definitions,* as is manifest in the example of "healthy."
> Now analogates of the second sort have the name in common and the *ratio* according to that name is in some way the same and in some way different, not because it is said simply of the first and of the others by relation to the first, but *they have the* ratio *in some way the same because of the identity of proportion, which is found in them, and they are in some way different because of the diversity of the natures of the supposits of those proportions.* For example: the form and matter of a substance and the form and matter of an accident are somehow analogates under the names "form" and "matter." Indeed, they have the common name, namely "form" and "matter," and the *ratio* according to the name "form" or "matter" is the same and diverse in this way, because the form of the substance is so disposed to the substance, as the form of the accident is to the accident; similarly the matter of the substance is so disposed to the substance,

as the matter of the accident is to the accident. Indeed both preserve the identity of proportion with the diversity of the nature and the unity of the name. This kind of analogy was mentioned by Averroës (*XII Met.*, com. 28), and more clearly by Aristotle (*Nich. Eth.* I, 6 [1096b29–30]).[9]

Cajetan here offers definitions of two sorts of analogy. In analogy of proportion, the analogous concept is "the same in some respect and different in some respect" in this way, that "the analogue is said simply, that is without addition of anything, of the first, and of the others it is only said with some relation to the first." In analogy of proportionality, the analogous concept is "the same in some respect and different in some respect" in this way, that the "*ratio* [is] in some way the same because of the identity of proportion, which is found in them, and they are in some way different because of the diversity of the natures of the supposits of those proportions."

Much will turn on what Cajetan has to say about "identity of proportion." But leaving aside until the next chapter what "identity of proportion" is, I highlight here the following points about Cajetan's presentation: *First*, the essentials of Cajetan's threefold division of analogy are already set out here in Cajetan's commentary on the *De Ente et Essentia*. What will three years later, in *De Nominum Analogia*, be called "analogy of inequality" is here described as signifying *per prius et posterius secundum esse*; what will be called "analogy of attribution" is here called "analogy of proportion"; and what will be called "analogy of proportionality" is here called by that name. The fact that this threefold division is articulated here without much fanfare suggests that Cajetan did not think he was setting out anything controversial or new; and the fact that it is done several years before *De Nominum Analogia* suggests that the purpose of the later work cannot have been merely to introduce and articulate that threefold division. Nor can the threefold division as presented in *De Nominum Analogia* have been some hasty or unconsidered proposal.

Second, only in one mode of analogy are secondary analogates defined in terms of the primary analogate (namely by some *relation* to the primary analogate). This is the mode that Cajetan will later call

analogy of attribution. In the analogy of proportionality, the secondary analogates are *not* defined in terms of the primary analogate, because they are not referred to by the analogical term just by reason of
a *relation* to the primary analogate.

Third, already it is clear that the same term can be analogous in
different ways, in different contexts. Cajetan's example in the passage
quoted above is "being." Said of God and creatures, "being" is analogous by proportionality. God is not called a being just because he is
somehow related to the being of creatures; nor are creatures called
beings just because they are somehow related to the being of God. But
being can be analogous by attribution, as when it is said of substance
and accident, for accident can be called being because of its relation to
the being of substance. Even more importantly, however, even as said
just of substance and accident "being" can be predicated *both* by analogy of attribution *and* by analogy of proportionality;[10] that is to say,
accident and substance can be considered as analogates insofar as one
is related to the other, and insofar as they are proportionally one.[11]

Fourth, Cajetan does not claim to be simply interpreting Aquinas. Cajetan does say that in giving the distinction between attribution and proportionality he is stating the position of Aquinas (*CDEE*
§17, "*ponetur opinio S. Thomae*"). And Cajetan eventually cites the
authority of *De Veritate* q. 2, a. 11, which describes different kinds
(*modi*) of analogy, one involving proportion, the other proportionality. However, the first authorities that Cajetan cites in support of his
distinction are Aristotle and Averroës. Furthermore, and more importantly, there is no mention here of *I Sent.* d. 19, q. 5, a. 2, ad 1, with
its contrast between analogy "*secundum esse*" and "*secundum intentionem*," a text usually cited as the basis of Cajetan's distinction between
modes of analogy.[12]

Fifth, in the *De Ente et Essentia* commentary Cajetan's discussion
of attribution (or proportion) and proportionality does not mention
intrinsic and extrinsic denomination. So it is manifest here that Cajetan does not define his modes of analogy in terms of intrinsic and
extrinsic denomination, as some of his interpreters have charged.

Sixth and last, Cajetan only asserts that analogy of proportionality
is sufficient for valid reasoning, but he does not explain how or why

this is true. Describing the unity that attends analogy of proportionality, Cajetan simply says that since such unity suffices for the object of science, according to Aristotle, being does not need to be univocal in order to be the basis for a contradiction.[13] So there is a concern to show, in response to the objections of Scotus, that a nonunivocal term can preserve the validity of scientific inferences.[14] But the response here is only by appeal to the authority of Aristotle, and there is no attempt to explain *why* what Aristotle says is true.

The Definitions from *De Nominum Analogia*

The above observations all suggest that the primary concern of *De Nominum Analogia* is not simply to present a threefold division of analogy. Instead, we will see that in the bulk of that text Cajetan is more concerned with explaining one member of his threefold division, analogy of proportionality, and accounting for how it can play a role in valid reasoning. This requires Cajetan to offer a more specific semantic analysis of analogy than he had offered in his commentaries on Aristotle's *Categories* or Thomas's *De Ente et Essentia*. So when Cajetan does present his threefold division, it is appropriate that his definitions of the three modes of analogy should take a more rigorous logical or semantic form, and that the bulk of his treatise is given over to a discussion of only one form, analogy of proportionality.

Turning to *De Nominum Analogia*, the first thing to notice is that, despite the claims of many of Cajetan's interpreters, Cajetan does *not* define analogy of attribution and analogy of proportionality in terms of extrinsic and intrinsic denomination.[15] As we will see, Cajetan does say that analogy of attribution involves extrinsic denomination, and that analogy of proportionality involves intrinsic denomination; but he presents these as properties or "conditions" (*conditiones*) that *follow from* the definitions of these kinds of analogy.[16] So before we can understand what Cajetan means by these conditions or properties, we must first attend to the proper definitions Cajetan offers for the various kinds of analogy.

Cajetan gives the following three definitions in *De Nominum Analogia*:

They are called analogous according to inequality whose name is common, and the *ratio* according to that name is wholly the same, but unequally participated.

They are analogous according to attribution whose name is common, and the *ratio* according to that name is the same with respect to a terminus, and different with respect to relations to that terminus.

They are called analogous according to proportionality whose name is common, and the *ratio* according to that name is proportionally the same.[17]

Note that even more strictly than those offered in *CDEE*, these definitions parallel the definitions of equivocation and univocation from Aristotle's *Categories. They are called . . . whose name is common, and the concept according to that name is . . .*[18] Again, Cajetan clearly wants to show how there are three different ways that we can understand a mean between equivocation and univocation, by showing that there are three different ways in which the concept(s) or *ratio(nes)* can be *aliquo modo eadem, et aliquo modo diversa seu secundum quid eadem, et secundum quid diversa.* To see the importance of these definitions, let us consider each of the three modes of analogy in turn—the first two in the remainder of this chapter, and the last, analogy of proportionality, in the following chapters.

ANALOGY OF INEQUALITY

Let us first briefly consider the case of analogy of inequality. We will need to clear up some common confusion about this controversial mode of analogy, and, in so doing, we will find that Cajetan's treatment of this mode confirms that in *De Nominum Analogia* Cajetan's interest in analogy is primarily semantic. In short, with his treatment of analogy of inequality we see that Cajetan excludes from the scope of his treatise metaphysical considerations that are irrelevant to his properly logical concerns.

Cajetan's "analogy of inequality" is sometimes taken as his own invention, but it is clear that it has precedence in a long tradition. Ashworth points to a phrase from Aristotle, translated into Latin as *"aequivocationes latent in generibus"* (equivocations are hidden in genera; *Physics* 249a22–25), and says, "Virtually every late thirteenth-century author felt obliged to fit this claim into the framework of equivocation and analogy, even if the consensus was that in the end the use of genus terms was univocal."[19] In both his *De Ente et Essentia* commentary and in *De Nominum Analogia*, Cajetan cites Averroës for the claim "that priority and posteriority of species does not impede the unity of the genus."[20]

According to Cajetan's definition of analogy of inequality, the *ratio* is "wholly the same" (*omnino eadem*), but it is "unequally participated" (*inaequaliter participata*). The example Cajetan uses is "body," and, as he says, "the *ratio* of all bodies, insofar as they are bodies, is the same." Nonetheless, that *ratio*, "corporeity," is not "in" all bodies equally. This is the position that sounds most odd, and has confused some commentators. But we can make sense of it if we remember the distinction made above in chapter 5, between what is predicated and what verifies that predication.[21]

Now consider why Cajetan would say that the same *ratio* can be in things unequally. When I predicate "body" of a stone and of a plant, I predicate exactly the same *ratio* or objective concept, the nature corporeity, in both cases. However, when I predicate "body" of stone, what verifies the predication is the particular corporeity of the stone, the individualized actuality by virtue of which the stone is a body. When I predicate "body" of a plant, what verifies the predication is the particular corporeity of the plant, the individualized act by virtue of which the plant is a body. But now, given the thesis of the unicity of substantial forms, and the fact that "body" (*corpus*) is a substantial predicate, we know that the corporeity of the stone is identical with the substantial form of the stone, and the corporeity of the plant is identical with the substantial form of the plant. Again, of course *what* is predicated of stone and plant is exactly the same, namely, the nature corporeity absolutely considered. But the corporeities that *verify* the predications—the individualized substantial natures actual in the stone and in the plant—are clearly not equal given that a plant's nature includes life. In this sense, although the general *ratio* of body applies equally to the plant and the stone, there is more to the particular "bodiliness" of the plant (as including life) than there is to the particular "bodiliness" of the stone. Thus Cajetan can say that "not only is the plant more noble than the stone, but the corporeity of the plant is more noble than the corporeity of the stone."[22]

Now we can see from this that in analogy of inequality, the way in which the different applications of analogous terms differ really does depend on metaphysics, on the state of things *in rerum natura* which verifies various predications. It depends on an order or hierarchy among actualizations in things, and this hierarchy does not affect the semantic properties of the term. There may be more or less actuality in particular instances of a given nature, but insofar as they are all instances of the same nature in general the relevant term always signifies those natures in virtue of exactly the same *ratio*. This is precisely why Cajetan says that analogy of inequality is only improperly called analogy. Here we may recall that "unequal participation" was one of the three inadequate accounts of analogical unity rejected at the beginning of *De Nominum Analogia*. While in one sense Cajetan is willing to count it as one kind of analogy, it is properly, from the logician's point of view, a case of univocation,[23] in truth "wholly foreign to analogy."[24]

That Cajetan dismisses analogy of inequality on these grounds, and does not treat it at all after the brief five paragraphs in the first chapter of *De Nominum Analogia*, should confirm that Cajetan is not interested in confusing his discussion of the *semantics* of analogous terms with *metaphysical* considerations of the things those terms name. To be sure, analogy of inequality counts as a kind of analogy at all only if we include metaphysical considerations; but this is why Cajetan quickly dismisses this kind of analogy, which is analogy only from the point of view of the natural philosopher, but not from the point of view of the logician.[25] But note further that Cajetan's original basis for distinguishing this particular mode of "analogy"—even if it turns out not to be a kind of analogy after all—is indeed properly *semantic* and not *metaphysical*. That is to say, Cajetan distinguishes this kind of "analogy" from the others by a semantic condition, namely, that its "*ratio*" is wholly the same. Indeed, this is precisely why it turns out to be not a kind of analogy at all, but rather an instance of univocation. So not only does this analysis make sense of what Cajetan says of analogy of inequality, but it confirms that Cajetan's interest in *De Nominum Analogia* is genuinely semantic.

This exposition of analogy of inequality should also help clear up some common confusion about it. Herbert Schwartz, for instance, was unable to see how Cajetan could claim that every univocal genus term could be said to be in some things more than others.[26] Schwartz's analysis ignores the fact that, for both Aquinas and Cajetan, when "body" is predicated of a material substance, the significate of the term in that substance is the substance's substantial form. Indeed, in general, when any genus term is predicated of one of its members, its significate in that member is that member's specific form. As explained above, then, a genus term can be more in one of its species than another to the extent that different species have different (higher and lower) substantial forms.[27]

ANALOGY OF ATTRIBUTION

According to Cajetan's definition, analogy of attribution involves a common name, and "the *ratio* according to that name is the same with respect to a terminus, and different with respect to relations to that terminus." In other words, in analogy of attribution there is community with respect to some one form, the form from which all the analogates are denominated. But that form is the proper significate of the analogous term only when predicated of the primary analogate. As predicated of a secondary analogate, the significate of the analogous term is not that form, but rather some relation to that form; that is to say, that form is the terminus of a relation, which relation is what is signified by the analogous term in the secondary analogates. So, Cajetan will say,

> "Healthy" is a name common to medicine, urine, and animal, and the *ratio* of all insofar as they are healthy, says different relations to one term (namely *health*). For if someone says, "What is *animal*, insofar as healthy?" one would say, "*subject of health*." But [one would say that] urine, insofar as healthy, is a *sign of health*; and for medicine, insofar as healthy, is given *cause of health*.[28]

So it is clear that, as predicated of its secondary analogates, a term analogous by attribution signifies a relation,[29] and elsewhere Cajetan will say just this.[30]

It is in this context that we must understand what Cajetan calls the first condition of analogy of attribution: that the secondary analogates are always denominated extrinsically.[31] Note again that, contrary to common interpretation, the distinction between attribution and proportionality is not made on the basis of the distinction between intrinsic and extrinsic attribution; Cajetan has not defined analogy of attribution in terms of extrinsic denomination.[32] Rather, Cajetan describes the extrinsic denomination of the secondary analogates as a "condition" that follows from the properly semantic definition of analogy of attribution.

This clarification helps us to see Cajetan's point here, that it is built into the semantics of the term, and is not dependent on extralogical, metaphysical considerations, that a term analogous by attribution denominates its secondary analogates extrinsically. In analogy of attribution, when we denominate the secondary analogates, we know the denominating form is extrinsic, i.e., is an actuality of another, because *ex hypothesi* there is a difference between the primary analogate (which has the form) and the secondary analogate (which is denominated with reference to that form in the primary analogate). So it follows from the definition of analogy of attribution that, when denominating secondary analogates, it signifies a relation, from which it follows that it denominates those analogates extrinsically. So saying that this kind of analogy involves the extrinsic denomination of the secondary analogates is here a properly semantic, as opposed to metaphysical, claim, as it follows from a strictly semantic specification of analogy of attribution.

In fact, Cajetan goes out of his way to clarify that his words about extrinsic denomination are meant to be taken as having logical, or semantic, as opposed to metaphysical, import. Thus he issues the following *caveat*, one that needs to be discussed at length because it has been so often misunderstood:

It must be carefully pointed out, that this condition of this kind of analogy—namely that it is not according to a kind of formally inherent cause, but always according to something extrinsic—is to be understood formally and not materially. That is, it is not to be understood by this that every name which is analogous by attribution is common to its analogates such that it only agrees with the first formally, and with the rest by extrinsic denomination—as happens with "healthy" and "medical." For universally this is false, as is clear from "being" [*ens*] and "good." Nor can it be had from what was said, unless it was understood materially. Rather, it must be understood from this that every name analogous by attribution *as such*, or *insofar as so analogous*, is common to its analogates such that it agrees with the first formally and with the rest by extrinsic denomination.[33]

Cajetan's qualification—which recalls the general distinction, discussed in the last chapter, between taking a relation *materially* and *formally*—is central to Cajetan's explanation of the occurrence of "mixed cases"—that is, cases in which there can be analogy of attribution, even if in fact the secondary analogates have an intrinsic form. To illustrate, Cajetan discusses the example of "being":

> *Being* [*ens*] indeed, though it formally agrees with all substances and accidents, etc., nevertheless, insofar as all are called beings from subjective being as such, only substance is formally being, while the rest are called *beings* because they are passions or generations, etc., *of* being—although they could be called beings formally for another reason.[34]

Cajetan's clarification and its application to mixed cases have been misunderstood or ignored by many commentators. Several commentators have expressed their puzzlement over Cajetan's position,[35] and some scholars have gone so far as to take this clarification as an implicit admission of weakness in Cajetan's analysis, a desperate attempt to patch up an incoherent theory. Thus McInerny, for instance, has argued that Cajetan here presents "tortured language needed to defend an indefensible position."[36] McInerny perceives here further evidence that the distinction between intrinsic and extrinsic denomination is irrelevant to analogy, thus vitiating Cajetan's very distinction between modes of analogy.[37]

A more charitable interpretation can be given to Cajetan's claim here, an interpretation that confirms Cajetan's consistent attention to logical or semantic, as opposed to metaphysical, concerns. According to Cajetan, "being" is analogous both by attribution and by proportionality: an accident does have its own inherent being, but is also related to the being of substance, and *insofar* as an accident is denominated a being by analogy of attribution—that is, insofar as it is denominated a being *because* of its relation to the being of substance—it is denominated a being by extrinsic denomination.

That is why Cajetan's reduplicative clause is so important: "Every name analogous by attribution *as such*, or *insofar as so analogous*, is common to its analogates such that it agrees with the first formally and with the rest by extrinsic denomination." Again, "*insofar as all are called beings from subjective being as such*, only substance is formally being."[38] As argued in the previous chapter, this is exactly the kind of qualification that is needed to ensure that the consideration of extrinsic denomination is properly logical and not metaphysical. Indeed, we can understand this as just an extension of Cajetan's distinction between interpreting a relation *formally* as opposed to *materially*. Because the analogous term as predicated of the secondary analogates signifies a relation, and because a relation can be understood formally, we can understand formally the claim that the analogous term as predicated of the secondary analogates signifies by extrinsic denomination.

In the previous chapter we used the example of the self-seeing eye to illustrate that extrinsic denomination can be understood as a semantic property. To consider the "mixed cases" of analogy is to do the same thing—that is, to consider a case in which something is extrinsically denominated despite having the relevant intrinsic form. Cajetan's examples of mixed cases are "being" and "good," but we can consider less portentous terms, and even more illustrative examples. Let us posit another scenario in which what is normally taken to be metaphysically extrinsic would in fact be metaphysically intrinsic, and yet its denomination would still be extrinsic. Take "healthy" as predicated of skin.[39] Although "healthy" is the traditional example of a term clearly analogous by attribution, and so exhibiting extrinsic denomination, it is possible, still within the framework of Cajetan's general theory, to attribute some intrinsic health not only to substantial organisms but also to some parts of substantial organisms—for example, organs—and this intrinsic health of living organs would be proportionally similar to the intrinsic health of living organisms. But then "healthy" as said of an animal organ would be like "being" as said of accidents, analogous by both attribution and proportionality. For example, a surgically removed kidney could be called "healthy" not only because it came from a healthy person but because it still exhibits its own well-ordered vital functioning (by virtue of which it could be a suitable candidate for transplant). In this case, we can say that there is an inherent health in the kidney, and in fact this may be why we normally call organs healthy. (It also may be that the intrinsic health of the organ is causally dependent on the health in the whole organism.)

Even in this case, however, *insofar as it is conceived of* as a *sign* or *effect* of health, an organ (like a kidney, or skin) is not denominated "healthy" because some health (even organ health) is in it, but because it is somehow related to (as sign or effect) the health of the organism; although as a matter of biological fact the health (of the organism) to which the organ is related may be intrinsically related to the organ (giving the organ its own health), this is a *metaphysical* (or merely physical) consideration irrelevant to the *semantics* of the term 'healthy' taken as denominating something as a sign or effect of health. Thus Cajetan's warning to take the rule about extrinsic denomination formally and not materially helps clarify why we can say that even in this case the term 'healthy' denominates extrinsically, and indeed, that it necessarily does, because it is a term analogous by attribution, denominating a secondary analogate insofar as it is a secondary analogate—that is, insofar as it is related to a primary analogate.[40]

It needs emphasizing that the Cajetanian tradition has always agreed that there are cases in which a term can be used by analogy of attribution and yet have secondary analogates that happen to possess an intrinsic form associated with that analogy. The point is that such a case is *logically* contingent, and depends on extralogical, *metaphysical* considerations. This was the position of John of St. Thomas, who conceded that in analogy of attribution, "it is possible that there be presupposed in the secondary analogates some intrinsic respect"; nonetheless that "intrinsic respect" is not that "by which [the secondary analogates] are denominated analogically and placed under the analogous form," rather it is that "by which they are related to that primary analogate, so that as a consequence they are denominated extrinsically and analogically from that [primary analogate]."[41] In other words, there may be some intrinsic metaphysical reason *why* a secondary analogate is related to a primary analogate, but if the secondary analogate is denominated by the analogous term just *as* so related to the primary analogate, as far as the logician is concerned the secondary analogate is denominated extrinsically. So even in mixed cases, from the logicians' point of view, *insofar as a thing is a secondary analogate of a term analogous by attribution*, the term denominates that thing extrinsically.[42]

This account of Cajetan's rule that in analogy of attribution secondary analogates are always denominated extrinsically, and of the clarification that this rule must be taken formally, puts in perspective the common complaint that certain "mixed cases" are left out of Cajetan's threefold division. It has long been objected against Cajetan that there are cases of *intrinsic* attribution. This was Suarez's famous criticism of Cajetan, and it has been voiced by others following Suarez.[43] Indeed, as Ashworth and Riva have shown, commitment to intrinsic attribution seems to have been the more traditional position before Cajetan.[44] The word most commonly thought to exhibit intrinsic attribution was "being" (*ens*). As Ashworth has noticed: "In general, it seems to be the case that people took it for granted that *ens* involved intrinsic denomination, and if '*ens*' was a term analogical by attribution, then obviously there were different kinds of attribution." Thus, Ashworth concludes, "Cajetan's claim that insofar as '*ens*' can be regarded as a term analogical by attribution it must be interpreted as involving extrinsic denomination strikes me as unprecedented."[45]

But Cajetan's position should hardly be surprising. Ashworth's wording is felicitous, because Cajetan only claims that *insofar as* a term is analogical by attribution its secondary analogates are denominated extrinsically; this does not preclude, what Cajetan had always acknowledged, that a term that is analogical by attribution could also, in some other capacity, denominate those things intrinsically. For *"ens"* may involve intrinsic denomination, and *"ens"* may also be analogical by attribution, but it just does not "obviously" follow that there are different kinds of attribution, some involving extrinsic denomination and others involving intrinsic denomination. Instead, we can conclude that there are things named analogously by attribution, which things also happen to have an intrinsic form, which form *can* be signified by that same term, but *not* insofar as that term is analogical by attribution, rather insofar as that term is analogical *in some other way*. If Cajetan is "unprecedented" in seeing this—and it seems that Ashworth is correct in so judging—it is because Cajetan is unprecedented in keeping logical or semantic considerations separate from metaphysical ones.

It is fitting then that Anderson has described the Suarezian criticism of Cajetan as involving a confusion between considering terms *in actu signato* and considering them *in actu exercito*. He says that in his treatment of mixed cases Cajetan is simply observing "the distinction between the order of specification, according to which analogy is considered formally (*in actu signato*), and the order of exercise, according to which analogy is considered materially (*in actu exercito*), as actually existing in the nature of things, as *exercised*."[46] Cajetan's *De Nominum Analogia* considers analogous terms *in actu signato*, while the Suarezians, according to Anderson, consider analogy *in actu exercito*.[47] Taking the forms as they are actually realized in things, rather than as they are signified by terms and conceived of in the mind, thus leads the Suarezians to insist on intrinsic cases of attribution—that is, cases where a secondary analogate's relation to a primary analogate entails something metaphysically inherent in that secondary analogate.[48]

As we have seen, then, not only does Cajetan's treatment of mixed cases require a distinction between considering terms "formally," as opposed to "materially," but even considering terms "formally" requires a distinction between different occasions of a term's use. For a term can be considered *insofar* as it is analogous by attribution (as "being," for example, can be predicated of accidents insofar as it signifies their having some relation to the primary being of sub-stance), or it can be considered in some other way (as "being" can also be predicated of accidents insofar as it signifies their own inherent accidental being). Based on Cajetan's treatment of mixed cases, then, it is clear that Cajetan is not guilty of some of the naive semantic assumptions Ashworth has detected in other medieval authors who tried to describe analogy. Ashworth notes that "medieval logicians . . . discussed analogy and equivocation as if they were properties of single terms, as if neither sentential context nor speaker use and intention were at issue."[49] Thus they tended to "take words as units, endowed both with their signification and their *modi significandi* before they enter sentences and independently of speaker intention on any given occasion."[50] But it is clear that if we can consider a word insofar as it denominates extrinsically, and then consider the same word insofar as it denominates intrinsically, then intrinsic and extrinsic denomina-tion will not be properties that terms have independent of sentential context or speaker intent. Likewise, on Cajetan's conception, being analogical by attribution just cannot be a fixed property of a term to be discerned independently of, and prior to, its use in actual sen-tences. The same term can be analogical by attribution, and analogical some other way, just as the same term can be analogical by attribution ("healthy" as said of the dog and his food) and univocal ("healthy" as said of Fido and of Spot).

Indeed, although Cajetan is trying to analyze analogy in terms of the relations of concepts signified by the analogous term, he is consistent in *not* treating the concept (or *ratio*) as a fixed property of a term independent of its sentential use. Thus, Cajetan does not ask about the *ratio* signified by "healthy," rather he asks, "What is the animal insofar as it is healthy?" and "What is urine insofar as it is healthy?"[51] In other words, what does "healthy" signify *when it is predicated of an animal*, and what does "healthy" signify *when it is predicated of urine*?

All the other properties (or *conditiones*) that Cajetan attributes to this mode of analogy, then, must be understood not as properties of isolated terms, but as properties of terms insofar as they are analogous by attribution—that is, insofar as they are being used to denominate something as being related to something else. And understood in this way, the properties do indeed follow just as Cajetan says they do. We have already seen that since, as predicated of secondary analogates, a term analogous by attribution always signifies a relation, it can be said always to denominate the secondary analogates extrinsically. As Cajetan notices, this also means that for a given analogous term, the terminus of the various relations signified in various secondary analogates (which terminus is directly signified by the analogous term as predicated of the primary analogate) is numerically one.[52] Furthermore, it will also follow that the first analogate is posited in the definition of the rest of the analogates. That is to say, the *ratio* of the significate of an analogous term, as predicated of the secondary analogates, includes reference to the primary analogate, in which the one terminus is signified.[53]

Lastly, it naturally follows from this, and almost goes without saying, that in this kind of analogy there is no significate common to all the analogates.[54] Different secondary senses of the analogous term will signify different relations to the primary sense; so secondary significates will be different from each other, and different from the primary significate. In other words, this is logically speaking a form of equivocation,[55] and indeed the Greeks did not call it analogy but rather a kind of equivocation, equivocation *to one*, or *from one*, or *in one*.[56]

It follows that analogy of attribution will behave in most respects like equivocation, even in causing the fallacy of equivocation. It should not be surprising, then, that Cajetan ends his discussion of analogy of attribution here. Cajetan had ended his discussion of analogy of inequality by noting that there is no need to determine other semantic features, since it will follow the rules for univocation.[57] Just so, he completes his discussion of analogy of attribution by noting that further semantic questions about it are already answered insofar as analogy of attribution will follow the rules of equivocation.[58]

In light of semantic principles presented in the previous chapter, we may now update the diagrams presented above in chapter 2 (figs. 1–3) and present somewhat more accurate diagrams of the relationships involved in the kinds of analogy presented thus far. In general, we may represent two uses of the same word, where the same word denominates different things by denominating forms conceived by their respective concepts, thus:

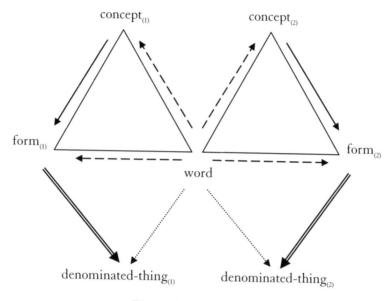

Figure 4. Equivocation

Here the "concept" is what Cajetan calls the formal concept, and the "form" is what he calls the objective concept. The solid arrow represents a relation of natural signification, the dashed arrow represents conventional signification, the double arrow represents the inherence relation, and the dotted arrow represents supposition or denomination. So, in the case of univocation, $concept_{(1)}$ = $concept_{(2)}$—that is, different things are denominated by forms that are the same in *ratio*. In pure equivocation (equivocation by chance), $concept_{(1)}$ and $concept_{(2)}$ are unrelated—two things are denominated by forms that are not connected in *ratio*.

In the case of analogy of inequality, $concept_{(1)}$ is identical with $concept_{(2)}$, while $form_{(1)}$ and $form_{(2)}$ are numerically distinct forms that unequally participate in the same *ratio*—that is, they are the same in *ratio* but different in their individual actualizations in their respective things. Thus:

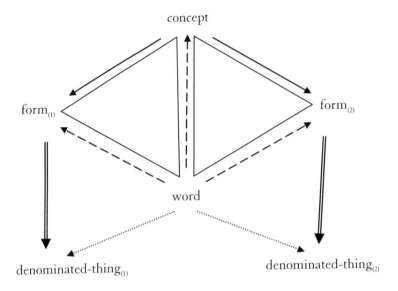

Figure 5. Analogy of Inequality

In analogy of attribution, on the other hand, concept$_{(1)}$ and concept$_{(2)}$ are not identical, but they are connected, insofar as the form by which one thing is denominated is some relation of that thing to the form by which the other is denominated. As a special case of equivocation, this can be depicted by figure 4 above, with the further stipulation that concept$_{(2)}$ is a function on concept$_{(1)}$, because form$_{(2)}$ in denominated-thing$_{(2)}$ is some relation of denominated-thing$_{(2)}$ to form$_{(1)}$ in denominated-thing$_{(1)}$.

This makes quite clear the need for a third way of describing a mean between equivocation and univocation, a third way that two concepts of analogous terms be the same in some respect (*unum secundum quid*) and diverse in some respect (*diversa secundum quid*). We have seen the first two possibilities for such a mean proposed by Cajetan. According to the first, the concepts are the same, full stop (*simpliciter*); they differ only in the character of their realization in things. According to the second, the concepts are diverse, full stop (*simpliciter*), but they are similar insofar as they share a common element— more precisely, one is analyzed in terms of a relation to the other.

The former mean between univocation and equivocation, analogy of inequality, is really a form of univocation. If two concepts are the same *simpliciter*, they will be univocal—no matter how they differ *secundum quid*. The latter mean, analogy of attribution, turns out to conform to the general rules of equivocation—including those rules about the use of those terms in discursive reasoning. If two concepts are diverse *simpliciter*, they will be equivocal, and if their unity *secundum quid* amounts to the *ratio* of one being included in the *ratio* of the other, they will still follow the general rules governing the semantics of equivocals. In particular, they will occasion a fallacy of equivocation if the different concepts are used in discursive reasoning as if they were really the same.

In short, neither mean between univocation and equivocation is a genuine mean—each is functionally equivalent to one or another of the extremes. Cajetan's analysis of analogy proceeds beyond the first two chapters of *De Nominum Analogia* because he discerns some other way that concepts distinct *simpliciter* can be the same *secundum quid*, and because he can argue that this alternative similarity *secundum quid* allows terms that signify those concepts not to follow all the other rules of equivocals. As a more genuine mean between univocation and equivocation, this third mode of analogy will require special treatment as regards such further logical questions as how it is "abstracted," and how it can play a role in reasoning. Only by addressing these issues can Cajetan answer the challenge to the very possibility of a mean between univocation and equivocation, and the very possibility of a nonunivocal term serving to mediate valid inferences.

Chapter Seven

The Semantics of Proportionality

The Proportional Unity of Concepts

We have seen that analogy of attribution is a species of equivocation in which the different concepts are related, so that the *ratio* of one appears in the definition of the others. This seems to be the most obvious mean between univocation and equivocation. But for Cajetan there is another mean: analogy of proportionality. This will turn out to be a truer mean between univocation and equivocation, so that the balance of Cajetan's treatise on analogy expounds the unique semantic characteristics of this analogy, which cannot be subsumed under univocation and equivocation. In the present chapter, we will begin to examine Cajetan's treatment of the definition of analogy of proportionality, and consider some common objections to the "proportional similarity" or "proportional unity" invoked in that definition.

" Analogy" Is an Analogous Term

In turning to analogy of proportionality we are, Cajetan says, "ascending from what is abusively to what is properly analogy."[1] Why this mode of analogy is the most "proper" we have already anticipated: it is expected to meet the semantic challenge that neither analogy of inequality nor analogy of attribution could meet. Our judgment of whether this mode of analogy meets this challenge in fact must be deferred until it has been presented in greater detail, but at the beginning it will be useful to clarify what Cajetan means by saying that certain uses of a term are "proper" and others are "abusive." This is especially important because Cajetan's mention of an "abuse" (*abusio*) of terms, or of things "abusively" (*abusive*) so-called, can help us better understand, if not the semantics, at least the genesis and use of analogous terms. This is also important, because Cajetan's language has the potential to mislead.

In *De Nominum Analogia*, Cajetan uses "*abusio*" or its cognates several times. For instance, he says that many names are called analogous "abusively" (*abusive*, §2); he says that it is an "abuse" (*abusio*) of vocabulary to treat signifying *per prius et posterius* as synonymous with signifying analogically (§7); he says that counting analogy of attribution as a kind of analogy is an "abusive" (*abusiva*) locution (§21); and, as noted, he says that to ascend from analogy of inequality, through analogy of attribution, to analogy of proportionality, is to ascend to the proper from the "abusive" (*abusive*) forms of analogy (§23). In all of these cases, the point seems to be that "analogy" is itself analogical.[2] Originally (in Greek) proper to mathematics and meaning "proportion," the term "*analogia*" was extended to cover other things.[3] Indeed, Cajetan implies that part of the difficulty of explaining what the term means is that it has been extended to cover such a variety of things that it would be confusing to try to unify them with a common definition.[4] What is being discussed is the development of language, a term's being stretched to cover things that it would not cover in its original, or strict, sense. Cajetan's "*abusio*," then, need not call to mind the moral connotations of English "abuse." To say that a term is used *abusive* ("abusively") is not to say that people who so use it are "abusers of language."[5] It is not even to say that the term is used illicitly, but only irregularly, loosely, or in a manner at some remove from its most proper use.[6] That employing an improper sense of a term is not abusing language, or misusing language, is obvious from the legitimacy of poetic or metaphorical usage.[7]

This is especially true if a particular use of a term is abusive or improper only from the etymological, or strictly technical point of view, but not from the point of view of established use. This observation, and Cajetan's discussion of the meaning of "analogy" in general, illuminates a general point about the genesis of analogous terms. Terms become analogical by a process of extension; they are extended from one, original signification to cover another, new signification. Some of these extensions are more fitting than others. What determines the fittingness or "propriety" of such an extension is not only the original meaning of the term, or its etymology, but the similarity of what is signified in what is originally denominated by the term to what is signified in that which the term is stretched to denominate. Etymology and established use may provide a clue to what is primarily, properly, or originally signified, but they do not determine the matter.

We might say that here is an obvious role for judgment in analogy—that is, in discerning the proper signification of a term. Another role for judgment is in discerning the similarity of this primary or original signification to the new signification that the term is extended to cover. Analogy of attribution works because we can extend a word from its original signification to cover something that is related to that original signification. Thus 'healthy' is extended from the animal to the food, because the latter is the cause of the health in the animal originally (and still primarily) signified by the term 'healthy.' But do we judge other kinds of similarities? Here we are back to the question with which we started this chapter. For this is just another way to ask the question: Can two *rationes* be the same *secundum quid* in some way other than one being a relation to the other? Cajetan answers affirmatively, and to see how, we need to turn to his definition of the other form of analogy, analogy of proportionality.

SIMILIS SECUNDUM PROPORTIONEM

Cajetan's definition of analogy of proportionality is as follows:

> They are called analogous according to proportionality, whose name is common, and the *ratio* according to that name is proportionally the same. Or this: they are called analogous according to proportionality, whose name is common and the *ratio* according to that name is similar according to proportion.[8]

On the face of it, this seems like a straightforward formulation, especially given the kind of question Cajetan has posed for himself. How, besides in the manner described for analogy of attribution, can two concepts be the same *secundum quid*? Cajetan's answer is that they can be the same according to proportion (*secundum proportionem*)—that is, proportionally the same. Proportional unity, or proportional sameness, is a perfectly respectable variety of unity or sameness; in the Aristotelian tradition of metaphysics, proportional unity is considered alongside of numeric, specific, and generic unity.[9] According to the terminology introduced earlier, proportional unity is a nongeneric likeness. It is the kind of unity that describes what is common between two things that share no one common element or quality but still bear a commonality or similarity that must therefore be nonunivocal or nongeneric.

It is not yet clear that "proportional unity" answers the further question that Cajetan wanted to answer: How does proportional unity make this kind of deliberate equivocation different enough from other cases of equivocation that it follows its own semantic rules—in particular, how does analogy of proportionality avoid the fallacy of equivocation? Indeed, it is not yet clear that being the same according to proportion is *different* from being the same because of reference to one.[10] Cajetan has not begun to address this yet, but just so far, it seems reasonable that, in looking for a kind of unity or sameness, he should invoke proportional sameness.

To illustrate the analogy of proportionality, Cajetan uses the traditional example of "seeing" (*videre*), which is predicated of bodily vision and of intellectual vision, "because, just as understanding exhibits a thing to the soul, so seeing exhibits a thing to an animated body."[11] Thus, we can predicate "seeing" of the soul because:

(1) *understanding:soul::seeing:body*

Here we use the well-known schema representing proportionality 'A:B::C:D.' However Cajetan quickly points out that the proportional similarity expressed by this schema—the similarity between 'A:B' and 'C:D'—is not enough to ensure genuine analogy of proportionality. Cajetan must distinguish between improper and proper analogy of proportionality—that is, between metaphor and genuine analogy. Taking a conventional example of a metaphor, Cajetan tells us that we can predicate "smiling" of a field, because:

(2) *blooming:field::smiling:man*

How does the case represented by (2) differ from that represented by (1)? Cajetan says that a predication is metaphorical "when that common name has one formal *ratio* absolutely, which is saved in one of the analogates, and is said of others by metaphor." By contrast, analogy of proper proportionality occurs "when that name is common to both of the analogates without metaphor"—that is, so that the signified *ratio* is "saved" in all of the analogates and "said of them proportionally."[12]

Cajetan's explanation here is very cursory, and raises a few difficulties. First, Cajetan seems open to the objection that his definitions are circular: a proportional predication is metaphorical when it is said by metaphor, and a proportional predication is proper when it is not said by metaphor. So we can understand the difference between metaphor and proper proportionality only if we already understand metaphor. Second, one may object that Cajetan's distinction between proper proportionality and metaphor is not based on semantic considerations but on metaphysical ones, namely, on whether or not the relevant formality or *ratio* is or is not realized in all of the analogates.

Responding to the second objection first, I think we can understand why the distinction between metaphor and analogy of proper proportionality is not irrelevant from the logician's point of view. A metaphor is not literally true; it is a predication made by "poetic license"—license, that is, to use words in ways other than their proper sense. Any predication *expresses* the inherence of the form signified by the predicate in the subject. This is true even in predicating "smiles" of a field. But properly speaking the *ratio* signified by "smiles" is not *actually* in the field; rather, there is something in the field (its blooming) that is proportionally similar to what "smiles" signifies in a face (its smiling).[13] But then, strictly speaking there is nothing in the field that verifies the proper *ratio* of "smiles" in it, which just is why we say that the predication is not *literally* true. This is why, properly speaking, the *ratio* of a metaphorical term is not verified of those things of which it is said metaphorically. When it is *known* that a term's *ratio* is not properly verified of certain things but is predicated of them anyway because it is *as if* there were something that verified the predication, then that term is predicated metaphorically. It is not a false predication, because although there is nothing in the field that verifies the form signified by the metaphorical term, there is something in the field that is somehow like what is signified by the metaphorical term. The intention of a metaphorical predication is not to say what is literally true, or to say what is false, but to express some truth by way of an improper terminology.

Still, by distinguishing between what is predicated, and what verifies the predication, it might seem that Cajetan is finally stepping outside of strict logical or semantic considerations, and importing metaphysics. Shouldn't metaphor and proportionality be the same from the logician's point of view? Cajetan apparently thought not. A thing named by metaphor does not just happen to differ in that it lacks the relevant intrinsic form. Rather, naming something by metaphor is an intention different from naming it by proper proportionality—the two are different from the logician's point of view, because they do not involve the same intention—that is, the intention to treat a thing as having a signified form. Metaphor works because, while on the surface it appears as if something is being described by an intrinsic property, the speaker—and the listener—consciously treats this as "just a manner of speaking."[14]

But now, if this much is understood, we have an implicit answer to the first objection, namely that Cajetan's definition of metaphorical predication is circular. For we just do know what a metaphor is, at least insofar as it is a predication not to be taken literally. Cajetan's distinction between metaphor and analogy of proportionality clearly assumes that we already have some sense of what it means for something to be predicated by metaphor—that is, not literally but by poetic license. What Cajetan wants us to learn from his discussion of metaphor is not that it is metaphorical, but that it has something in common with analogy of proportionality, namely, that it depends on the recognition of proportional similarity. In analogy of proportionality, we recognize proportionally similar things and signify them *each* with the same word. In metaphor, we recognize proportionally similar things and signify *one* of the similar things with a word, which word we then use *as if* it signified the other thing, in order to call to mind that other thing's similarity to that first thing that the word properly signifies. In either case, what makes the predication possible is the recognition of proportional similarity, the nongeneric likeness captured by the classic four-term schema A:B::C:D.

To illustrate this, one may use again the diagram of equivocation given in the previous chapter:

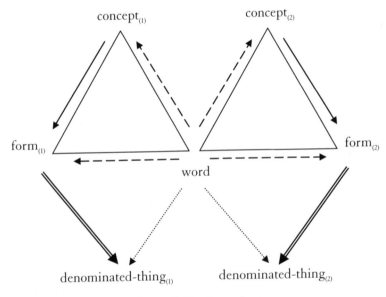

Figure 4. Equivocation

Analogy of proportionality in general occurs when concept$_{(2)}$ is not identical with, but is proportionally the same as, concept$_{(1)}$. Since a concept's ratio determines which forms it naturally represents, we may say that concept$_{(1)}$ and concept$_{(2)}$ are proportionally similar when:

$$form_{(1)}\text{:}denominated\text{-}thing_{(1)}\text{::}form_{(2)}\text{:}denominated\text{-}thing_{(2)}$$

Furthermore, such analogy of proportionality is a case of *metaphor* when the word does not really signify concept$_{(2)}$, but what it does signify, concept$_{(1)}$, is proportionally similar to concept$_{(2)}$. On the other hand, there is analogy of *proper proportionality* when the word genuinely signifies both concept$_{(1)}$ and concept$_{(2)}$.

Some Objections to Proportionality

Proportional similarity is a perfectly respectable variety of similarity in the Aristotelian philosophical tradition, but it is a challenging notion. Puzzles associated with it in the context of analogy can be grouped under two species of objection, one having to do with the usefulness of analogy in its theological applications, and one having to do with the usefulness of it more generally. These objections shall be considered in turn.

Proportionality and Divine Names: The "Two Unknowns" Objection

A common criticism of Cajetan's analysis of analogy of proportionality is that "proportional unity" can only be described by the schema A:B::C:D, and that this schema is not useful in theology, one of the areas where it is supposed to have special application.

According to this objection, analogy is supposed to explain how it is possible to learn about God from creatures, but this is impossible with the schema A:B::C:D. This is because presumably the schema is like a sort of equation, in which one unknown term can be calculated from the other three. But in filling in the schema with an analogy between God and creatures, one gets something like the following example:

(man):(being of man)::(God):(being of God)

and in this case, there is not just one unknown, but two unknowns: God, and the being of God, both of which are beyond our knowledge and are the sorts of things we were supposed to be able to learn about only by analogy in the first place.

This objection is especially invited by the practice of expressing the proportionality in quasi-mathematical form,[15] thus:

$$\frac{man}{being\ of\ man} = \frac{God}{being\ of\ God}$$

What this form suggests is that we have here an equation, which can be solved by a kind of calculation. But such an equation cannot be solved if there are two unknowns, and since both God and his being are beyond human knowledge, it appears that both terms on the right-hand side of the equation are unknown, and cannot be solved for just on the basis of our knowledge of the terms on the left-hand side of the equation.[16]

To this objection, there have been two common replies. One is that there is really only one unknown, not two, and so the "calculation" can, in fact, be performed. This was the strategy of Garrigou-Lagrange, who argued that

> there are not two unknown elements in each of these proportions, but two terms known immediately with their created mode, one term expressing the uncreated analogue which is mediately known (the first cause), whence we infer the presence of the fourth term, which until then remained unknown. It may be expressed by saying that there is a similarity of proportion between the creature with its mode of being and the first cause with its mode of being.[17]

James F. Anderson replies to the two-unknowns objection similarly, saying that we can prove that God exists (i.e., that there is a First Being), so there are not really two unknown terms after all.[18]

The more common response to the "two unknowns" objection has been to point out that an analogy, or proportion, is not meant to be an equation to be solved in the first place. Thus it is properly pointed out that the proportion '::' should not be interpreted as a mathematical identity '=' and that the schema is not intended to be computational.[19]

Putnam has offered another argument against using the schema to calculate an unknown:

> If . . . *analogia* is understood by taking literally the notion of 'proportion,' that is, by employing such a formula as:
>
> > (1) *God's Knowledge is that F which is to God exactly as Socrates' knowledge is to Socrates*
>
> then the explanation seems to be wholly inadequate. There is no clear sense of 'A is to B as C is to D' that I am aware of which will justify supposing that such a formula as (1) has a unique solution. Just to consider the right hand of the formula, *is there* a single way in which Socrates' knowledge *is to* Socrates? Surely God's knowledge isn't to God in *every* way just as Socrates' knowledge is to Socrates![20]

Putnam's objection is made with reference to the use of analogy in religious discourse, but obviously the question applies to nontheological uses of analogy as well. In general, if the proportionality schema is not supposed to help us compute a fourth term given the three others, what are we supposed to learn from it? If '::' does not mean '=' then what *does* it mean? With this question, we move beyond the particular objection to the use of analogy in theology, to a more general objection to the schema A:B::C:D and the meaning of proportionality.

The Circularity Objection

By far the most common objection brought against analogy of proportionality is that it involves a vitiating circularity. Since the Latin '*analogia*' is just a transliteration of the Greek word for proportion, circularity appears even at the level of vocabulary. What kind of unity does an analogical concept have? Proportional, which is to say, analogical, unity.[21] But the problem is not only verbal.

For instance, one proposed solution to the "two unknowns" objection is that one of the unknowns can in fact be grasped, *by analogy*.[22] But more generally, we have seen that we seem to face circularity as soon as we try to clarify that '::' does not mean '=' but some other relation. For on the one hand the schema A:B::C:D seems to have been offered as an explanation of analogy, and on the other hand it seems that we cannot understand the '::' without again invoking analogy.

Eric Mascall considers this objection, although he frames it as a problem of infinite regress rather than a problem of circularity. We can say that the life of a cabbage is analogous to the life of man. So we deny the univocity suggested by the equation

$$life\ of\ cabbage = life\ of\ man$$

replacing it with an analogy, which we can represent with the equation

$$\frac{life\ of\ cabbage}{essence\ of\ cabbage} = \frac{life\ of\ man}{essence\ of\ man}$$

But the point of analogy is that the '=' of this quasi-mathematical equation does not mean identity but only a kind of similarity. After all, "the point is not that the life of the cabbage is determined by the essence of the cabbage in the same way as that in which the life of the man is determined by the essence of the man, but that the way in which cabbage essence determines cabbage life is proper to cabbagehood, while the way in which the human essence determines human life is proper to manhood."[23] So denying the univocity suggested by this equation, we substitute for it:

$$\frac{way\ in\ which\ life\ of\ cabbage\ is\ determined\ by\ essence\ of\ cabbage}{essence\ of\ cabbage} = \frac{way\ in\ which\ life\ of\ man\ is\ determined\ by\ essence\ of\ man}{essence\ of\ man}$$

But even here the '=' deceptively implies univocity, and what this equation really means is something more like:

$$\frac{\begin{array}{c}\textit{way in which way-in-}\\ \textit{which-life-of-cabbage-is-}\\ \textit{determined-by-essence-of-}\\ \textit{cabbage is determined by}\\ \textit{essence of cabbage}\end{array}}{\textit{essence of cabbage}} = \frac{\begin{array}{c}\textit{way in which way-in-}\\ \textit{which-life-of-man-is-}\\ \textit{determined-by-essence-of-}\\ \textit{man is determined by}\\ \textit{essence of man}\end{array}}{\textit{essence of man}}$$

It is clear that these qualifications would go on infinitely,

> at each successive stage denying progressively more complicated relationships between cabbages and men, and never managing to assert a relationship which we shall not immediately have to deny. . . . Our proportionality has completely collapsed, and all we are left with is the fact that cabbages have nothing in common with men except for the fact that, for no valid reason, men have described them both as being alive.[24]

Though he frames this objection forcefully, Mascall actually believes that some sense can be made of the proportionality schema.[25] David Burrell is far less sanguine. According to Burrell, "proportionality is a bag of tricks,"[26] and the schema A:B::C:D "won't work."[27] "The '::' relating *a:b* with *c:d* may not be interpreted as '=', and this discrepancy signals the limits of any promise of systematic clarity."[28]

> To say that the respect in which they are similar is itself proportional, where this cannot be specified, introduces an irremediable circularity into the use of 'similar.' What is really being said here is that two or more things are similar in similar respects; and when one asks how the respects are similar, one is told that such a question cannot be asked in this case. This is not an ordinary similarity but a proportional one, and irreducibly proportional so that the proportion cannot even be granted the relative invariance of a mathematical function, for that would introduce sameness.[29]

Burrell will have none of this circularity. "If one needs to speak of similitude, it had best be a single one and not a proportional one."[30]

ANSWERING THE OBJECTIONS: TWO CONDITIONS FOR AN ACCEPTABLE ANALOGY THEORY

In chapter 3, we considered a variety of objections to the notion of a semantic analysis of analogy. The threat seemed to be that semantic analysis would be a procrustean bed that could not accommodate analogy without violating its integrity. Some have found it especially inappropriate to analyze analogy in terms of *concepts* insofar as a concept seems to be, by its nature, univocal.

From these worries about the limits of semantic analysis, and from the objection to proportionality just considered above, we can discern two distinct conditions of any acceptable analysis of analogy. According to one, an analysis of analogy should not dissolve analogy into univocity; let us call this the *nonreductionist* condition. According to the other, an analysis of analogy should not be circular (or lead to an infinite regress); let us call this the *explanatory* condition.

On first glance these two conditions might appear to be in irresolvable tension. Indeed, they seem to pull in directly opposite directions. It is hard to see how both conditions could be satisfied at once: a noncircular *explanation* of analogy would not contain analogy in its explanans, yet if this were the case it would seem that analogy had been reduced to other, presumably univocal, terms. In fact, the desire to satisfy the explanatory condition can push one to violate the nonreductionist condition. Take the proposal articulated by Paul C. Hayner, which has not been an uncommon approach to analogy. Considering a traditional Thomistic account of the relationship between God and creatures, Hayner finds that it still does not account for how predicates can be true of God and creatures. He says: "To invoke the use of analogy [in order to explain how perfections are predicated of God and creatures] is merely to beg the question. . . . [To predicate perfections commonly of God and creatures] in the absence of any specific or generic likeness, [is] to invoke another analogy to explain the analogy in question, and thus to fall into an infinite regress of analogical explanations." Hayner's proposal is to escape this circularity by insisting that in things analogically related there is, after all, some "one property" had in "common." Analogically related things, then, are after all members of the same "class."[31] Though Hayner does not realize it, on his analysis analogical terms turn out to be genus terms, predicated of diverse things in light of a common significate in each, and so analogy has been reduced to univocity. But he is pushed to this position by a reasonable desire that his treatment of analogy not be circular.

The kind of proposal Hayner offers is what Yves Simon called the mistake of the "beginner" who assumes that in analogy "some common feature will be disclosed."

> In the beginner's understanding, to say that a term is not purely equivocal but analogical is the same as to say that, in spite of all, the meanings do have in common some feature, albeit a very thin one, which survives the differences and makes it possible for a term, whose unity is but one of analogy, to play the role of syllogistic term.[32]

In Simon's treatment of analogy, by contrast, we have exemplary attention to the nonreductionist condition. Analogates involve irreducible plurality, and we should not expect it to go away upon analysis; indeed, a proper analysis of analogy is one that respects, and elucidates, the nature of this plurality.

That the nonreductionist and the explanatory conditions can be insisted upon at the same time is evident from the work of Burrell. Attention to the explanatory condition is manifest in Burrell's criticism that proportionality will not deliver "systematic clarity," and in his complaint that proportionality exhibits "irremediable circularity" if it cannot be further "specified." And yet, as we saw in chapter 3, Burrell is also a strong defender of the irreducibility of analogy, warning against a semantic approach that might analyze analogy away. Thus he appreciates Simon's sensitivity to the "irreducible plurality" of analogates, and his qualification of the sense in which "one concept" can be "abstracted" from diverse analogates.

ANALOGY OF PROPORTIONALITY AND
PROPORTIONAL UNITY

Is Cajetan's analysis of analogy both explanatory and nonreductionist? As this study has been arguing, what Cajetan is offering is an
analysis of the semantics of analogical signification. Once this key fact
is held in mind, it is also easy to see that the analysis is not circular.
Cajetan does not claim to offer an explanation of what proportionality
is, or to describe proportional unity in terms of something else; what
he offers is an explanation of what it is for a term to be analogous
in a way that is neither univocal nor equivocal. He appeals to proportional unity to explain the semantics of signification in this mean
between univocation and equivocation.[33] Most of those who charge
that the teaching is circular focus their arguments on the circularity
of defining proportional unity in terms of a schema (A:B::C:D) that
itself *does* require an understanding of proportional unity. But while
Cajetan does elucidate proportional unity by reference to the schema
(as Aristotle and so many others had done), this is not the accom-
plishment of his theory, and it is not the central point of his analysis
of what it is for a term to be analogous by analogy of proportionality.
Cajetan's contribution is to use the notion of proportional unity to explain the semantics of a mean between univocation and equivocation,
and specifically to explain how two concepts can be the same *secundum quid* in some way other than occurs in the *pros hen* equivocation
that is analogy of attribution. Proportional unity, or proportionality,
is thus included only in the explanans, and is not the explanandum.
His account is thus noncircular, satisfying the explanatory condition.

From this we can also see that Cajetan is not guilty of violating
the nonreductionist condition. For the analysis of analogical signification does not analyze away analogical similarity. Analogical similarity (as Simon had argued) is irreducible, and despite criticisms
from those who fear that semantic analysis might do violence to the
irreducibility of analogy, Cajetan's semantic analysis in fact confirms
that irreducibility.

This defense of Cajetan's theory might raise a further objection. Even if Cajetan's analysis may not be formally circular, because
proportional unity is not what is being explained, this mysterious

proportional unity still does appear in the explanans. So it might seem that what Cajetan offers is either not helpful—if we wanted to understand the nature of proportional unity—or it is just vacuous—if proportional unity just doesn't mean anything to us.

To this objection, the first thing to point out is again that Cajetan was not attempting to give an account of proportional unity; indeed, it is quite clear that he assumes our ability to recognize proportional unity, and makes no attempt to defend its place in the Aristotelian philosophical tradition. And within that tradition, unity is the domain of metaphysics; as "being," so too "one" is said in many ways. As already noted, proportional unity, as a variety of unity, is something considered by the metaphysician, along with numerical, specific, and generic unity. Cajetan assumes this, and does not defend it.

Even if proportional unity is a respectable object of metaphysical attention, it is still difficult to give conditions for recognizing it. Ross remarks that "rules" for identifying proportionality "are difficult to imagine," and judges that this is a "deficiency" of analogy theories thus far. According to Ross, "a fully accurate and adequate analogy theory will have to contain a practicable criterion of similarity of relations."[34] From the context of Ross's remark, it is clear that by an "analogy theory" he means specifically a theory of the semantics of analogical signification. But in that context, it is not at all clear that it is a defect that we lack "rules" for identifying proportional similarity; what we want is some account of the relations between the relevant semantic entities, which will distinguish analogy from univocation and equivocation. And in any case, it is difficult to see how "a practicable criterion of similarity of relations"—that is, a criterion that did not itself contain any reference to proportional similarity—might satisfy the nonreductionist condition.[35]

To reiterate then, Cajetan is *not* trying to offer an analysis of proportional unity or proportional similarity, nor is he even describing conditions under which proportional unity or similarity can be recognized. And this is well and good, because he is limiting himself to giving semantic conditions that must obtain for a term to be used to signify proportional similarity in things. This does assume our ability to recognize the proportional unity that we signify. Not only is proportional unity assumed in the analysis of how terms signify analogically—by means of diverse *rationes* proportionally the same—but it is assumed in the phenomenon that leads us to use words analogically—for we use words analogically only having recognized that two things are proportionally the same.

If this is in part intended as a response to the Scotistic objections to the very possibility of analogy, it is reasonable at this point to ask to what extent Cajetan's theory could be expected to satisfy a Scotist. Scotus effectively denied the possibility of proportional unity in metaphysics. His reasoning was that 'being' is not an analogical term, because it is semantically impossible for a term's multiple significations to have a relationship that is a genuine mean between univocation and equivocation. Where there is more than one concept corresponding to one term, there is equivocation, and so the possibility of the fallacy of equivocation in using that term. By contrast, where only one concept corresponds to a given term, there is univocation. Indeed, for Scotus, univocity is defined as involving a concept that is sufficiently unified to found contradiction and avoid the fallacy of equivocation.

Cajetan's response is to defend the logical space denied by Scotus and his followers, by showing how one could give an account of a mean between univocation and equivocation. This account did require him to invoke the metaphysical notion of proportional unity. So while Scotus and his followers had argued against the possibility of analogy in metaphysics by denying the semantic possibility of analogical signification, Cajetan's response is that analogical signification is semantically possible, because analogical relationships are metaphysically real.

Put another way, the challenge Cajetan faced was to characterize the unity of the analogical concept. As a question about the relationships between words, concepts, and things signified, this is a properly semantic question—a question about how to explain occasions of associated meaning. But to the extent that the question concerns unity, the question has an inescapably metaphysical component. Unity, like being, is said in many ways; and it is metaphysics, and not semantics as such, that is concerned with elucidating unity and its varieties, including the variety of nongeneric or proportional likeness.

In this sense, it would be fair to say that Cajetan's distinction between kinds of analogy does depend on metaphysical considerations.

I have argued that Cajetan's distinction between modes of analogy is not based on the kinds of metaphysical considerations that other commentators have emphasized—consideration of the inherence or noninherence of forms in things. But in answering the semantic question of the unity of the analogical concept, Cajetan must invoke metaphysical distinctions between kinds of unity. In this sense, however, it is not a criticism of Cajetan's semantic analysis to say that it depends on metaphysical considerations. Given the nature of the semantic challenge of analogy, it is only proper for a semantic analysis of analogy to appeal to metaphysical distinctions between kinds of unity.

If this discussion cannot satisfy, that is to say persuade, the Scotist, we are tempted to say that it is nonetheless precisely the kind of answer that a Scotist merits. For as the Scotistic argument shows, and Cajetan's response to it confirms, the Scotist simply refuses to recognize something that is, in fact, real: proportional sameness, analogical unity. Although Scotus argues against the analogy of "being" by denying the logical possibility of analogy, we can see based on these considerations that in fact Scotus's logical assumptions are just an attempt to shore up his denial of the metaphysical category of proportional unity; that is why he must define univocation in terms of its capacity to serve as the basis for contradictory statements and so to preserve inferences from the fallacy of equivocation. While plausible enough at first sight, this is a radical innovation;[36] but Scotus could do it only because he refused to countenance the reality of proportional unity.

Privileging Analogy of Proportionality

Cajetan is clear and consistent about the privileged place enjoyed by analogy of proportionality. It alone is "properly" called analogy; and it precedes all the other forms of (improperly so-called) analogy.[37] Many of Cajetan's interpreters have puzzled over Cajetan's reasons giving priority to analogy of proportionality in this way. The issue has been made all the more urgent by the fact that recent scholarly consensus finds Cajetan's order a departure from Aquinas. To the extent that a distinction between analogy of attribution and analogy of proportionality can be found in Aquinas at all, it seems to most commentators that the Angelic Doctor's preferred type was analogy of attribution. Many commentators thus take Cajetan's preference for proportionality as an interpretive gaffe, giving too much weight to an idiosyncratic text of Aquinas (*De Veritate* 2.11) and ignoring other more consistent and representative passages.

We have already seen that Cajetan's analogy theory should not be dismissed as a bad interpretation of Aquinas if it isn't primarily intended as an interpretation of Aquinas in the first place. Cajetan's purpose is instead to answer questions about the possibility of a mean between univocation and equivocation, questions that Aquinas himself never answered or even explicitly asked. Cajetan gives priority to analogy of proportionality because doing so helps him to answer these questions—and so this priority cannot be evaluated by a simple comparison with texts in Aquinas.[38]

Apart from the charge of mistaken interpretation, most commentators explain that Cajetan preferred analogy of proportionality because it involves the *intrinsic* denomination of all of its analogates. Let us be clear what this means: the term denominates the analogates on account of something intrinsic to each analogate. For instance, *seeing* can denominate the eye on account of its grasp of visible objects, and it can denominate the intellect on account of its grasp of intelligible objects. Now this obviously does not entail that the term denominates two analogates insofar as the analogates are *intrinsically related*, although this has been a point of confusion for some commentators. Although there are proportionally similar relationships between the intellect and its act and the eye and its act (the eye is to ocular vision as the intellect is to intellectual vision), there is no intrinsic connection between the two; the proportional relationship between physical and intellectual vision is not caused by one's acting on the other. It may be that for other cases of proportionality, we would account for the proportional relationship of the analogates by reference to an intrinsic causal relationship between them: for instance, as an accident's being, proportionate to the being of substance, is causally dependent on the being of substance and could not have being without the being of substance; or as the goodness of creatures, caused by the goodness of God, is good insofar as it is caused by the goodness of God and would not be good without the goodness of God. One should not object, then, as does Klubertanz, that proportionality does not adequately describe the relationship between God and creatures because it doesn't refer to their intrinsic causal relationship, but is based on only "extrinsic comparisons."[39] Much like the Suarezian objection that Cajetan's classification does not allow for mixed cases of "intrinsic attribution," this objection results from a failure to appreciate Cajetan's explicit focus on semantic (formal) rather than metaphysical (material) considerations.

Even with the clarifications and corrections offered here, however, it is not quite precise to say that Cajetan regards analogy of proportionality as superior because it denominates all analogates intrinsically, whereas analogy of attribution denominates its secondary analogates only extrinsically. It is true that Cajetan occasionally encourages this reading, saying that analogy of proportionality precedes the others because "this occurs according to the genus of formal inherent cause—since it predicates those which inhere in singulars, while the other [kinds of analogy] occur according to extrinsic denomination" (*DNA* §27). Furthermore, he says: "We know, according to this analogy, something in things of intrinsic entity, goodness, truth, etc., which is not known from the prior analogy [i.e., analogy of attribution]" (*DNA* §29).

But the problem with such an explanation is that it has tempted some commentators to conclude that proportionality is preferred for metaphysical, as opposed to logical or semantic, reasons. It leads us away from the questions that motivated Cajetan's theory of analogy, and the way in which analogy of proportionality serves to answer those questions. Analogy of proportionality is preferred, not because of its metaphysical properties, but because it is best able to serve a particular semantic role: a mean between univocation and equivocation.

As we have seen from our discussions of Cajetan's definitions of the modes of analogy, in analogy of proportionality the intrinsic denomination of all of the analogates is not part of the definition but a feature consequent on its definition: it only follows from the fact that different concepts of the analogues are proportionally the same. And it is this proportional similarity that is key to the superiority of analogy of proportionality. That two things are denominated intrinsically by an analogous term is not enough, without the denominating forms signified by the analogous term being proportionally the same. So while, loosely speaking, intrinsic denomination is a part of the reason Cajetan prefers analogy of proportionality, it is not the full reason; the full reason is that the concepts by which the denominating term signifies, and thus the intrinsic "forms" by which the analogates are denominated, are proportionally one.

Now, while proportional unity is itself a metaphysical notion, the real reason Cajetan prefers analogy of proportionality to analogy of attribution has to do not with metaphysics but with logic: for proportional unity allows for a true mean between univocation and equivocation. The "mean" of analogy of inequality turns out to be closer to univocity—indeed, from the logician's point of view, it just is a case of univocity. The "mean" of analogy of attribution turns out to be closer to equivocation—indeed, Cajetan's treatment of it implies that as far as the logician is concerned it behaves in most circumstances just like equivocation. By contrast, analogy of proportionality seems to be a truer mean. A term analogous by proportionality signifies by means of (diverse but proportionally similar) concepts that are more unified than the (diverse but related) concepts signified by a term analogous by attribution, and yet not so unified as the (one) concept signified by a term analogous by inequality. This is why it is the true analogy, the true mean between univocation and equivocation; and the key to this is the relation of proportional unity.

Chapter Eight

The Semantics of Proportionality

Concept Formation and Judgment

If analogy of proportionality is superior because its diverse concepts are proportionally the same, it remains the case that what it means to have two concepts proportionally the same is obscure—as Cajetan himself admits at the end of the third chapter of *De Nominum Analogia*.[1] As a true mean between univocation and equivocation, analogy of proportionality has semantic properties that cannot be subsumed under those of equivocation or univocation. Thus more than three-quarters of *De Nominum Analogia* (§§31–125) is taken up with elucidating further what is entailed by analogy of proportionality—that is, analogy in which two concepts are proportionally the same.

The organization and arguments of these chapters becomes intelligible if we remember not only Scotus's particular objections to analogy but the traditional structure of logic. Scotus objected that the terms of a scientific metaphysics and theology could not be analogical, for, according to him, nonunivocal terms cause the fallacy of equivocation in scientific demonstrations. This objection touches on all three dimensions of logic. If equivocal terms cause the fallacy of equivocation (in discursive reasoning), it is because they do not predicate the same *ratio* of those equivocated things (in the second act of reasoning, composing and dividing); and this is because they do not allow the abstraction of a common *ratio* from the equivocated things (simple apprehension). Cajetan must show how analogy differs from equivocation in each of these respects, and yet remains different from univocation as well. So he describes in turn the ramifications of proportional unity in the context of simple apprehension (chaps. 4–5), composing and dividing (i.e., judgment, chaps. 6–9), and reasoning (chaps. 10–11),[2] laying the groundwork for, and finally formulating, a response to the objection of Scotus that no nonunivocal term could avoid causing the fallacy of equivocation.

THE ANALOGUE: PERFECT AND IMPERFECT CONCEPTS (*DNA* CHAP. 4)

In explicating equivocation in his commentary on the *Categories*, Cajetan had clarified that both names and things can be called equivocals. Therefore, he said, we must distinguish between the equivocal equivocating (*aequivocum aequivocans*) and the equivocals equivocated (*aequivoca aequivocata*). The distinction is between what is shared by the things named equivocally (the equivocal name), and the things named equivocally themselves (the equivocated things).[3] Cajetan makes a similar distinction with regards to the univocal and its univocates,[4] but of course in univocals there is more than just a name in common; not just a name but also a *ratio* can be considered as the univocal, common to all the univocates.

This is the background for the question Cajetan raises in his fourth chapter: How is the analogue distinguished from the analogates? The question arises because Cajetan wants to explain how analogy is a mean between univocation and equivocation. In equivocation, the equivocal (what equivocates) is just the common word; the equivocated things are the things denominated by that word. In univocation, the univocal (what univocates) can be understood as not only the common word, but the common formal concept by which that word signifies, and the common *ratio* which that word signifies as its objective concept. Analogy, as a mean between equivocation and univocation, will have more in common than is found in the purely equivocal (just the word) but less in common than is found in the univocal (the word, and the objective and formal concept). Thus his fourth chapter clarifies analogy with respect to the three elements of the semantic triangle, considered in turn: word, concept, and thing—where the "thing" is not the analogate that is denominated by the analogous term, but the objective concept that is signified by the analogous term.[5] All of these can be considered as the analogue, to be distinguished from the analogates, and in this respect, analogy is similar to univocation (where word, concept, and thing are common) and unlike equivocation (where only the word is common). Thus the bulk of the chapter is an attempt to clarify the difference between analogy and univocation. Cajetan's concern here is not just how the analogue is distinguished from the analogates, but how this differs from the way that the univocal is distinguished from the univocates.

Just on the basis of Cajetan's third chapter, we know that in analogy of proportionality, there are diverse analogates, denominated with respect to diverse *rationes* that are proportionally the same. Cajetan explicates this in his fourth chapter by considering the difference between the foundation of univocation and the foundation of equivocation. What it is in diverse things that founds a univocation, while many insofar as they are individuated in those diverse things, is entirely the same in *ratio*. "The things founding univocation are like themselves in such a way that the foundation of similitude in one is of wholly the same *ratio* as the foundation of similitude in the other; so that the *ratio* of one contains in itself nothing that the *ratio* of the other does not contain." By contrast, what it is in diverse things that founds an analogy is not of wholly the same *ratio*.

> The things founding analogy are similar in such a way that the foundation of similitude in one is different *simpliciter* from its foundation in the other; so that the *ratio* of one does not contain what the *ratio* of the other contains. And because of this, the foundation of analogical similitude in neither of the extremes can be abstracted from them; but they remain distinct foundations, nevertheless similar according to proportion.[6]

This may sound somewhat redundant: the foundation of analogy is analogical similarity. But what Cajetan is doing here is showing how the general notion of analogical similarity works itself out in the semantic details. We started with the claim, in Cajetan's chapter

3, that the *rationes* in analogy are proportionally the same. Here we see further that this means that whatever there is in things that have those *rationes*, from which those *rationes* are abstracted, must themselves be proportionally the same; indeed, that is just why the *rationes* are proportionally the same, because they are the *rationes* of forms that are themselves proportionally the same.

Cajetan illustrates with examples of univocation and analogy. The word 'animal' is univocally said of man, cow, and lion, because each has in it an individual sensitive nature. These natures, though diverse in being, are so alike that the *ratio* of animality abstracted from any one contains nothing more or less than the *ratio* of animality abstracted from any other; this is just what it means to say that 'animal' is univocal.[7] The word 'being,' however, is said of substance, quantity and quality, not because each has in itself an individualized nature from which some one, generic *ratio* can be abstracted.[8] Rather, each analogate has a different nature, which is nonetheless similar enough—proportionally similar—to found an analogy.[9]

It is in discussing mental concepts that Cajetan makes an important distinction, crucial to an appreciation of the course he steers between univocation and equivocation. It is the distinction between "perfect" and "imperfect" concepts. The proportionally similar but nonetheless distinct natures signified in analogy of proportionality are each properly conceived of by distinct "perfect" concepts. These perfect concepts are themselves proportionally the same, so that while each represents[10] one of the diverse natures properly and perfectly, it represents the others proportionally and imperfectly. Thus Cajetan says that while there is no perfect concept common to all the analogates, we can speak of an imperfect concept that is common to all the analogates. His point could be depicted as in Figure 6. Here, $concept_{(1)}$ and $concept_{(2)}$ are perfect concepts; $concept_{(1)}$ properly represents $form_{(1)}$ and $concept_{(2)}$ properly represents $form_{(2)}$. But $concept_{(1)}$ and $concept_{(2)}$ are proportionally similar (as are $form_{(1)}$ and $form_{(2)}$), and this proportional similarity allows us to speak of another, "imperfect" concept ($concept_{(3)}$), a concept that imperfectly represents *both* $form_{(1)}$ *and* $form_{(2)}$.

Cajetan's introduction of this common, imperfect concept raises a question. Is what we call the imperfect concept *another* concept,

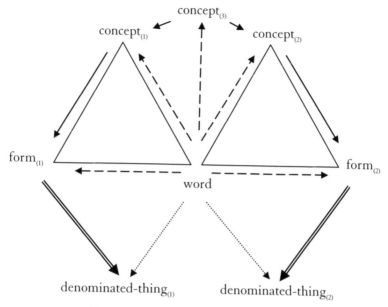

Figure 6. Analogy of Proportionality

in addition to the distinct perfect concepts (as fig. 6 suggests)? Or, is what we call the imperfect concept really just (any) one of the (many) perfect concepts, *considered insofar as* it imperfectly represents the other analogates of which it is not a perfect concept? (In other words, is it possible that $concept_{(3)}$ is not a third concept but is really just $concept_{(1)}$ or $concept_{(2)}$, considered insofar as $concept_{(1)}$ and $concept_{(2)}$ can imperfectly represent that which is proportionally similar to that which they perfectly represent?) The latter alternative is suggested by Cajetan's claim that "one concept perfectly representing one analogate imperfectly represents the rest."[11] But in favor of the former alternative, Cajetan seems to say that there is just *one* imperfect concept.[12] This wouldn't seem to be the case if each perfect concept could be considered as an imperfect concept, for then there would not be only one imperfect concept but exactly as many as there are perfect concepts.

In fact the two alternatives may not be so different: the many imperfect concepts implied by the latter alternative—each a perfect concept of a distinct analogate, imperfectly representing other analogates—may be regarded as *proportionally* one imperfect concept—insofar as they all represent all analogates imperfectly—as implied by the former alternative.

In any case, Cajetan does speak of something at least logically distinct from the perfect concepts: the imperfect concept, a concept that would imperfectly represent all the analogates rather than perfectly representing one and imperfectly representing the others. It is also true that any perfect concept, insofar as what it is a concept of is proportionally similar to other things, is imperfectly a concept of those other things. (For example, insofar as intellectual apprehension is proportionally similar to physical sight, the perfect concept of physical sight is imperfectly a concept of intellectual apprehension.) So in a sense it seems that Cajetan does not need to find these two alternatives mutually exclusive, and indeed can endorse them both.[13] In any case, it seems unreasonable to press this question too far, especially in light of Cajetan's warning that there is a sense in which there is not a common concept *at all*. Cajetan cautions that we need to tailor our characterization of analogous concepts to different audiences. He thinks it is most proper *not* to say that there is a common concept, but to say that there are many concepts, proportionally similar. However, in some contexts—presumably when speaking with those who deny the unity that is involved in analogy—it can be appropriate to speak of a common concept. Given this, Cajetan says, "one ought to be in the habit of using discretion when it is found written that the analogates agree in one *ratio*, and when it is found said elsewhere that the analogates do not agree in one *ratio*,"[14] for these apparently different claims do not necessarily contradict each other; they may just be attempts to emphasize different aspects of a consistent, delicately balanced analogy theory.[15]

THE "ABSTRACTION" OF THE ANALOGUE AND THE CONFUSION OF THE ANALOGUES (*DNA* CHAP. 5)

In discussing the proportional unity of the objective and mental concepts, Cajetan had already introduced the issue of abstraction; because proportionally similar things are not generically similar, a

single common *ratio* cannot be abstracted from them.[16] Cajetan turns
to discuss abstraction more directly in his fifth chapter ("How there
is abstraction of the analogue from the analogates"). Cajetan believes
that despite what was said in his previous chapter, it still might appear
that there is some one thing abstractable, as there are in univocals.
Since abstraction always involves "understanding one [thing] while
not understanding others,"[17] Cajetan says, "to treat the abstraction of
the analogue from the analogates is nothing other than to ask and determine how the thing signified by the name of the analogue may be
understood without also understanding the analogates, and how its
concept can be had, without the concepts of those [analogates]."[18]

Cajetan agrees that the common analogue can be understood separately, and thus it can be said to be abstracted, but it is not abstracted
in the manner that a generic concept is abstracted in univocation.[19]
There is not a third, separate simple concept, which can be abstracted
from the two analogous concepts.[20] Rather, in analogy, there is a kind
of abstraction by confusion: the diverse proper analogues are considered *as similar*, and their diversity is ignored or "confused." What
is confused (blurred, or made indistinct) is the distinction between
the proportionally similar *rationes*, so that what is considered is their
proportional similarity. This means that in one sense abstraction is
possible; indeed, just as Cajetan says that there both is and is not one
concept, Cajetan says that there both is and is not abstraction.[21]

But, it may be asked, if this kind of quasi abstraction is possible,
why is proper abstraction not possible? If in this quasi abstraction it is
the similarity of the diverse analogical *rationes* which is being considered, why is there not some common property, with respect to which
they are similar, and which can be properly abstracted from them?[22]
Yves Simon called it the "beginner's mistake" to look for a common
element—but why is this a mistake? Must not there be some common element with respect to which similar things are similar? As
Burrell put it:

> If one needs to speak of similitude, it had best be a single one and
> not a proportional one. For whether we think of a similitude as
> a kind of template or prefer to be guided by a careful use of lan-
> guage, the upshot will have to be something invariant, else why

invoke the expression? Careful attention to language would note that '*x* is similar to *y*' is an ellipsis which must furnish 'in respect of *z*' on demand.[23]

Of course, if Burrell's '*z*,' in respect of which things are supposed to be similar, must always be a common, shared element, it is hard to see how Burrell could have a place for analogy, without denying that analogues are similar; and yet analogues *are* similar. If there cannot be a common element by virtue of which analogically similar things are similar, why not?

Interestingly, Cajetan's response to this question is that it can't be answered, because it is inappropriate to ask; it is just the nature of proportional similarity that it is genuine similarity and yet there is not some commonly abstractable element. Those who do not see that, and ask why it is the case, ask what does not fall under question, like asking why man is a rational animal.[24]

I take it that this is why Bochenski, in his formal analysis of analogy, found it necessary to introduce the notion of "isomorphy." As Bochenski saw, there could not be one common element between two proportionally similar things. Indeed, two things are only proportionally similar insofar as they find themselves in proportions which are similar—A is proportionally similar to C insofar as A is to B as C is to D. But there cannot even be a common element in these similar proportions of the form '*x* is to *y*'; nor could there be a more general relation that contained the two relations, for in that case there would be, after all, some univocal element. Bochenski's "isomorphy" just allows for two relations to be similar without their being specifications of some more general, common, and so univocal relation.[25]

Indeed, it seems that Bochenski's 'isomorphy' means nothing more than this. Though its provenance (it is taken from *Principia Mathematica*) gives it a technical connotation, making it suitable for inclusion in Bochenski's highly formalized arguments, 'isomorphy' appears to mean just exactly what Cajetan meant by proportional similarity—that is, genuine similarity of proportions which yet does not allow the abstraction of a common, general relation.[26] If so, the traditional explication of "isomorphy" is illuminating: assume two "structures" S_1 and S_2, whose elements have a one-to-one correspondence, and for any relation R_1 between elements a_1 and b_1 of structure S_1, there is a corresponding relation R_2 between elements a_2 and b_2 of structure S_2. Relations R_1 and R_2 are not the same relation, but are said to be similar just insofar as they relate corresponding elements of their respective structures. In this case, S_1 and S_2 can be said to be isomorphic, as can R_1 and R_2. We could also say that they are proportionally similar. By extension, corresponding elements a_1 and a_2 can also be said to be proportionally similar—that is, analogous. But to understand this is not to understand some common element shared by a_1 and a_2, rather it is to understand a_1 and a_2 as playing corresponding roles in their respective (and so proportionally similar) structures $(S_1{:}R_1a_1b_1{::}S_2{:}R_2a_2b_2)$.

In short, the primary lesson that Cajetan would have us learn about analogy on the level of simple apprehension is that there cannot be a concept or *ratio* that captures one common element shared by diverse analogates, but there can be a kind of quasi abstraction—abstraction-by-confusion—of an *imperfect* concept, which is an apprehension of diverse things in their proportional similitude.

Predication: Universal but Not Univocal (*DNA* Chap. 6)

The exposition of the semantics of analogy of proportionality at the level of simple apprehension leads to questions at the level of composing and dividing. Because it involves only the quasi abstraction of a quasi concept (the "confusion" that produces an "imperfect" concept), it is difficult to understand what is involved in predicating a term analogous by proportionality of its subjects. After all, in general what is predicated is supposed to be a common nature or *ratio*, considered absolutely, which is signified by a term as its objective concept. And yet, in analogy of proportionality, there is no one proper objective concept of all the analogates, but instead a proper objective concept of one analogate (physical sight, for instance), and a different, albeit proportionally similar, proper objective concept of another analogate (such as intellectual apprehension). Though it seems to play the role of a universal predicated of diverse individuals, can there be "one" analogue here, understood as something unified and common to many? Analogy thus raises its own problem of universals. This particular difficulty, with which Cajetan is concerned in the sixth chapter of *De Nominum Analogia*, is: how can a term analogous by proportionality be predicated of diverse analogates as a superior predicated of its inferiors?

We say that a univocal term is predicated of its univocates as a superior of inferiors, because what is predicated of one is wholly the same as what is predicated of the other, namely the common *ratio* abstractable from each univocate and signified as the *ratio* or objective concept of that term. The foundation of the "superiority" of the univocal is the identity of the *rationes* in the diverse univocates. Not surprisingly, Cajetan insists that there is a difference between univocal and analogical superiority. Just as the foundation of similarity should not be confused with the foundation of univocation,[27] so the foundation of superiority should not be confused with the foundation of univocation. The foundation of univocation is the complete identity of *rationes*; the foundation of superiority is the identity of *rationes*, where identity here can include even *proportional* identity.[28] So while univocates have both the foundation of superiority and the foundation of univocity, in analogates there is not the foundation of univocity, but there is still the foundation of superiority, just insofar as the diverse *rationes* of the analogates are the same *proportionally*. And the proportional identity of the *rationes* is enough to found superiority, because it is almost as if there is a common *ratio* of all analogates, insofar as the *ratio* of one analogate is *proportionally* the *ratio* of another analogate.[29]

Here again, then, we see that the logical space between univocation and equivocation, namely the space for a common and superior but nonunivocal *ratio*, can be defended only by appeal to the metaphysical space between sameness and difference, and specifically to the metaphysical recognition of proportional sameness. And although Cajetan does not name Scotus in this chapter of *De Nominum Analogia*, his distinction between the foundation of superiority and the foundation of univocity provides some of the response necessary to the Scotistic criticism of analogy. Cajetan describes a fallacy of concluding from a *ratio*'s being superior or universal to its being univocal.

The fallacy results from failing to distinguish between identity and mode of identity, and thus failing to distinguish between the foundation of superiority and the foundation of univocity.[30] While a fallacy about logic, it is clear that it is rooted in a failure to appreciate the metaphysical category of proportional identity. "For identity and unity contain under themselves not only complete unity and identity, but proportional."[31]

By this point in his discussion, Cajetan believes he has made good on the promise at the very beginning of *De Nominum Analogia* that he would expose as false three popular characterizations of the unity of the analogical concept.[32] True analogy cannot involve one precise concept unequally participated (although this is a fair description of analogy of inequality). Nor can it involve diverse concepts unified as a disjunction, or as an ordered set (although the latter alternative might be a fair description of analogy of attribution, with the secondary analogues ordered to, by their relation to, the primary analogue). Rather, genuine analogy, which allows for something common to be abstracted and predicated as a universal, requires that there be diverse concepts that are the same *by proportion*.[33] Cajetan does not offer further explanation, but he does not need to. If there were only one precise concept, it would necessarily be a form of univocation; and if the diverse concepts were not proportionally one, then there could not even be the kind of confused, or quasi, abstraction that allows the analogical term to be predicated as a superior of inferiors.

DEFINITION: SIGNIFYING THE FOUNDATION
OF A RELATION (*DNA* CHAP. 7)

It is clear that just showing the falsity of three popular characterizations of the analogical concept(s) is not enough for Cajetan. These alternative characterizations mentioned at the beginning may sound like the occasion of his work, but Cajetan does not spend much time discussing them, and comes back to them again only as a kind of aside. Cajetan's real aim is to elucidate the nature of the unity of the analogical concept, and the three incorrect proposals are only symptoms of contemporary confusion about the subject, pointing to the need to treat it fully. And Cajetan's own appeal to proportional unity still requires further elucidation, for he still has not directly addressed the Scotistic concern that a nonunivocal term will *ipso facto* cause the fallacy of equivocation. Thus Cajetan continues by raising a question that has to do with *definition*. Since there are diverse perfect *rationes*, how are the different definitions of each *ratio* related?

More specifically, must one *ratio* be defined in terms of another? This had been the case with analogy of attribution, at least with its secondary analogates, since those secondary analogates are defined in terms of their relation to the primary analogate. But in analogy of proportionality, two things are not analogous because one has some determinate relation to another, but because both are proportionally the same.

It is in this context that Cajetan makes the important but often overlooked claim that in analogy of proportionality what is signified is not a relation but the foundation of a relation[34]—a distinction invoked again in Cajetan's *Summa* commentary.[35] In analogy of attribution, the analogical term, as predicated of the secondary analogates, signifies a relation, namely, the relation between the secondary analogate and the primary analogue. In analogy of proportionality, however, this is not the case; the analogical term—as predicated of any analogate, secondary or primary—signifies not a relation but the foundation of a relation.

How so? Actually, we can discern two senses in which the analogical term signifies the foundation of a relation, for there are two different orders of relation in analogy of proportionality. There is the proportional relation between two analogates (the relation represented by the double colon [':'] in 'A:B::C:D'), and, on either side of this proportional relation, there is the relation of the analogate to its analogue (the relation represented by the single colons [':'] on either side of 'A:B::C:D'). Which of these two relations does Cajetan have in mind when he says that a term analogical by proportionality signifies the foundation of a relation? Cajetan is in fact not entirely clear, although at *DNA* §83 it seems that he has in mind the former relation, the "relation of identity or similarity" between two analogates. But whichever relation Cajetan has in mind, we can see that the same thing can be considered as its foundation. Consider the example of "sees," which is predicated of the intellect by analogy with the seeing of an eye. The proper operation of the intellect, its grasping of its proper object, is a foundation of the relation that holds between it and the intellect. And of course this "intellectual vision" is also a foundation of the relation of proportional similitude between the intellect and the eye; it is insofar as the intellect has this "vision" that it is said to be proportionally similar to the eye and its "vision." And this same thing that is the foundation of both relations we have considered is in fact what is signified by the analogous term in the analogate; and the *ratio* of the analogous term is the *ratio* of that vision itself, and not some relation that that vision has to something else.

In light of this we can understand Cajetan's further point that in analogy of proper proportionality, one analogous *ratio* can be known without knowing the others. Though one *ratio* of an analogous term does *have* a relation to others, namely the relation of proportional similarity, that *ratio* can be *known* without knowing the other *rationes* to which it is proportionally similar. In this sense, the *ratio* of an analogue is like the *ratio* of a univocal; for a *ratio* is univocal if it is the same as the *ratio* of another thing, and yet one does not have to know that relation to the other thing to know the univocal *ratio*. The *ratio* of "animal," for example, is univocal to man and cow, and so the *ratio* of animal, as predicated of man, is related to the *ratio* of animal as predicated of the cow; and yet, when we say that man is an animal, we do not predicate of man that his *ratio* has some relation to the *ratio* of a cow. This is the point that Cajetan makes by introducing the logician's distinction between considering a term in the signified act (*in actu signato*) and in the exercised act (*in actu exercito*):

> As "animal" said of *man* and *horse* implies univocation *in the exercised act*, it does not *predicate* of man, all this, namely "sensitive nature entirely the same according to *ratio* as the sensitive nature of horse and cow," but [rather it predicates] "sensitive nature" simply. However, since the predication *is* univocal, it must *be* wholly the same according to *ratio*, as the sensitive nature of horse and cow. Just so, "being" [*ens*], implying proportionality *in the exercised act*,

does not *predicate* of quantity all this, namely "having itself to being [*esse*] proportionally as substance or quality to their being [*esse*]"; but [it predicates] "having itself to being [*esse*] in such a way," without any other addition; nevertheless it is necessary that, for the predication to *be* analogous, it must *be* the same proportionally with the other [*rationes*] "having itself to being in such a way," which being [*ens*] predicates of substance or quality.[36]

This is why in analogy of proper proportionality, one analogue can be known without the other, and does not need to be defined by reference to another.

Cajetan is careful at this point to clarify that this same rule does not hold for metaphor. In metaphor, "the analogue taken metaphorically predicates nothing other than that *this* has itself by similitude to *that*, so that without the other extreme it cannot be understood."[37] In other words, similarity to something else is included in the *ratio* of the metaphorical analogue, not only *in actu exercito* but also *in actu signato*. And because of this, the metaphorical analogue *is* defined by reference to the other analogue, so that "the one properly taken must be included in the *ratio* of the one taken metaphorically; since it is impossible to understand what something is according to a metaphorical name without knowing that to which the metaphor refers. Nor indeed can it happen that I understand what a field is insofar as it is smiling, without knowing what the name 'smile' signifies properly taken, by similitude to which the field is said to smile."[38]

In this respect, metaphor is like analogy of attribution, in that the secondary analogue cannot be understood without the primary analogue,[39] and the *ratio* of the primary analogue appears in the definition of the *ratio* of the secondary analogue. Indeed, this is just why it is so easy to distinguish, in both metaphor and analogy of attribution, what is primary and what is secondary. But this raises a question about the issue of priority in analogy of proportionality. If one is not defined in terms of the other, how can we tell which is the primary analogate? Indeed, how can there *be* a primary analogate? What, if anything, can be the criterion for "primacy" in analogy of proportionality?

In order to address this question Cajetan introduces another distinction at this point of *De Nominum Analogia*. We can say that there is an order of things considered under one name, but we must distinguish between the order on the part of the thing, and that on the part of the imposition of the name.[40] While it had appeared difficult to see how there could be priority and posteriority at all, with this distinction Cajetan reminds us that there are actually two ways order can occur. That can be considered the primary analogue that the name was first imposed to signify. (In this sense creatures, for example, are the primary analogates under the term 'good,' which is secondarily said of God.) However, at the same time that can be considered a primary analogate which is said to have the analogue in a metaphysically higher, or primary way. (In this sense, God is the primary analogate of "good," which is only secondarily said of creatures.)[41]

Comparison, Division, Resolution (*DNA* Chaps. 8 and 9)

It is easy to judge priority in the order of imposition of names, for names are conventional, and as a matter of human intention it will generally be known what a term was originally or primarily imposed to signify. But how is it possible to judge priority in the order of things? We have just said that God has the analogue of goodness "in a metaphysically higher, or primary way"—how is this discerned? Of course, in the case of terms analogous between God and creatures, we have easy theological and metaphysical reasons to grant God primacy, but what about in other, nontheological cases of proportionality? How will we be able to discern order then?[42]

This is the kind of difficulty that prompts Cajetan's eighth chapter, about "how there is comparison in the analogue." But the question here is even more basic, not just how we can *discern* priority in the order of things, but how there can even *be* such priority and posteriority. Since there is no common element in analogy, it seems that there is no basis for comparison of analogues, and so we could not say, for instance, that one is *greater* than another in some respect. And yet this seems necessary if, as we know, analogy involves an order of primary and secondary analogates, not just in the order of imposition but in the order of reality. How could there be primary and secondary analogates if there is no basis of comparison between them, no common element that they both share to a greater or lesser extent?

Cajetan addresses this problem with a distinction. As with superiority,[43] the foundation of comparison is not *absolute* identity or unity, which is the foundation of univocation, but *any manner* of identity or unity.[44] So it is sufficient for comparison in analogy that the different analogues are *proportionally* one.[45] This does not preclude one of the proportionally similar *rationes* from being "more perfect" than another; and such difference would occur if one thing has more perfect being according to the proportionally common *ratio* than another thing. Discerning these degrees of perfection is what is required for identifying what is more prior in itself, and not just on the part of the imposition of the name.

The analogue can thus be said to be *divided* into the analogates—that is, divided according to the different ways the analogates take up the *ratio* of the analogue. Cajetan says that the various different analogates are already contained in the analogue, in a way that the univocates are not contained in the univocal. The univocates require something else added, a difference from outside the genus. But the analogates do not need something else added, rather their confused inclusion needs to be made more precise.[46] Cajetan had already spoken of the quasi abstraction allowed of analogues that happened "by sort of hiding the diversity" of the perfect concepts,[47] so that "not so much the concepts as their diversity is confounded" in the analogical concept.[48] So the "division" of the common analogue into its analogates involves not the addition of differences, as to a univocal genus, but the uncovering, or bringing into focus, of hidden diversity.[49]

The process of division thus has a complementary process that moves in the opposite direction, bringing together distinct things and ignoring their diversity. Though the *ratio* of one analogate is not defined in terms of the *ratio* of another, still one *ratio* (a proper concept) can be analyzed into the common analogue. This process is called *resolution*; the distinct analogate is resolved into the common analogue.[50]

At first glance, it would seem that what Cajetan says about *division* and *resolution* here in chapter 9 does not add much to his earlier discussions of *distinction* and *abstraction* in chapters 4 and 5 respectively. In both resolution and abstraction, a common *ratio* of diverse subjects is discerned; in both division and distinction, the diversity of analogates within the common ratio is discerned. But chapter 9 does offer further explanation and more precise characterization of what was earlier only described in terms of a quasi abstraction. We have already seen that the quasi abstraction possible in analogy must differ from proper abstraction in not having an abstractable *common element* in the diverse things. But a further consequence of this is that diverse analogates do not differ from each other by *differences* separable from and added to a common (generic) nature. Such differences would necessarily be outside the common nature, so analogates can differ only by something that is *included* in the common analogical *ratio*. As Cajetan points out,[51] this is one of Aristotle's arguments why *being* is not a genus: the "differences" that are "added" to being to constitute the categories themselves have being, and so are not outside of the common "nature" they differentiate.

In general, then, the reason there cannot be genuine abstraction in the case of analogy is that the common analogue is in principle inseparable from those features that constitute the diversity of the analogates. Cajetan appears to offer "division" and "resolution" as alternative technical terminology, since, properly speaking, there is no "differentiation" and "abstraction" in analogy. Resolution is the mind's capacity to give attention to the proportional unity of necessarily diverse *rationes*, whose necessary diversity is not constituted by the addition of differences to a genus absolutely one; and since resolution is attention to proportional unity *as such*, even this attention must be accompanied by awareness of the necessary diversity of the analogates—otherwise, the analogue would collapse into a univocal *ratio*, absolutely one. And since the analogous *ratio* so "resolved" is not absolutely one, it necessarily includes an order of priority, according as the analogous *ratio* results from adding to one *ratio* (of the primary analogate) qualifications that allow it to be extended to secondary analogates, resulting in a modified *ratio* proportionally one with the original *ratio*. To take again the crucial example from metaphysics:

being cannot be regarded as abstractable from substance (*substantial being*) and from quantity (*measurable being*) as a genus from species, because *substantial* and *measurable* are not differences constituting diverse species of absolutely one genus; rather, they are qualifications constituting diverse yet proportionally one *ratio/rationes* of *being*.

Chapter Nine

The Semantics of Proportionality

Syllogism and Dialectic

In the middle chapters of *De Nominum Analogia*, with their continued emphasis on concepts, Cajetan at first glance seems to be primarily concerned with matters of epistemology or philosophical psychology. The concern, however, remains properly logical or semantic. The common theme is the acquisition, structure, and deployment of analogical concepts. Analogy of proportionality was given its formal definition on the level of the first act of apprehension, in terms of the semantic triangle. And yet the unique relation of proportional unity required an exploration of its ramifications through the activities of the second act of apprehension, loosely called judgment, but which we have seen involves the definition, predication, and formation of analogical concepts—everything that arises from the use of predicates that are neither purely equivocal nor purely univocal. This leaves the semantics of analogy on the level of the third act of apprehension— discursive reasoning—to the final chapters of the treatise. In these chapters Cajetan takes up the challenge of how analogical terms can mediate syllogistic inference, and he reflects on other hermeneutic challenges raised by the use of analogical terms in argument.

Scientific Reasoning (*DNA* Chap. 10)

How can a term used nonunivocally in different premises of a syllogism avoid causing the fallacy of equivocation? That was the question pressed by Scotus's objections to analogy. It is the question that Cajetan's treatise on analogy finally addresses directly in the tenth of its eleven chapters.

By now we can rephrase the question, in light of Cajetan's semantic analysis of analogical concepts: How can an analogical term avoid causing the fallacy of equivocation when that term, occurring in different premises in a scientific demonstration, signifies different perfect concepts? Cajetan considers the example of wisdom, in the syllogism "Every simple perfection is in God, wisdom is a simple perfection, therefore [wisdom is in God]."[1] It seems that this cannot be a scientific demonstration, because in the minor premise, "wisdom" signifies the *ratio* of creaturely wisdom, while in the conclusion it signifies the *ratio* of divine wisdom.

Cajetan attributes this objection to Scotus (*I Sent.* d. 3, q. 1), and responds that those who follow this argument "are deceived . . . , because seeing in the analogue the diversity of *rationes*, they do not consider that unity and identity which it conceals."[2] Only when we accept the proper *rationes* in themselves, as perfect concepts of their respective analogates, do they lead to the fallacy of equivocation; but accepting them *as proportionally the same*—as imperfect concepts representing many analogates—they do not. As Cajetan explains:

> Whatever agrees with one, agrees also with the other proportionally; and whatever is denied of one, is denied of the other proportionally; because whatever agrees with a similar, insofar as it is similar, agrees also with that to which it is similar, while always saving the proportionality.[3]

So in responding to the claim that analogy would cause the fallacy of equivocation, Cajetan invokes a principle that we may call transitivity by likeness: if something applies to a likeness, insofar as it is a likeness, it applies also to the thing of which the likeness is a likeness (*quidquid convenit simili, in eo quod simile, convenit etiam illi, cui est simile*).[4] (The principle is so obvious as hardly to need articulating: if you call a picture of a puppy cute, it follows that you think the puppy of which it is a picture is cute.)[5] It is on the basis of this principle that our syllogism can move from claims about creatures to claims about God, for although not univocal, the different *rationes* signified by the analogical term are sufficiently similar to each other, indeed they are proportionally one. Indeed, that is just why, according to Cajetan, proportional unity is numbered among varieties of unity, for what is proportionally one is "affirmable and deniable, and consequently distributable and knowable, as subject, middle term, and predicate."[6]

Applying the principles laid out in early chapters of *De Nominum Analogia*, we can say that in analogy of proportionality, the different *rationes* of the term do not cause the fallacy of equivocation because the proportional similarity of those different *rationes* as predicated of their different subjects allows for a superior, imperfect concept that can be predicated of both subjects. This concept is said to be "imperfect," however, because it is not a definite, univocal concept, of which the diverse proper *rationes* are specifications derived by the addition of differences. Rather it is a "confused"—that is, indeterminate—concept of both of those *rationes* considered *in their proportional similarity*. Of course, in the example above, the individual premises are true because the word 'wisdom' as predicated of creatures does signify creaturely wisdom; and as predicated of God, it signifies divine wisdom. But because creaturely wisdom and divine wisdom are proportionally the same, the truth of those premises is also saved if we consider not two different *rationes* of wisdom, but the superior, confused apprehension of them both in their proportional similarity. In other words, the two different *rationes* of wisdom are, in fact, proportionally the same, and their proportional similarity is a sufficient similarity to avoid the fallacy of equivocation. So we can, after all, understand the syllogism as involving three terms, not four.

It is not surprising that in response to Scotus's argument to the contrary, Cajetan is pressed to clarify what constitutes contradiction. According to Scotus, contradiction was affirmation and negation of a univocal of a univocal—indeed, Scotus defined univocation and contradiction in terms of each other. Cajetan replies that contradiction is "affirmation and negation of the *same* of the *same*," where sameness can obviously include *proportional* sameness. "Identity, as much in thing as in *ratio*, as is repeated many times, is extended to proportional identity."[7]

Again, then, in the example above "the word 'wisdom' does not stand for this or that *ratio* of wisdom, but for wisdom proportionally one, that is, for both *rationes* of wisdom, not conjoined or disjuncted, but insofar as they are proportionally undivided, and one is proportionally the other, and both constitute a *ratio* proportionally one."[8] And this proportional identity means that the word 'wisdom' does not signify different things, but the same thing—albeit analogically or proportionally the same—in each of its occurrences in the syllogism.[9]

So we can see that just as Scotus's argument against analogy involves a confusion of the foundation of univocation with the foundations of similarity and superiority, it also involves a confusion of the foundation of univocation with the foundation of contradiction. As Cajetan puts it, "Scotus . . . either poorly explained the univocal concept, or contradicted himself" when he defined a univocal concept as one sufficing to found contradiction. If this is univocation, then 'being,' although analogical, would satisfy the definition of a univocal. Scotus, however, thought his argument proved that 'being' had one concept simply and undivided—that is, that it was not analogical. But if Scotus intended to exclude proportional unity from his definition of univocation, then he was wrong to define a univocal concept as one that suffices to found a contradiction.[10]

Cajetan believes his position is supported not only by the authority of Aquinas but by the "daily exercise" of analogy in scientific reasoning. He also finds it supported by Aristotle's explicit claims in *Posterior Analytics* that an analogue is an adequate mean in a scientific demonstration (98a20ff.; 99a16ff.). Indeed, according to Aristotle's example, this does not even require that there already be an analogical term common to many things, so long as the many things are understood to be analogically related. For, as Cajetan quotes Aristotle, "There is not accepted one and the same [word] that ought to name sepion, spine, and bone. However, there are those [attributes] which follow as if there were one existent nature of this kind."[11]

CAJETAN'S PARTING ADVICE (*DNA* CHAP. II)

Cajetan's discussion of scientific reasoning includes a warning: even though a term analogous by proportionality can, like a univocal term, serve in scientific reasoning without causing the fallacy of equivocation, still its proportionality must be kept in mind, and it must not be treated as if it were a univocal term. For the unity of an analogical term does hide equivocations, and if one were to forget these, and treat the analogical term as univocal, one might falsely attribute to one analogate something that is proper only to another analogate.[12] While analogical terms can be used in scientific reasoning, it is obviously not an easy or unproblematic matter. So it is appropriate that Cajetan not end his treatise on analogy without providing some cautions and helpful practical advice. By signaling possible mistakes in reasoning with and about analogical concepts, the final chapter of *De Nominum Analogia* is effectively a brief *de fallaciis* to conclude the logical *organon* of the preceding chapters.

Cajetan's first piece of advice is that we should not assume that just because a term is univocal with respect to some things, it will be univocal with respect to all. The example Cajetan uses is "wisdom," which originally was univocal as applied to different wise men. Yet as extended to apply to God, the word is not univocal but analogical.[13]

A second piece of advice is that we shouldn't be misled by there being one or many names, for what is important is that there are proportionally similar *rationes*. Cajetan's example here is again Aristotle's example of the *ratio* of *what supports flesh*, which is found in bone, sepion, and spine, although there is no common word that is applied to all three of these things.[14] Diverse things that lack a common name may in fact have a common nature; and diverse things that do share a common name may still be only analogically one.

Cajetan's third piece of advice is another reminder not to be misled into thinking that an analogical term is univocal. Not only can we be misled by the unity of the term, but also by the apparent unity of the analysis or definition of the *ratio* signified by that term. Cajetan's example is that the term 'principle' may be analyzed as *that from which a thing becomes* (or *is*, or *is known*), and this itself might seem to apply univocally to different things conceived of as principles. Yet the mere "vocal unity" of this analysis should not disguise the fact that the analysis itself is analogical, which is obvious when it is realized that it contains analogical terms: "neither *to become*, nor *to be*, nor *to be known*, nor the word 'from,' is wholly one in *ratio*, but [each] is saved proportionally."[15]

A fourth bit of advice is for those interpreting what others have said about analogy: Cajetan says that we should not be bothered by the diversity of what has been said about analogy by "doctors." Indeed, diverse kinds of claims should be expected, for insofar as analogy is a mean between univocation and equivocation, it may appear especially like or unlike one or another extreme, depending on what feature is being emphasized. As we have already seen in Cajetan's own presentation, sometimes the unity of the analogue will be emphasized, other times the diversity, and these emphases are not contradictory.[16] It is with this in mind that Cajetan says we can see the essential consistency of apparently contradictory things said by Aristotle[17] and by Aquinas.[18]

This leads to Cajetan's last piece of advice, which is meant to conclude the discussion of how to interpret remarks about analogy, and yet applies to the general difficulty of interpreting any remarks involving the use of analogical terms. Cajetan commends us to interpret individual claims with an eye to the context in which they are made: "If someone does not wish to err, he ought habitually to consider the occasion of the speech."[19] This is the warning mentioned above in chapter 3, in response to those who feared that Cajetan's semantic analysis of analogy would necessarily ignore context and the requirement of using judgment in applying and interpreting analogical terms. By now we can see that Cajetan's advice to pay attention to context is consistent with the whole of his teaching—that is, with his semantic principles in general, and with his semantic analysis of analogy in particular.

De Conceptu Entis

Although written eleven years later, Cajetan's letter *De Conceptu Entis* (On the Concept of Being) is usually reproduced with the treatise *De*

Nominum Analogia. This is appropriate, although not for the reasons that many have assumed. The letter addresses certain questions about the concept of *being*, and has contributed to the tendency of some interpreters to insist that Cajetan's teaching on analogy is the teaching of a metaphysician, rather than a logician. However, as the title rightly indicates, the letter treats not being, nor the analogy of being, but the *concept* of being. And even if Cajetan had not said so explicitly, we would have known from the semantic principles laid out in his *Categories* commentary that "it is the same to speak of the concept of being as to speak of the signification of 'being.'"[20]

The letter is appropriately paired with *De Nominum Analogia*, then, not because it clarifies metaphysical issues ("the analogy of being") but because it clarifies semantic issues ("the analogy of 'being'"). The letter fits well with *De Nominum Analogia* because within the context of the letter's concern with a particular concept (being), it reiterates several of the treatise's doctrines about analogy in general. The letter can also be understood as an application and illustration of the advice Cajetan offered at the end of his treatise, about how to interpret different and apparently contradictory claims about analogy.

In the letter, Cajetan responds to two interpretive problems raised by his fellow Dominican Francis of Ferrera. The first problem is that Cajetan seems to contradict himself on the subject of whether there are one or many mental concepts (formal concepts, as opposed to objective concepts) of being. The second is that Cajetan's claim that a concept of being cannot be abstracted from individual beings seems to contradict Aquinas's claim that being is the most simple concept. In both cases, Cajetan's response reminds us that because analogy is a mean between univocation and equivocation, learned men have said and will say apparently contradictory things about it, claims that can be reconciled when we remember the nature of analogy itself, and the context in which claims about it are made.

So in response to the question of whether there are one or many mental concepts of being, Cajetan first reminds Francis of transitivity by likeness: "Whatever is the image of something which is similar to another, is also the image of that other insofar as it is similar to the first."[21] It follows that numerically one concept existing subjectively in the mind represents what is one not numerically but analogically;[22]

so there is one mental concept in the mind,[23] but this is not one perfect and adequate concept. It is when speaking of perfect and adequate mental concepts and what they represent that Cajetan says that in analogy there cannot be numerically one.[24]

In response to the second question, Cajetan reiterates his point from *De Nominum Analogia* that a perfect and adequate concept of a common analogue cannot be abstracted from the diverse analogates. This is because properly speaking abstraction implies the separation of a distinct *ratio* common to those things from which it is abstracted. Indeed, this is why there can be no perfect and adequate concept of the common analogue. Nonetheless, there can be an imperfect concept of the common analogue; it is possible to resolve a proper *ratio* of an individual analogate into a "confused" concept that imperfectly represents the diverse analogates.[25] In the case of *being*, this means that a concept can be resolved that is not the concept of one particular being, or even of one category of being, but of all being. Indeed, anything, insofar as it is a being, can be resolved into this concept of being, which is why *being* is said to be the first known, and the most simple.[26] So Cajetan can say that a perfect and adequate concept of being cannot be abstracted, and yet being is a simple concept, the first known, and into which all resolution is made.[27]

Insofar as Cajetan's clarifications—especially the second—concern the concept of *being*, they are, no doubt, important for the metaphysician. Anyone looking for insight into Cajetan's understanding of metaphysics would do well to consider the discussion in *De Conceptu Entis*, a discussion that supplements, for example, what Cajetan says about the primacy and simplicity of the concept of being at the beginning of his commentary on *De Ente et Essentia*. Yet Cajetan's discussion, compressed as it is,[28] is primarily a clarification of the semantic analysis given in *De Nominum Analogia*. To be sure, it involves an application of that theory to the concept of being, but it is nonetheless made up of essentially semantic clarifications, clarifications about the different senses of concepts, about which kinds can be abstracted and how, about the nature of resolution, and, again, about the care that must be taken in interpreting different remarks about analogy.

—AT THIS POINT, THEN, WE CAN SUMMARIZE CAJETAN'S treatment of analogy of proportionality. The initial chapters of *De Nominum Analogia* describe, and then set aside, two descriptions of how a term can signify *rationes* that are partly the same and partly different. Only a third proposal, in which diverse *rationes* are proportionally one, cannot be subsumed under the semantic rules that govern equivocals and univocals, and so the balance of Cajetan's treatise, the heart of Cajetan's theory of analogy, is an analysis of the semantic ramifications of proportional unity at all semantic levels—simple apprehension, judgment, and inference. From the beginning this requires Cajetan to qualify the sense in which there is and is not one analogue, which leads to his distinction between the "perfect" mental concept, which adequately represents only one of the diverse, precise analogues, and the "imperfect" mental concept, which somehow represents one common analogue, by representing the diverse analogues in their unity. This naturally leads to a discussion of the special circumstances of "abstraction" in the case of analogy. Properly speaking, there can be no abstraction, insofar as this implies the isolation of a common and univocal element. But there can be a kind of quasi abstraction, by which the commonness of the analogates is considered without their diversity. This involves a making indeterminate, or a "confusion," of their distinctness, leaving only attention to their (proportional) unity.

Moving from simple apprehension to judgment, Cajetan explains that because there can be this kind of quasi abstraction of a common analogue, so that it is apprehended by one imperfect concept, the analogue can be predicated as a superior of inferiors. Here again, its universality must not be conflated with univocity; for the foundation of univocity is absolute sameness of *rationes*, while the foundation of superiority is merely sameness of *rationes*, where this can include even proportional sameness. If the analogue is to be defined, however, this proportional sameness will not enter into the definition of the analogue. This is why Cajetan clarifies that a term analogous by proportionality signifies not a relation, but the foundation of a relation. In other words, because analogy of proportionality involves diverse, proportionally similar relations (the relations between the diverse analogues and their respective analogates), a term analogous by proportionality signifies one of the relata (one of the analogues) of one of the proportionally similar relations. But not all of the relata of these relations, nor the relations themselves, are included in the definition of the analogue; or, to put it another way, one of the proportionally similar *rationes* is not defined in terms of another. In this respect, analogy of proportionality differs from analogy of attribution, and from metaphor, in which the *ratio* of a secondary analogue necessarily includes reference to a primary analogue.

Nonetheless, priority and posteriority are present in analogy of proportionality, in two ways. First, there is the priority of the original signification of a term subsequently extended analogically; this is priority in the order of imposition. Second, there is the priority in the order of the thing signified; for diverse, proportionally similar analogues can have more or less excellence, and their respective analogates can have priority or posteriority in the order of being. But the fact that we can make such comparisons does not imply that there is some univocal element in virtue of which they are compared, for the foundation of comparison, like the foundation of superiority, is not absolute sameness, but any sameness, which can include proportional sameness.

Lastly, Cajetan describes the implications of proportional unity at the level of inference, and it is here that he finally addresses the infamous arguments of Scotus, that any nonunivocal term would cause a fallacy of equivocation. In short, Scotus's semantic objections ignored the metaphysical classification of proportional unity, and failed to recognize that the kind of unity that is the foundation of contradiction, like that which founds superiority and comparison, includes this proportional unity. So *rationes* proportionally one are unified enough to preserve the validity of inferences. An analogous term can be used in different senses in different parts of the syllogism, and yet the common term does not disguise an equivocation, for the term signifies an analogue proportionally one.

By ending with some general advice about employing analogical terms, and about how to make sense of the sometimes seemingly contradictory claims others have made about the nature of analogy, Cajetan reminds us that semantic analysis alone is not sufficient to guarantee the right use and interpretation of analogical terms. We might say that here is a recognition of the limits of semantic analysis, and a clear acknowledgment of the role of judgment in analogy. But for Cajetan, it is clear that properly exercising that judgment requires us to keep in mind the semantic details of analogical terms, and especially to keep in mind the nature of proportional unity and its implications in all three parts of reasoning governed by logic.

Conclusion

Modern scholarly discussions of Cajetan's *De Nominum Analogia* have focused on the question of Cajetan's fidelity to Aquinas. But in seeking an answer to that question, the scholarly debate lost sight of the question or questions that motivated Cajetan to write *De Nominum Analogia*, and so lost sight of the most appropriate perspective from which to interpret, and then to evaluate, the intention and significance of Cajetan's analogy theory.

Cajetan's *De Nominum Analogia* offers a semantic analysis of analogy—that is, an analysis of the semantic properties of terms that exhibit associated meaning, considered as a mean between univocation and pure equivocation. Cajetan's starting point was a tradition that had described analogy as a kind of equivocation (*aequivocatio a consilio*), involving diverse *rationes* that are similar "in some respect" (*secundum quid*). Latent in the tradition, but brought out and made inescapable by the objections of Scotus, were two difficulties. First, how can the sameness *secundum quid* be further specified? And second, how can any nonunivocal term, exhibiting not sameness *simpliciter* but only sameness *secundum quid*, avoid causing the fallacy of equivocation?

The two central doctrines of Cajetan's teaching on analogy must be understood as responses to these two questions. Cajetan's threefold division of "modes" of analogy is a description of three different ways that *rationes* signified by a term can be somehow the same. And Cajetan's preference for analogy of proportionality is based on the conviction that, of the three modes, only this one is a true mean between univocation and equivocation, a nonunivocal term that is nonetheless sufficiently unified to preserve the validity of inferences.

The centerpiece of Cajetan's theory of analogy, then, is his appeal to a special category of sameness or unity. By appealing to non-generic likeness or proportional unity—*analogia* in the original Greek sense—Cajetan only draws on another part of the same Aristotelian philosophical tradition within which the semantic difficulties about analogy had taken shape. Just in this respect it must be acknowledged that proportional unity is a perfectly legitimate variety of unity *secundum quid*. Moreover, proportional unity seems especially suited to answer the question of how diverse *rationes* in an *aequivocatio a consilio* could be unified enough to respond to the Scotistic objections against the possibility of a true mean between univocation and equivocation.

In one sense, Cajetan's theory is not a startling innovation. He pursues, perhaps with greater rigor, the strategy already common in the earlier commentary tradition on the *Categories*, of appealing to proportionality as one of several relationships possible in deliberate equivocation. The innovation is in seeing that this helps to answer challenges to the Aristotelian framework that had not been pressed before Scotus. Proportional unity, as opposed to the relational unity of attribution, is sufficient to preserve the validity of inferences in scientific reasoning, and for this reason analogy of proportionality is the most proper form of analogy—the most genuine mean between univocation and equivocation—and so superior to other kinds of *pros hen* equivocation.

Cajetan's appeal to proportional unity also has the advantage of respecting and confirming the limits of semantic analysis. In light of the present interpretation, we can understand why Cajetan is preoccupied with describing the unity of the analogical concept—a preoccupation that heretofore has seemed inappropriate to many of Cajetan's interpreters—and at the same time we can appreciate that by describing the unity of the analogical concept as *proportional*, Cajetan refused to follow the Scotistic temptation to regard semantic analysis as requiring a reduction to univocal concepts. Furthermore, Cajetan's analysis of what a proportionally unified concept entails for the rest of logic confirms the importance of context, and the necessary role of judgment, in the use and interpretation of analogical terms.

Cajetan, apparently unlike some of his contemporaries, does not hold that words have fixed semantic properties independently of their role in sentences; rather they must be understood and analyzed in light of propositional and inferential context.

Undoubtedly the most difficult, and alien, aspects of Cajetan's semantic analysis of analogy are the discussions of the logical and psychological implications of proportionally unified concepts—for example, in the distinction between "perfect" and "imperfect" concepts, and the distinction between proper abstraction and a kind of abstraction by "confusion." For many interpreters, these discussions have seemed obscure and overly technical. And yet at the very least we can now see the motivation behind them; they no longer need to seem like unaccountable preoccupations, but can be understood as necessary expansions of traditional logical and psychological frameworks to accommodate the phenomenon of analogy.

Indeed, while the present study does not claim to be an exhaustive exploration of Cajetan's teaching on analogy, it does claim to set out the terms within which further fruitful exploration must take place. Most of the history of interpretations of Cajetan's *De Nominum Analogia* can be described, as in chapter 1, as representing a more-or-less coherent "paradigm," approaching *De Nominum Analogia* as if it were an interpretation or systematization of Aquinas, or a generically "Thomistic" exposition of analogy. Recent historical scholarship, and reflection on the text of *De Nominum Analogia* itself, suggested the exhaustion of that paradigm, and pointed to the emergence of a new one, which approaches *De Nominum Analogia* as a text intending to answer the particular and focused questions recapitulated here.

Of course, when an old paradigm gives way to a new one, it is because the new one accounts for all those things that the old paradigm had tried to account for, and accounts for further things that the old one could not account for. But an old paradigm also gives way to a new one because that new one opens up space for new inquiry. The new paradigm, which this study advocates and tries to embody, brings with it its own new "puzzles." Among these puzzles are some relating to the relevant psychology and epistemology of analogical concept formation and reasoning. How can we better understand the nature of an "imperfect" concept and its acquisition? How can we better understand the psychological process of abstraction-by-confusion? Among other puzzles are those concerning the articulation, and even formalization, of the semantics of analogy. Is Bochenski's "isomorphy" an appropriate and useful translation of proportional unity? Can it contribute to a rigorous formal analysis of analogy?

And of course there will be puzzles about how Cajetan's teaching on analogy applies to particular questions or theses, for instance about the divine names, about being as the first object of knowledge, and about the use of argument by analogy in the special sciences.

And finally, we may return to the question of how Cajetan's theory of analogy relates to the thought and writings of Aquinas. That question is not fully addressed here, largely because in describing a new interpretive paradigm it was necessary to set aside as ill-formed the question of whether Cajetan's theory was "an authentic interpretation of Aquinas." Only by setting that question aside could we try to make sense of Cajetan's theory on its own terms. But once introduced, the new paradigm may return to the question of how Cajetan's analysis of analogy is related to Aquinas's own teaching. It may even ask, in a new way, to what extent Cajetan's theory is "Thomistic." We now see that a responsible evaluation of the "Thomism" of Cajetan's theory of analogy must take into account the significant development, between the times of Aquinas and Cajetan, in the terms of Thomistic logic and psychology (the distinction between formal and objective concepts is only the most rudimentary example of this). And as we have seen, strictly speaking, Aquinas did not answer, and did not try to answer, the specific semantic questions that *De Nominum Analogia* addresses. But Aquinas did appreciate the importance of proportional unity, as a special kind of unity, and one that was not the same as a determinate relation of one to another. The question of the Thomism of Cajetan's theory will depend at least in part on whether we judge that Thomas himself would have invoked proportional unity if he, like Cajetan, had attempted to analyze the relationships that hold between the semantic properties of analogical terms.

Notes

The epigraphs are from R. G. Collingwood, *An Autobiography* (Oxford: Oxford University Press, 1939), 39, and H. G. Gadamer, *Truth and Method*, 2nd ed. (New York: Crossroad, 1992), 429.

   1. *CPA* 11: "Quot autem modis contingat variari analogiam et quomodo, nunc quum summarie loquimur, silentio pertransibimus, specialem de hoc tractatum, si Deo placuerit, cito confecturi."
   2. "Difficultates de analogia, quae satis metaphysicae sunt, ita copiose et subtiliter a Caietano disputate sunt opusc. de Analogia nominum, ut nobis locum non reliquerit quidquam aliud excogitandi."*Ars Logica*, p. 2, q. 13, a. 2 (481b30–35).
   3. A brief biography of Cajetan, with further references, is in James A. Weisheipl, "Cajetan (Tommaso de Vio)," in *New Catholic Encyclopedia*, vol. 2, 2nd ed., ed. Bernard L. Marthaler et al. (Detroit: Gale/Catholic University of America Press, 2003), 852–55.

   1. A recent suggestion of the ubiquity of metaphor in everyday discourse is George Lakoff and Mark Johnson, *Metaphors We Live By* (Chicago: University of Chicago Press, 1980). The authors apparently don't realize that their thesis is not new, and could be attributed to Aristotle: see Mary Hesse, "Aristotle's Logic of Analogy," *Philosophical Quarterly* 15 (1965): 328–40.
   2. There is no comprehensive study of the history of analogy. One reason is that there are diverse phenomena to be taken into account besides the two highlighted here, such as the related but arguably distinct issue of analogy as a form of reasoning or argument (cf. G. E. R. Lloyd, *Polarity and Analogy: Two Types of Argumentation in Early Greek Thought* [Cambridge: Cambridge

University Press, 1966] and Mary Hesse, *Models and Analogy in Science* [Notre Dame, Ind.: University of Notre Dame Press, 1966]). Second, a history would have to cover the many logical, epistemological, and metaphysical issues that arise in connection with analogy in different fields of thought, from the natural sciences to politics and theology. (Consider how the issues raised in the works by Lloyd and Hesse just referenced would differ from the relevant topics in works on analogical reasoning in jurisprudence or political history, not to mention the topics treated along with analogy in works on natural theology and divine naming). Moreover, the very approach to analogy itself varies according to the methods and conventions of the various disciplines that have taken an interest in it: in addition to logic, metaphysics, and theology, there is linguistics, epistemology, cognitive psychology, legal theory, social and political philosophy, philosophy of science, etc. The history traced briefly here is that typically thought essential for understanding scholastic considerations of analogy in logic, metaphysics, and theology; a longer version of such a history (although with some important gaps, e.g., Boethius) has recently been traced by Joël Lonfat, "Archéologie de la notion d'analogie d'Aristote à saint Thomas d'Aquin," *Archives d'Histoire Doctrinale et Littéraire du Moyen Age* 71 (2004): 35–107. A more thorough history is in the third volume of Jacobus M. Ramirez, *De analogia*, tom. 2 of his *Opera omnia* (Madrid: Instituto de Filosofia "Luis Vives," 1970).

3. The point is well established, but see G. L. Muskens, *De vocis* ἀναλογίας *significatione ac usu apud Aristotelem* (Groningen: Wolters, 1943) and Pierre Aubenque, "Les origines de la doctrine de l'analogie de l'être: Sur l'histoire d'un contresens," *Les Études Philosophiques* 33 (1978): 3–12.

4. On nongeneric likeness in Aristotle, see M.-D. Philippe, "*Analogon* and *Analogia* in the Philosophy of Aristotle," *The Thomist* 33 (1969): 1–74. On associated meaning, see Christopher Shields, *Order in Multiplicity: Homonymy in the Philosophy of Aristotle* (Oxford: Oxford University Press, 1999).

5. C. Luna, "Paronymie, homonymie πρὸς ἕν et analogie: A propos d'un article de J. Hirschberger," app. 2 in *Simplicius: Commentaire sur les Catégories*, ed. Ilsetraut Hadot, Philosophia Antiqua 51, fasc. 3 (Leiden: Brill, 1990), 153–59.

6. For discussion see Joseph Owens, *The Doctrine of Being in the Aristotelian "Metaphysics": A Study in the Greek Background of Medieval Thought*, 3rd ed. (Toronto: Pontifical Institute of Medieval Studies, 1978), 118–25.

7. On focal meaning, see G. E. L. Owen, "Logic and Metaphysics in Some Early Works of Aristotle," in *Aristotle and Plato in Mid-Fourth Century*, ed. Ingemar Düring and G. E. L. Owen (Göteborg: Studia Graeca et Latina Gothoburgensia, 1960), 163–90.

8. See Philippe, "*Analogon* and *Analogia* in the Philosophy of Aristotle," and Muskens, *De vocis* ἀναλογίας *significatione ac usu apud Aristotelem*. Even Leszl, who insisted on treating analogy as a function of terms (a "logical device") like focal meaning, conceded that "what Aristotle himself normally means by ἀναλογία is not the logical device itself, but only the proportion [of things] on which it is based." Walter Leszl, *Logic and Metaphysics in Aristotle: Aristotle's Treatment of Types of Equivocity and Its Relevance to His Metaphysical Theories* (Padua: Editrice Antenore, 1970), 126–27.

9. Typically *analogia* was taken to describe quantities in a *geometric* harmony (e.g., 2:3::6:9), although it seems that even in a mathematical context *analogia* was a somewhat flexible notion that could apply to other sorts of relationships, such as succession (2:3::8:9) or the relation of a number to its square (2:4::8:64).

10. This extension of the technical mathematical term *analogia* to other uses is itself a result of discerning nongeneric likeness: qualitative comparison is somehow like quantitative comparison; strict *analogia* is to relationships of numerical quantity as *analogia* more broadly speaking is to nonmathematical relationships. So, as a word that gets extended to a new context, the case of *analogia* in Greek is also an instance of a term becoming subject to diverse but associated meanings. But with this observation we are getting somewhat ahead of ourselves.

11. Simplicius, Ammonius, and Porphyry each take Aristotle's discussion of equivocation or homonymy as an occasion to distinguish between deliberate and chance homonyms, and then further distinguish homonyms "according to analogy" as a subdivision of deliberate homonyms. On Simplicius's treatment of analogy in the context of equivocation in Aristotle's *Categories*, see Lonfat, "Archéologie," 63–68.

12. Boethius, *In Categorias Aristotelis Libri Quatuor* (*PL*, vol. 64), 166.

13. See the commentary in Jean-Yves Guillaumin's edition and translation of Boethius, *Institution arithmétique* (Paris: Les Belles Lettres, 1995), 215–16.

14. Given the schema X:Y::Y:Z, Y is the mean of an arithmetic proportion if $Y-X = Z-Y$. Y is the mean of a geometric proportion if $X/Y = Y/Z$. Y is the mean of a harmonic proportion if $Z/X = (Z-Y)/(Y-X)$.

15. For instance, see Avicenna, *Metaphysica*, in *Liber de Philosophia Prima sive Scientia Divina*, ed. S. Van Riet (Leiden: Brill, 1977, 1980), I.5, p. 40, and V.5, p. 272. For secondary literature, in addition to some of the historical studies already mentioned, see the work of E. J. Ashworth, for instance: "Medieval Theories of Analogy," in *The Stanford Encyclopedia of Philosophy*, ed. Edward N. Zalta, Winter 1999 ed. (URL = http://plato.stanford.edu/archives/win1999/entries/analogy-medieval/); "Analogical Concepts: The Fourteenth-Century Background to Cajetan," *Dialogue* 31 (1992): 399–413, esp. 401; and "Analogy and Equivocation in Thirteenth-Century Logic: Aquinas in Context," *Mediaeval Studies* 54 (1992): 94–135, esp. 102–3. On especially the Arabic influence, see H. A. Wolfson, "The Amphibolous Terms in Aristotle, Arabic Philosophy, and Maimonides," *Harvard Theological Review* 31 (1938): 151–73. On the development of analogy theories in the Middle Ages also see Lonfat, "Archéologie,"; Alain de Libera, "Les sources gréco-arabes de la théorie médiévale de l'analogie de l'être," *Les Études Philosophiques* (1989): 319–45; and Jean-François Courtine, *Inventio analogiae: Métaphysique et ontothéologie* (Paris: Vrin, 2005).

16. Compare the two articles by Philip L. Reynolds, "Bonaventure's Theory of Resemblance," *Traditio* 58 (2003): 219–55, and "Analogy of Names in Bonaventure," *Mediaeval Studies* 65 (2003): 117–62.

17. Two studies of analogy outside of the more common fields of logic, metaphysics, and theology are Richard Padovan, *Proportion: Science, Philosophy, Architecture* (London: Spon, 1999), and John E. Murdoch, "The Medieval

Language of Proportions: Elements of the Interaction with Greek Foundations and the Development of New Mathematical Techniques," in *Scientific Change: Historical Studies in the Intellectual, Social and Technical Conditions for Scientific Discovery and Technical Invention, from Antiquity to the Present*, ed. A. C. Crombie (New York: Basic Books, 1963), 237–71.

18. Anne Moyer, *The Philosopher's Game: Rithmomachia in Medieval and Renaissance Europe* (Ann Arbor: University of Michigan Press, 2001).

19. One could cite numerous works on analogy in the theology of St. Thomas, but two recent studies are Seung-Chan Park, *Die Rezeption der mittelalterlichen Sprachphilosophie in der Theologie des Thomas von Aquin: Mit besonderer Berücksichtigung der Analogie* (Leiden: Brill, 1999), and Gregory Philip Rocca, *Speaking the Incomprehensible God: Thomas Aquinas on the Interplay of Positive and Negative Theology* (Washington, D.C.: Catholic University of America Press, 2004).

20. Compare for instance the logical emphasis in Ralph McInerny, *Aquinas and Analogy* (Washington, D.C.: Catholic University of America Press, 1996), with the metaphysical emphasis in James F. Anderson, *The Bond of Being: An Essay on Analogy and Existence* (St. Louis: Herder, 1949). A recent entry in this ongoing debate is Laurence Dewan, "St. Thomas and Analogy: The Logician and the Metaphysician," in *Laudemus viros gloriosos: Essays in Honor of Armand Maurer*, ed. R. E. Houser (Notre Dame, Ind.: University of Notre Dame Press, 2007), 132–45.

21. Cf. George P. Klubertanz, *St. Thomas Aquinas on Analogy: A Textual Analysis and Systematic Synthesis* (Chicago: Loyola University Press, 1960).

CHAPTER ONE

1. M. T.-L. Penido, *Le rôle de l'analogie en théologie dogmatique* (Paris: Librairie Philosophique J. Vrin, 1931), 143n2: "En réalité Cajetan ne prétendait aucunement innover, mais *restituer* la théorie aristotélico-thomiste. . . . Il ne veut pas innover mais restaurer."

2. Ibid., 35–36.

3. Aloys Goergen, *Kardinal Cajetans Lehre von der Analogie; Ihr Verhältnis zu Thomas von Aquin* (Speyer a. Rh.: Pilger-Druckerei, 1938).

4. *I Sent.* 19.5.2 ad 1: "aliquid dicitur secundum analogiam tripliciter: vel secundum intentionem tantum, et non secundum esse. . . . Vel secundum esse et non secundum intentionem. . . . Vel secundum intentionem et secundum esse."

5. Reginald Garrigou-Lagrange, *La synthèse Thomiste*, nov. ed. (Paris: Desclée de Brouwer and Cie., 1950), 144–55; Garrigou-Lagrange, *The One God: A Commentary on the First Part of St. Thomas' Theological Summa*, trans. Bede Rose (St. Louis: Herder, 1943), 396–400; Garrigou-Lagrange, *God: His Existence and His Nature*, 2 vols., trans. Bede Rose (St. Louis: Herder, 1934/1936), vol. 1, 214, 224–27; vol. 2, 203–21.

6. Jacques Maritain, *Distinguish to Unite, or The Degrees of Knowledge*, trans. Gerald B. Phelan (New York: Charles Scribner's Sons, 1959), 418–21

("Appendix 2: Analogy"). (Maritain called *De Nominum Analogia* "authentically Thomistic"; 420.)

7. Gerald B. Phelan, *St. Thomas and Analogy* (Milwaukee: Marquette University Press, 1941).

8. Yves Simon, "On Order in Analogical Sets," in *Philosopher at Work: Essays by Yves R. Simon*, ed. Anthony O. Simon (Lanham, Md.: Rowman and Littlefield, 1999), 135–71 (reprinted from *New Scholasticism* 34 [1960]: 1–42). But note that Burrell portrays Simon as departing from the Cajetanian tradition. Burrell, *Analogy and Philosophical Language* (New Haven: Yale University Press, 1973), 202–9; Burrell, "A Note on Analogy," *New Scholasticism* 36 (1962): 225–32. The position of Simon and the interpretation of Burrell are considered in chaps. 3 and 8 below.

9. James F. Anderson, *The Bond of Being: An Essay on Analogy and Existence* (St. Louis: Herder, 1949); Anderson, *Reflections on the Analogy of Being* (The Hague: Martinus Nijhoff, 1967); Anderson, "Some Basic Propositions Concerning Metaphysical Analogy" (with comments and responses), *Review of Metaphysics* 5 (1952): 465–72; Anderson, "Mathematical and Metaphysical Analogy in St. Thomas," *Thomist* 3 (1941): 564–79; Anderson, "Bases of Metaphysical Analogy," *Downside Review* 66 (1948): 38–47.

10. Edward A. Bushinski and Henry J. Koren, trans., *The Analogy of Names and the Concept of Being*, by Cajetan (Pittsburgh: Duquesne University Press, 1953), ix, 7.

11. Jacobus M. Ramirez, "De analogia secundum doctrinam Aristotelico-Thomisticam," in *Ciencia Tomista* 24 (1921): 20–40, 195–214, 337–57; 25 (1922): 17–38.

12. Jacobus M. Ramirez, "En torno a un famoso texto de Santo Tomas sobre analogia," reprinted as an appendix to Ramirez, *De analogia*, in Ramirez, *Opera omnia*, tom. 2 (Madrid: Instituto de Filosofia "Luis Vives," 1970), vol. 4, 1811–50. (The article originally appeared in *Sapientia* 8 [1953]: 166–92.)

13. Ramirez, *De analogia*, 1400–17.

14. George P. Klubertanz, *St. Thomas Aquinas on Analogy: A Textual Analysis and Systematic Synthesis* (Chicago: Loyola University Press, 1960).

15. Bernard Montagnes, *La doctrine de l'analogie de l'être d'après Saint Thomas d'Aquin* (Louvain/Paris: Publications Universitaires/Béatrice-Nauwelaerts, 1963). There is now an English edition, *The Doctrine of the Analogy of Being According to Thomas Aquinas*, trans. E. M. Macierowski (Milwaukee: Marquette University Press, 2004).

16. P. Pedro Descoqs, *Praelectiones Theologiae Naturalis*, 2: 758ff. Descoqs, *Institutiones Metaphysicae Generalis*, vol. 1, 262–71.

17. Hampus Lyttkens, *The Analogy Between God and the World: An Investigation of Its Background and Interpretation of Its Use by Thomas of Aquino* (Uppsala: Almqvist and Wiksells Boktrycheri AB, 1952).

18. E. J. Ashworth, "Suárez on the Analogy of Being: Some Historical Background," *Vivarium* 33 (1995): 57; Ashworth, "Analogical Concepts: The Fourteenth-Century Background to Cajetan," *Dialogue* 31 (1992): 401; Ashworth, "Analogy and Equivocation in Thirteenth-Century Logic: Aquinas in

Context," *Mediaeval Studies* 54 (1992): 128; Ashworth, "Language, Renaissance Philosophy of," in *Routledge Encyclopedia of Philosophy*, vol. 5 (New York: Routledge, 1998), 411–15, §4.

19. Edward P. Mahoney, "Cajetan (Thomas De Vio)," in *Routledge Encyclopedia of Philosophy*, vol. 2 (New York: Routledge, 1997), 171–75, §2.

20. Jean-Luc Marion, *Sur la théologie blanche de Descartes: Analogie, création des vérités éternelles et fondement* (Paris: Presses Universitaires de France, 1981), 88, 92.

21. Ralph J. Masiello, "The Analogy of Proportion According to the Metaphysics of St. Thomas," *Modern Schoolman* 35 (1958): 91–105.

22. Copleston denies that Aquinas "ever abandoned analogy of proportionality"; Frederick C. Copleston, *A History of Philosophy*, vol. 2, *Medieval*, part 2, *Albert the Great to Duns Scotus* (Garden City, N.Y.: Image, 1962), 74. But Copleston also says, "I venture to doubt whether [Cajetan's teaching on analogy] represents the view of St. Thomas"; *A History of Philosophy*, vol. 3, *Late Medieval and Renaissance Philosophy*, part 2, "The Revival of Platonism to Suarez" (Garden City, N.Y.: Image, 1963), 158.

23. Ramirez, "En torno a un famoso texto de Santo Tomas sobre analogia." Cf. Ramirez, *De analogia*, 1473, 1482–88.

24. Suarez, *Disputationes metaphysicae*, vol. 2 (Hildesheim: Georg Olms, 1965), disp. 28, sect. 3, nn. 14, 17; disp. 32, sect. 2, n. 14, pp. 17, 19, 323.

25. Descoqs, *Institutiones metaphysicae generalis*, vol. 1, 260–69; Descoqs, *Praelectiones theologiae naturalis*, vol. 2, 765ff. On Descoqs' "slightly modified Suarezianism" see Lyttkens, *The Analogy Between God and the World*, 238–40. Descoqs discusses Suarez at *Praelectiones theologiae naturalis* 2: 768.

26. George P. Klubertanz, "Analogy," in *New Catholic Encyclopedia*, vol. 1 (New York: McGraw Hill, 1967), 462–63.

27. Ralph McInerny, *The Logic of Analogy: An Interpretation of St. Thomas* (The Hague: Martinus Nijhoff, 1961); McInerny, *Aquinas and Analogy* (Washington, D.C.: Catholic University of America Press, 1996). McInerny's criticism of Cajetan is addressed below in chap. 6.

28. For references to Gilson and those who have followed him, see chap. 3 below where this criticism is addressed. For another discussion of this issue see Gregory Philip Rocca, *Speaking the Incomprehensible God: Thomas Aquinas on the Interplay of Positive and Negative Theology* (Washington, D.C.: Catholic University of America Press, 2004), 154–95.

29. David Burrell, *Analogy and Philosophical Language* (New Haven: Yale University Press, 1973). Cf. Burrell, "A Note on Analogy," *New Scholasticism* 36 (1962): 225–32; Burrell, "Beyond the Theory of Analogy," *Proceedings of the American Catholic Philosophical Association* 46 (1972): 114–21.

30. Battista Mondin, *The Principle of Analogy in Protestant and Catholic Theology*, 2nd ed. (The Hague: Martinus Nijhoff, 1968), 36.

31. Ibid., 40.

32. Ibid., 42.

33. Ibid.

34. Montagnes, *La doctrine de l'analogie de l'être d'après Saint Thomas d'Aquin*, 126: "La doctrine de Cajetan sur l'analogie est-elle conforme à celle de S. Thomas?"

35. Ibid., 126–27.

36. John F. Wippel, *The Metaphysical Thought of Thomas Aquinas: From Finite Being to Uncreated Being* (Washington, D.C.: Catholic University of America Press, 2000), 73n30; 90n87.

37. Leo O'Donovan, "Methodology in Some Recent Studies of Analogy," *Philosophical Studies* (Dublin) 16 (1967): 78. Cf. Michael McCanles, "Univocalism in Cajetan's Doctrine of Analogy," *New Scholasticism* 42 (1968): 18–47.

38. Burrell, *Analogy and Philosophical Language*, 122.

39. Paul G. Kuntz, "The Analogy of Degrees of Being: A Critique of Cajetan's *Analogy of Names*," *New Scholasticism* 61 (1982): 72.

40. Jean-Luc Marion, *God Without Being: Hors-Text*, trans. Thomas A. Carlson (Chicago: University of Chicago Press, 1991), 81.

41. Lyttkens, *The Analogy Between God and the World*, 205; Edward A. Bushinski, "Introduction" to *The Analogy of Names and the Concept of Being*, by Thomas de Vio Cardinal Cajetan, trans. Edward A. Bushinski and Henry J. Koren (Pittsburgh: Duquesne University Press, 1953), ix, 5; Edward Mahoney, "Cajetan," in *The Routledge Encyclopedia of Philosophy*, vol. 2, 171; Mondin, *The Principle of Analogy in Protestant and Catholic Theology*, 36–42; Burrell, *Analogy and Philosophical Language*, 11; Robert E. Meagher, "Thomas Aquinas and Analogy: A Textual Analysis," *The Thomist* 34 (1970): 231, 237; James F. Ross, "Analogy as a Rule of Meaning for Religious Language," in *Aquinas: A Collection of Critical Essays*, ed. Anthony Kenny (Garden City, N.Y.: Anchor Books, 1969), 93 (this essay also appears in *International Philosophical Quarterly* 1 [1961]: 468–502, and in *Inquiries into Medieval Philosophy: A Collection in Honor of Francis P. Clarke*, ed. James F. Ross [Westport, Conn.: Greenwood, 1971], 35–74); Jean-François Courtine, *Inventio analogiae: Métaphysique et ontothéologie* (Paris: Vrin, 2005), 163, 339. But cf. Ralph McInerny, *Aquinas and Analogy*, 24: "It is not at all clear that Cajetan in his opusculum intends to give an account of St. Thomas's teachings on analogous naming . . ."

42. Frank R. Harrison, "The Cajetan Tradition of Analogy," *Franciscan Studies* 23 (1963): 180; Ralph J. Masiello, "The Analogy of Proportion According to the Metaphysics of St. Thomas," *Modern Schoolman* 35 (1958): 92; Michael McCanles, "Univocalism in Cajetan's Doctrine of Analogy," *New Scholasticism* 42 (1968): 18.

43. A typical presentation is Mondin, *The Principle of Analogy in Protestant and Catholic Theology*, 35–40.

44. As already noted, Penido and Goergen invoke this claim in defense of Cajetan's fidelity to Aquinas. The claim that Cajetan's classification is *based on* the *Sentences* passage is made in: Lyttkens, *The Analogy Between God and the World*, 205; Harrison, "The Cajetan Tradition of Analogy," 182; Ralph J. Masiello, "The Analogy of Proportion," 93, 105; McInerny, *Aquinas and Analogy*, 5, 11, 12, 17; McInerny, *The Logic of Analogy*, 2–4, 22, 80; Robert E. Meagher,

"Thomas Aquinas and Analogy," 231; George P. Klubertanz, *St. Thomas Aquinas on Analogy: A Textual Analysis and Systematic Synthesis* (Chicago: Loyola University Press, 1960), 7; Kevin Flannery, S.J., review of McInerny, *Aquinas and Analogy*, in *Fellowship of Catholic Scholars Quarterly* 20 (1997): 34; Rocca, *Speaking the Incomprehensible God*, 113; Mondin, *The Principle of Analogy in Protestant and Catholic Theology*, 42; Seung-Chan Park, *Die Rezeption der mittelalterlichen Sprachphilosophie in der Theologie des Thomas von Aquin: Mit besonderer Berücksichtigung der Analogie* (Leiden: Brill, 1999), 358, 404. The passage from Aquinas "inspired" Cajetan's division, according to Montagnes, *La doctrine de l'analogie,* 136, and Henry Chavannes, *The Analogy Between God and the World in Saint Thomas Aquinas and Karl Barth*, trans. William Lumley (New York: Vantage Press, 1992), 52. Ian Wilks, "Aquinas on Analogy: The Distinction of Many-to-One and One-to-Another," *Modern Schoolman* 75 (1997): 40n12, says that Aquinas's text "gives rise to the Cajetanian classification in the first place." And Cajetan "follows" Aquinas's division, according to Vernon J. Bourke, "Cajetan, Cardinal," in *The Encyclopedia of Philosophy*, vol. 2, ed. Paul Edwards (New York: Macmillan, 1967), 5.

45. Penido and Goergen both invoke this in defense of Cajetan's theory, and the claim is also maintained by the now classic critics of Cajetan (Klubertanz, Montagnes, and Lyttkens) who have been followed since by McInerny, Wippel, and many others. To cite some recent works, see Courtine, *Inventio analogiae*, 339n3 ("C'est sur ce passage du corpus thomasien que se fonde toute la doctrine de Cajétan"), and Park, *Die Rezeption*, 396–97, 404.

46. On intrinsic and extrinsic denomination, see chap. 5 below; on their role in Cajetan's theory of analogy, see chaps. 6 and 7.

47. Park, *Die Rezeption*, 452.

48. E.g., Anderson, who takes himself to be following Cajetan, emphasizes the metaphysical dimension of analogy. See Anderson, *The Bond of Being*. Marion is typical of critics of Cajetan who say that Cajetan preferred analogy of proportionality because it involves intrinsic denomination. Marion, *Sur la théologie blanche de Descartes*, 93. On the priority of proportionality, see chap. 7 below.

49. Meagher, "Thomas Aquinas and Analogy: A Textual Analysis," 240.

50. Cajetan's discussion of analogy in *CDEE* is taken up again in chap. 6 below.

51. Both Capreolus and Soncinas cited *I Sent.* 19.5.2 ad 1 in connection with their proposed threefold divisions of analogy. Michael Tavuzzi, "Some Renaissance Thomist Divisions of Analogy," *Angelicum* 70 (1993): 100–102. Fifteenth-century Thomists apparently found the passage compatible with a threefold division of analogy made by a late thirteenth-century anonymous commentator on the *Sophistici Elenchi*. See Ashworth, "Suárez on the Analogy of Being," 59–61. Ashworth concludes that "neither Cajetan's use of Aquinas's *Sentences* commentary nor his threefold division of analogy were novel" (61). Chap. 2 will further pursue the historical background to Cajetan's division; more will be said about the philosophical, as opposed to textual, basis of Cajetan's threefold division in chap. 6.

52. Philip L. Reynolds's study of Bonaventure leads him to conclude that with respect to the priority of proportionality, we "should construe Cajetan's position rather as one of several traditional options than as a misreading of Thomas." Philip L. Reynolds, "Analogy of Names in Bonaventure," *Medieval Studies* 65 (2003): 161–62.

53. This criticism is addressed in chaps. 3 and 5, below.

54. McInerny, *Aquinas and Analogy*, 21, 30, 36, 46.

55. Anderson, *The Bond of Being*.

56. *DNA* §1.

57. However, I will argue in chaps. 5 and 6 below that even this is still a properly semantic and not strictly metaphysical consideration.

58. E.g., Maritain, *The Degrees of Knowledge*, 418; Anderson, "Bases of Metaphysical Analogy," and "Some Basic Propositions Concerning Metaphysical Analogy."

59. Ashworth, "Analogical Concepts: The Fourteenth-Century Background to Cajetan," 409.

60. Ibid., 399.

61. Ashworth, "Analogy and Equivocation in Thirteenth-Century Logic: Aquinas in Context," 94. Cf. Ashworth, "Equivocation and Analogy and Fourteenth Century Logic: Ockham, Burley, and Buridan," in *Historia Philosophiae Medii Aevi: Studien zur Geschichte der Philosophie des Mittelalters*, vol. 1, ed. Burkhard Mojsisch and Olaf Pluta (Amsterdam: Gruner, 1991), 24. Ashworth also considers views of Dominic of Flanders, Capreolus, and Soncinas in "Suárez on the Analogy of Being," 68–72.

62. Ashworth, "Analogical Concepts, 402.

63. Ibid., 402–3.

64. Tavuzzi, "Some Renaissance Thomist Divisions of Analogy," 93.

65. Tavuzzi defines the period as extending from 1444 to 1545—i.e., from the death of Capreolus to the opening of the Council of Trent. Tavuzzi, "Hervaeus Natalis and the Philosophical Logic of the Thomism of the Renaissance," *Doctor Communis* 45 (1992): 132.

66. Franco Riva, *Tommaso Claxton e l'analogia della proporzionalità* (Milan: Vita e Pensiero, 1989).

67. Montagnes suggests that Thomas Sutton and Thomas Claxton are "precursors" of Cajetan, especially that Cajetan "developed" Claxton's correllation of attribution with extrinsicality, and proportionality with intrinsicality. Montagnes, *La doctrine de l'analogie*, 124, 125n33.

68. Tavuzzi, "Some Renaissance Thomist Divisions of Analogy," 94.

69. Michael Tavuzzi, "Hervaeus Natalis and the Philosophical Logic of the Thomism of the Renaissance," *Doctor Communis* 45 (1992): 133–34.

70. Tavuzzi, "Some Renaissance Thomist Divisions of Analogy," 94.

71. Ibid. Tavuzzi cites Luciano Gargan, *Lo studio teologico e la biblioteca dei Domenicani a Padova nel tre e Quattrocento* (Padua: Editrice Antenore, 1971), 150–51.

72. Tavuzzi, "Some Renaissance Thomist Divisions of Analogy," 99. Dominic studied under John Versorius (d. 1485), who himself discussed analogy in a

work published in Cologne in 1494 (96n11). Tavuzzi notes that Dominic died in 1479 and so, contrary to the speculations of Marega (*CPI* xv) and Pinchard (*Métaphysique et semantique* [Paris: Vrin, 1987], 30, 96n11), could not have been one of Cajetan's teachers. However, according to Tavuzzi it is likely that Dominic would have taught Soncinas. Tavuzzi, "Some Renaissance Thomist Divisions of Analogy," 97.

73. Tavuzzi, "Some Renaissance Thomist Divisions of Analogy," 100–102. Tavuzzi suggests that Soncinas was following Capreolus in his use of *I Sent.* 19.5.2 ad 1.

74. Franco Riva, *Analogia e univocità in Tommaso de Vio "Gaetano"* (Milan: Vita e Pensiero, 1995). See also Riva, *L'analogia metaforica: Una questione logico-metafisica nel tomismo* (Milan: Vita e Pensiero, 1989); Riva, *Tommaso Claxton e l'analogia della proporzionalità* (Milan: Vita e Pensiero, 1989); Riva, "L'analogia dell'ente in Dominico di Fiandra," *Rivista di Filosofia Neo-scolastica* 86 (1994): 287–322; and Riva, "Il Gaetano e l'ente come «primum cognitum»," *Rivista di Filosofia Neo-scolastica* 85 (1993): 3–20.

75. With my overview of Cajetan's interpreters, compare the more detailed, but also schematic and essentially compatible, overviews in Riva, *Analogia e univocità in Tommaso de Vio "Gaetano,"* 3–17 and 343–49.

76. I will explore further what Riva describes as the polemic context of *DNA* in chap. 2, below.

77. Ashworth, "Suárez on the Analogy of Being: Some Historical Background."

78. Duns Scotus, *Librum Praedicamentorum Quaestiones*, in *Opera omnia*, vol. 1 (Hildesheim: Georg Olms, 1968; reprint of Lyon, 1639), 129b–130b.

79. Ashworth, "Suarez," 75, concludes by considering whether Cajetan or Suarez is "the correct interpreter of Aquinas."

80. This is not a criticism of Riva. To the contrary, Riva's scholarship provides much more historical detail than the present study, and the claims that will be offered here about how to interpret *De Nominum Analogia* could be vindicated only by the kind of thorough and nuanced research presented in Riva's *Analogia e univocità in Tommaso de Vio "Gaetano."* Yet as a history, Riva's book is more concerned with reading Cajetan in the context of his immediate contemporaries and less concerned with isolating Cajetan's distinctive theoretical concern.

CHAPTER TWO

1. The list of expected elements in a scholastic prologue is not fixed; this one is taken from A. J. Minnis, *Medieval Theory of Authorship: Scholastic Literary Attitudes in the Later Middle Ages* (London: Scholar Press, 1984), 19. Compare, for instance, Cajetan's own prologue to *CPA*, which, following the advice of Averroës' *Physics* commentary, lists "intention, utility, order [i.e., place among other works in the same subject; alternatively, the end or purpose the work is "ordered" to], division [i.e., order of parts], proportion [i.e., the relation to other

works and subjects], way of teaching [i.e., method of proceeding], name of the book, and subject of the author" (*CPA* 1). Other scholastic lists include such elements as the purpose or end (*causa operis, finis,* or *causa finalis*).

2. *CPA* 5: "si quaeratur, de vocibus an de rebus principaliter hic tractetur, respondendum est quod de rebus non absolute sed incomplexe conceptis et consequenti necessitate significatis." While this may sound like a reversal of the Porphyrian/Boethian tradition, which held that the *Categories* is about "words insofar as they signify things," Cajetan argues that his position is in fact the same. *CPA* 4–5: "Idem enim est tractare de rebus ut conceptis simplici apprehensione, et de vocibus ut significant illas sic conceptas, quoniam quicquid attribuitur uni, attribuitur reliquo, servata tamen proportione, quia res sic conceptae et significatae attribuitur ut rei, voci vero ut signo." For a more extended discussion of this argument, see Joshua P. Hochschild, "Words, Concepts and Things: Cajetan on the Subject of the *Categories,*" *Dionysius* 19 (2001): 159–66.

3. *DNA* §31. Cf. *CPA* 10–11, 13, and *CDEE* §21.

4. Aristotle himself apparently had a somewhat different equivocation in mind: the Greek word *zôon* could mean both *animal* and *picture.* But the commentary tradition soon mistook the intended sense, and even sometimes replaced the example, taking *anthrôpos* as equivocal between a picture of a man and an actual man. The misunderstanding (finding an analogy or *pros hen* equivocation where Aristotle probably intended only pure equivocation) does not make it any less appropriate that analogical usage be addressed in the context of Aristotle's discussion of univocation and equivocation. In the medieval Latin tradition the notion of analogy as a mean between univocation and equivocation can be traced to Porphyry (transmitted by Boethius, *In Categorias Aristotelis*), to Pseudo-Augustine (*Categoriae Decem*), and to Simplicius's commentary on the *Categories* (in the translation of William of Moerbeke).

5. *CPA* 11: "Quot autem modis contingat variari analogiam et quomodo, nunc quum summarie loquimur, silentio pertransibimus, specialem de hoc tractatum, si Deo placuerit, cito confecturi."

6. On translating *"ratio"* as "concept," see chap. 5.

7. *CPA* 8.

8. *CPA* 11.

9. Indeed, it is the precision of Cajetan's parallel definitions that allowed Bochenski to apply the tools of twentieth-century formal mathematical logic to articulate Thomistic notions of analogy. I. M. Bochenski, "On Analogy," *The Thomist* (1948): 425–77. Bochenski's paper was reprinted with corrections in *Logico-Philosophical Studies,* ed. Albert Menne (Dordrecht: D. Reidel, 1962), and in *Inquiries into Medieval Philosophy: A Collection in Honor of Francis P. Clarke,* ed. James F. Ross (Westport, Conn.: Greenwood, 1971), 99–122.

10. "Pour mieux situer le lecteur, si besoin est, rappelons que le présent Traité est un traité de *Logique.*" Hyacinthe-Marie Robillard, *De l'analogie et du concept d'être de Thomas de Vio, Cajetan: Traduction, commentaires et index* (Montreal: Les Presses de l'Université de Montréal, 1963), 218.

11. Robert Meagher, "Thomas Aquinas and Analogy: A Textual Analysis," *The Thomist* 34 (April 1970): 240, 241.

12. Meagher cites pages 35, 91, 93, and 98 of Ralph McInerny, *The Logic of Analogy* (The Hague: Martinus Nijhoff, 1961). The views articulated there appeared subsequently as well in McInerny, *Studies in Analogy* (The Hague: Martinus Nijhoff, 1968), 105–6, 108; McInerny, "The Analogy of Names Is a Logical Doctrine," in *Being and Predication: Thomistic Interpretations* (Washington, D.C.: Catholic University of America Press, 1986); McInerny, "Saint Thomas on *De hebdomadibus*," in *Being and Goodness: The Concept of the Good in Metaphysics and Philosophical Theology*, ed. Scott MacDonald (Ithaca: Cornell University Press, 1991), 90; McInerny, *Boethius and Aquinas* (Washington, D.C.: Catholic University of America Press, 1990), 238; McInerny, *Aquinas and Analogy* (Washington, D.C.: Catholic University of America Press, 1996), 11.

13. Against the exaggerated claims of Robert Meagher, see for instance McInerny, *The Logic of Analogy*, 34, 75. McInerny's criticism of Cajetan will be addressed in chap. 6.

14. Edward A. Bushinski and Henry J. Koren, *The Analogy of Names and the Concept of Being* (Pittsburgh: Duquesne University Press, 1953), 6.

15. Not surprisingly, other commentators have described Cajetan's concern in *De Nominum Analogia* as semantic. James F. Ross, "Analogy as a Rule of Meaning for Religious Language," in *Inquiries into Medieval Philosophy*, 36, says "'being analogous' will signify a semantical property of a term in several of its instances." David Burrell, in "Religious Language and the Logic of Analogy: Apropos of McInerny's Book and Ross' Review," *International Philosophical Quarterly* 2 (1962): 643, in a note to the claim that analogy is a "logical doctrine," says: "'Logical' is used here in the comprehensive scholastic sense of the science of the argumentation whereby one proceeds from what is known to what is unknown. . . . As such it includes the study of words and their meanings as preliminaries to reasoning, as well as formal deductive procedures. We should say rather: 'analogy is a semantic doctrine.'" See also Bruno Pinchard, *L'Analogie des Noms*, in *Métaphysique et sémantique: La signification analogiques des termes dans les Principes Métaphysiques* (Paris: Vrin, 1987), although Pinchard's approach to "semantics" is itself idiosyncratic. For the point that medieval logic in general is closer to what we today call semantics than to the mathematical formalism often associated with modern logic, cf., e.g., E. J. Ashworth, "Logic, Medieval," in *Routledge Encyclopedia of Philosophy* (New York: Routledge, 1998), §4: "The purpose of logic had nothing to do with the setting up of formal systems or the metalogical analysis of formal structures. Instead, it had a straightforwardly cognitive orientation." Cf. also Ernest A. Moody, "The Medieval Contribution to Logic," *Studies in Medieval Philosophy, Science, and Logic: Collected Papers, 1933–1969* (Berkeley: University of California Press, 1975), 387–90: "The historical significance of medieval logic seems to lie in the part it played in disclosing the insecure semantical presuppositions of the Aristotelian logic of terms. . . . What medieval logic has to contribute, to the further development and enrichment of modern logic, is [a] semantical bridge between the abstract, axiomatically derived, formal system of modern mathematical logic, and the concrete, empirically oriented forms in which natural languages exhibit the rational structure of experience on its phenomenological level."

16. *CDEE* §21: "Univocata sunt, quorum nomen est commune, et ratio secundum illud nomen est eadem simpliciter. Pura aequivocata sunt, quorum nomen est commune, et ratio secundum illud nomen est diversa simpliciter. Analogata sunt quorum nomen est commune, et ratio secundum illud nomen est aliquo modo eadem, et aliquo modo diversa seu secundum quid eadem, et secundum quid diversa. . . . Unde analogum est medium inter purum aequivocum et univocum, sicut inter idem simpliciter et diversum simpliciter cadit medium idem secundum quid et diversum secundum quid." It is worth remarking that, although he has replaced Aristotle's "dicuntur" with "sunt" in rephrasing the definitions of univocals and equivocals, Cajetan should not thereby be assumed to have ignored or failed to appreciate the import of Aristotle's wording. Cf. *CPA* 9: "Signantur quoque dixit «dicuntur» et non dixit «sunt», quia rebus non convenit aequivocari ut sunt in rerum natura, sed ut sunt in vocibus nostris. Aequivocari enim praesupponit vocari, quod rebus ex nobis accidit."

17. E. J. Ashworth, "Analogical Concepts: The Fourteenth-Century Background to Cajetan," *Dialogue* 31 (1992): 403.

18. Boethius, *In Categorias Aristotelis*, lib. I (*PL*, vol. 64, 166b–c); Pseudo-Augustine, *Categoriae Decem*, §17 (*PL*, vol. 32, 1421–22).

19. I. M. Bochenski, "On Analogy," *The Thomist* (1948): §16.

20. See chap. 4 for a discussion of what Aquinas has to offer on this matter.

21. The influence of Scotus's arguments on the development of Thomistic theories of analogy, including Cajetan's, has been widely noted. See, e.g., Bernard Montagnes, *La doctrine de l'analogie de l'être d'après Saint Thomas d'Aquin* (Louvain/Paris: Publications Universitaires/Béatrice-Nauwelaerts, 1963), 125, 154; Jean-Luc Marion, *Sur la théologie blanche de Descartes: Analogie, création des vérités éternelles et fondement* (Paris: Presses Universitaires de France, 1981), 79ff.; Joseph J. Przezdziecki, "Thomas of Sutton's Critique of the Doctrine of Univocity," in *An Etienne Gilson Tribute*, ed. Charles J. O'Neil (Milwaukee: Marquette University Press, 1959), 189; Patrick J. Sherry, "Analogy Today," *Philosophy* 51 (1976): 443; E. J. Ashworth, "Equivocation and Analogy in Fourteenth Century Logic: Ockham, Burley and Buridan," in *Historia Philosophiae Medii Aevi: Studien zur Geschichte der Philosophie des Mittelalters*, vol. 1, ed. Burkhard Mojsisch and Olaf Pluta (Amsterdam: Gruner, 1991), 25; Aloys Goergen, *Kardinal Cajetans Lehre von der Analogie; Ihr Verhältnis zu Thomas von Aquin* (Speyer a. Rh.: Pilger-Druckerei, 1938), 31–32; Michael Tavuzzi, "Some Renaissance Thomist Divisions of Analogy," *Angelicum* 70 (1993): 93–94; Ashworth, "Analogy and Equivocation," 121. The influence on Cajetan of some particular followers of Scotus is considered by Franco Riva, *Analogia e univocità in Tommaso de Vio "Gaetano"* (Milan: Vita e Pensiero, 1995), 25–36, 89; see also Ashworth, "Analogical Concepts," 401, and Ashworth, "Medieval Theories of Analogy," in *Stanford Encyclopedia of Philosophy*, ed. Edward N. Zalta (Winter 1999 ed.), URL = http://plato.stanford.edu/archives/win1999/entries/analogy=medieval/, §7.

22. Accordingly most other attempts to give historical context to Cajetan's treatise emphasize the controversy over the concept of *being*. Cf., e.g., Montagnes, *La doctrine de l'analogie de l'être d'après Saint Thomas d'Aquin*, 150ff.

23. Robert Prentice, "Univocity and Analogy According to Scotus's *Super Libros Elenchorum Aristotelis*," *Archives d'Histoire Doctrinale et Littéraire du Moyen Age* 35 (1968): 42–47.

24. Duns Scotus, *Commentaria Oxoniensia*, I, d. 3, qq. 1 & 2, a. 4, ¶346, ed. Marianus Fernandez Garcia (Florence: Collegii S. Bonaventurae, 1912), 309: "conceptum univocum dico qui ita est unus, quod eius unitas sufficit ad contradictionem affirmando et negando ipsum de eodem: sufficit etiam pro medio syllogistico, ut extrema unita in medio sic uno sine fallacia aequivocationis concludantur inter se uniri."

25. As Franco Riva has noted, Trombetta's Scotistic defense of univocity rests in part on the denial that a nonunivocal concept can be the subject of a science. Franco Riva, *Analogia e univocità in Tommaso de Vio "Gaetano,"* 32: "La difesa dell'univocità da parte di Antonio Trombetta si lascia cogliere secondo . . . la negazione che un concetto non univoco possa essere soggetto di scienza."

26. Duns Scotus, *In Librum Praedicamentorum Quaestiones*, q. 1: "ubi est idem conceptus, ibi est univocatio." Cf. *In Libros Elenchorum Quaestiones*, 2 (Paris: Vives, 1891), 20a–25a. For more references and discussion see Prentice, "Univocity and Analogy According to Scotus's *Super Libros Elenchorum Aristotelis*," 39–64.

27. Ashworth, "Equivocation and Analogy in Fourteenth Century Logic," 25. Cf. Burrell, "A Note on Analogy," 226: "Any concept, in so far as it is one concept, is univocal."

28. Ross, *Portraying Analogy*.

29. Burrell, *Analogy and Philosophical Language*.

30. Actually, as suggested in the previous chapter, the polemic context is more complicated. As Riva has shown, Cajetan is responding not only to Scotus but to other Thomists. But Cajetan (implicitly) criticizes the alternative "attributionistic" Thomistic school because he finds the analogy of attribution insufficient to satisfy Scotus's semantic challenge.

31. For citations and excerpts of texts, see Tavuzzi, "Some Renaissance Thomist Divisions of Analogy." Tavuzzi also cites Soncinas, *Super artem veterem* (f. 19 r–v), published in 1499—the year after Cajetan's *De Nominum Analogia*—which explictly addresses the fallacy of equivocation. On Dominic, see Franco Riva, "L'analogia dell'ente in Dominico di Fiandra," *Rivista di Filosofia Neo-scolastica* 86 (1994): 287–322, and Riva, *Analogia e univocità in Tommaso de Vio "Gaetano,"* 140–46, 154–59, 344.

32. Thomas Sutton, *Quaestiones ordinariae*, q. 33 (5th objection and reply), ed. Johannes Schneider (Munich: Verlag der Bayerischen Akademie der Wissenschaften, 1977), 911, 929.

33. *CDEE* §21: "quod cum talis unitas apud Aristotelem (IV Metaph. [6], text. com. II) sufficiat ad objectum scientiae, ens non oportet poni univocum ad hoc quod passiones habeat et contradictionem fundet, et reliqua hujusmodi habeant sibi convenientia."

34. Cajetan's remarks on analogy in *CDEE* are discussed at greater length in chap. 6.

35. Cf. *DNA* chap. 10, esp. §§104, 106, 113. Bochenski noticed the importance of this issue in *De Nominum Analogia* and in considerations of analogy

generally, and concluded his application of modern methods of formal analysis to the issue of analogy by evaluating different conceptions of analogy on the basis of whether they allow for the validity of syllogisms with analogical middle terms. Bochenski, "On Analogy," §§12, 14–19. Among those others who have noted that Cajetan was interested in avoiding the fallacy of equivocation are Frederick C. Copleston, *A History of Philosophy*, vol. 3, part 2 (Garden City, N.Y.: Image Books, 1963), 158, and James F. Anderson, *The Bond of Being: An Essay on Analogy and Existence* (St. Louis: Herder, 1949), 260.

36. Patrick J. Sherry seems to have missed the connection between the motivation to respond to Scotistic arguments and the necessity of characterizing the unity of the analogical concept. After noting, in more detail than most scholars, that Cajetan specifically wanted to respond to Scotus's argument that nonunivocal concepts cause the fallacy of equivocation, Sherry immediately says that Cajetan's "promising logical approach is marred by Cajetan's 'ideational' theory of meaning, which leads him to devote a disproportionate amount of time to explaining how there can be a single analogical concept." Sherry, "Analogy Today," 443.

37. Robillard is sensitive to the semantic concerns of *De Nominum Analogia*, noting that the text is organized to treat analogy with respect to all three parts of medieval logic: simple apprehension (*DNA* chaps. 3–5), judgment (chaps. 6–9), and reasoning (chap. 10). Robillard, *De l'analogie et du concept d'être de Thomas de Vio, Cajetan*, 253. Among the few others who have already read Cajetan in light of the explicit semantic concerns described here are Bochenski ("On Analogy") and Ross ("Analogy as a Rule of Meaning for Religious Language"). However, Bochenski's article "On Analogy" did not so much argue for a particular interpretation of Cajetan as formalize some of Cajetan's conclusions. Furthermore, though the article has been reprinted a few times, it remains somewhat inaccessible: a compressed style, obscure symbolic language, and apparently parochial Thomistic interests have reduced the exposure of Bochenski's important analysis. Ross's article also formalizes a Cajetanian theory of analogy, with results similar to Bochenski, but he frames it as a particular issue regarding *religious* language; and Ross's later criticisms of the Cajetanian tradition have undoubtedly diminished the authority of what he accomplished in this article. In any case, in neither article would it be apparent to the average reader that what is being offered is a particular *interpretation* of *Cajetan's* theory of analogy, viz., as a theory addressing the semantic puzzles described above.

CHAPTER THREE

1. E. J. Ashworth, "Equivocation and Analogy in Fourteenth Century Logic: Ockham, Burley and Buridan," *Historia Philosophiae Medii Aevi: Studien zur Geschichte der Philosophie des Mittelalters*, vol. 1, ed. Burkhard Mojsisch and Olaf Pluta (Amsterdam: Gruner, 1991), 28. Ashworth makes similar observations in Ashworth, "Signification and Modes of Signifying in Thirteenth-Century Logic: A Preface to Aquinas on Analogy," *Medieval Philosophy and Theology* 1 (1991): 45–46; Ashworth, "Analogy and Equivocation in Thirteenth-

Century Logic: Aquinas in Context," *Mediaeval Studies* 54 (1992): 107; and Ashworth, "Language, Renaissance Philosophy of," in *The Routledge Encyclopedia of Philosophy*, in which she writes that in the period she considers "there was little discussion in logic texts of how words relate to each other in propositional contexts" (411).

2. Ashworth, "Equivocation and Analogy in Fourteenth Century Logic," 42–43.

3. Ashworth, "Signification and Modes of Signifying in Thirteenth-Century Logic," 67.

4. E. J. Ashworth, "Analogical Concepts: The Fourteenth-Century Background to Cajetan," *Dialogue* 31 (1992): 400.

5. E. J. Ashworth, "Analogy, Univocation, and Equivocation in Some Early Fourteenth-Century Authors," in *Aristotle in Britain During the Middle Ages*, ed. John Marenbon (Turnhout: Brepols, 1996), 246–47.

6. James F. Ross, *Portraying Analogy* (Cambridge: Cambridge University Press, 1981).

7. Ibid., ix.

8. Ibid.

9. Josef Stern makes similar observations on the limitations of Ross's book in his review in *Journal of Philosophy* 84 (1987): 392–97.

10. Armand Maurer, "St. Thomas and the Analogy of Genus," *New Scholasticism* 29 (April 1955): 143. Maurer's claims are considered in Michael P. Slattery, "Concerning Two Recent Studies in Analogy," *New Scholasticism* 31 (1957): 237–46.

11. Armand Maurer, *Medieval Philosophy*, 2nd ed. (Toronto: Pontifical Institute of Medieval Studies, 1982), 351.

12. Patrick J. Sherry, "Analogy Today," *Philosophy* 51 (1976): 443.

13. Étienne Gilson, *Jean Duns Scot: Introduction à ses positions fondamentales* (Paris: Librairie Philosophique J. Vrin, 1952), 101–2: "La doctrine thomiste de l'analogie est avant tout une doctrine du *jugement* d'analogie. C'est en effet grâce au jugement de proportion que, sans en altérer la nature, on peut faire du concept un usage tantôt équivoque, tantôt analogique, tantôt univoque. . . . L'analogie à laquelle pense Duns Scot est beaucoup plutôt une analogie du *concept*. Or, sur le plan du concept et de la représentation, l'analogie se confond pratiquement avec la ressemblance. Il ne s'agit plus alors de savoir si deux termes jouent un rôle analogue dans un jugement de proportion, mais si le concept désigné par un terme est ou n'est pas le même que le concept désigné par l'autre." Gilson advances this interpretation of Thomistic analogy in terms of judgment versus concepts elsewhere as well: Gilson, *The Christian Philosophy of St. Thomas Aquinas*, trans. L. K. Shook (New York: Random House, 1956), 106–9. Gilson, *Le Thomisme: Introduction a la philosophie de Saint Thomas d'Aquin*, 5th ed. (Paris: Vrin, 1944): "Sur le plan du concept, il n'y a pas de milieu entre l'univoque et l'equivoque" (155; the word 'concept' is translated as 'quiddity' in the English translation by L. K. Shook). See also Gilson, *Being and Some Philosophers*, 2nd ed. (Toronto: Pontifical Institute of Medieval Studies, 1952), 190–215.

14. In addition to Maurer, Sherry, and Ross, already mentioned, Gilson's interpretation on this point is followed by: George P. Klubertanz, *St. Thomas*

Aquinas on Analogy: A Textual Analysis and Systematic Synthesis (Chicago: Loyola University Press, 1960), 116 ("Analogy is primarily an affair of judgment rather than concept"); Henri de Lubac, *The Discovery of God*, trans. Alexander Dru (New York: P. J. Kennedy and Sons, 1960), 201; cf. E. L. Mascall, *Existence and Analogy* (London: Longmans, Green, 1949), 116–21; Gregory Philip Rocca, *Speaking the Incomprehensible God: Thomas Aquinas on the Interplay of Positive and Negative Theology* (Washington, D.C.: Catholic University of America Press, 2004). Battista Mondin has dissented from Gilson's interpretation, arguing for the compatibility of judgment and concept. Mondin, *The Principle of Analogy in Protestant and Catholic Theology*, 2nd ed. (The Hague: Martinus Nijhoff, 1968), 58n2; 60n2. Rocca also admits the compatibility of emphasizing judgment and concept (165–73). For a summary of the history of the emphasis on analogy as judgment, see Rocca, *Speaking the Incomprehensible God*, 154–59.

15. David Burrell, "From Analogy of 'Being' to the Analogy of Being," in *Recovering Nature: Essays in Natural Philosophy, Ethics, and Metaphysics in Honor of Ralph P. McInerny*, ed. Thomas Hibbs and John O'Callaghan (Notre Dame, Ind.: University of Notre Dame Press, 1999), 259–60. Cf. Burrell, *Analogy and Philosophical Language* (New Haven: Yale University Press, 1973), 204.

16. Burrell, *Analogy and Philosophical Language*, 5.

17. Burrell has in mind specifically Bochenski, "On Analogy," and James F. Ross, "Analogy as a Rule of Meaning for Religious Language"; this latter was written before Ross's own rejection of such approaches in *Portraying Analogy*.

18. Burrell, *Analogy and Philosophical Language*, 15.

19. Philip A. Rolnick, *Analogical Possibilities: How Words Refer to God* (Atlanta: Scholars Press, 1993), 101.

20. David Burrell, review of James F. Ross, *Portraying Analogy*, in *New Scholasticism* 59 (1985): 349.

21. Ibid., 347. In a footnote Burrell clarifies that he is speaking of "Peter Geach's observations in *Mental Acts* . . . regarding abstraction, together with Lonergan's comprehensive review of the matter in *Verbum*, explicitly designed to correct the vaguely Scotistic accounts which had paraded as standard Thomistic epistemology."

22. Bernard Lonergan does seem to be under the specific impression that Cajetan's view of concepts has been unduly influenced by Scotus; see Bernard Lonergan, *Verbum: Word and Idea in Aquinas*, ed. David Burrell (Notre Dame, Ind.: University of Notre Dame Press, 1967), 25n122. But cf. Lonergan, *Insight: A Study of Human Understanding*, 3rd ed. (New York: Philosophical Library, 1970), 368–71.

23. Cf. Michael McCanles, who has argued that "once . . . analogy is dealt with on the level of concepts, the pressure seems of necessity to push *esse* toward a univocal concept, as both Scotus and Ockham show. Cajetan's analogical concept cannot maintain its integrity." McCanles, "Univocalism in Cajetan's Doctrine of Analogy," *New Scholasticism* 42 (Winter 1968): 47. McCanles thus describes what he sees as the problem of a semantic analysis of analogy which makes reference to the analogical concept: "[Cajetan's] method of treating the problem is at odds with itself, and to a very large extent undercuts the very doctrine he is overtly trying to refine" (19). Unfortunately McCanles's argument is

complicated by a confusion; McCanles does not sufficiently distinguish the issue of analogical signification in general (which is Cajetan's main concern in *De Nominum Analogia*) from the metaphysical issue of describing "the analogy of being."

24. Yves R. Simon, "On Order in Analogical Sets," in *Philosopher at Work: Essays by Yves R. Simon*, ed. Anthony O. Simon (Lanham, Md.: Rowman and Littlefield, 1999), 135–71; originally in *New Scholasticism* 34 (1960): 1–42.

25. Ibid., 140.

26. As an example of one tempted by this naive assumption: "The suggestion here proposed is that, in order to employ analogical predication . . . we must hold that any two entities standing in an analogical relation to each other . . . must have a minimum of one property in common." Paul C. Hayner, "Analogical Predication," *Journal of Philosophy* 55 (1958): 860.

27. Simon, "On Order in Analogical Sets," 145.

28. Ibid., 143.

29. Ibid., 145.

30. Ibid., 156.

31. Burrell, "A Note on Analogy," *New Scholasticism* 36 (1962): 226.

32. Ibid., 225; cf. Burrell, *Analogy and Philosophical Language*, 203.

33. Burrell's emphasis on *use* is the most obvious manifestation of his (acknowledged) debt to Wittgenstein. Cf. Burrell, *Analogy and Philosophical Language*, 17, 122, 123.

34. Perhaps it could be argued that to insist on such a distinction is already to grant Cajetan too much, to separate analogy from the "context" of particular theological and metaphysical judgments. Nonetheless, the phenomenon of analogical signification does take place outside of theology and metaphysics, and it is reasonable to insist on the logical distinction between considering the phenomenon of analogical signification in general, and considering particular terms, such as 'being' or divine names, which can exhibit analogical signification.

35. *CDEE* §67: "res intelligitur quando ejus conceptum formamus. . . . conceptus formatio est factio rei extra actu intellectae."

36. Cajetan, *Commentaria in Summam Theologiae St Thomae*, I.13.1, n. 3: "voces significant res non nisi media conceptione intellectus; igitur significatio causatur ex conceptione."

37. Actually the "concept" discussed in this paragraph—that by which something is signified and understood—is by Cajetan and other Thomists in some contexts called by a more technical name, the formal concept, to distinguish it from the objective concept; cf., e.g., *CDEE* §14. Cf. Jacques Maritain, *Distinguish to Unite, or The Degrees of Knowledge*, trans. Gerald B. Phelan (New York: Charles Scribner's Sons, 1959), app. 1, "The Concept," 387–417. So, as will be discussed in chap. 5, Cajetan's use of *conceptus* thus does not always imply a *mental act*, but often (more like *ratio*) implies the *intelligible content* of a thing that might be conceived by a mental act.

38. Gabriel Nuchelmans offers as the standard definition of *"significare"* for late-scholastic philosophers: "representing some thing or some things or in some way to the cognitive faculty." Nuchelmans, *Late-Scholastic and Humanist*

Theories of the Proposition (Amsterdam: North Holland, 1980), 14. Paul Vincent Spade makes a similar point when he notes that "signification is a psychologico-causal property of terms" which is traced back to Boethius's claim that "'to signify' something was 'to establish an understanding of it.'" P. V. Spade, "The Semantics of Terms," in *The Cambridge History of Later Medieval Philosophy* (Cambridge: Cambridge University Press, 1982), 188–98, 188. Cf. Paul Vincent Spade, *Thoughts Words and Things: An Introduction to Late Medieval Logic and Semantic Theory,* version 1.0, chap. 3: the interpretation of *significare* as "to establish an understanding" (from Boethius, "*constituere intellectum*") is "the predominant one throughout the Middle Ages." Cf. Ashworth, "Signification and Modes of Signifying in Thirteenth-Century Logic," 44: "to signify is to establish an understanding (*significare est intellectum constituere*)."

39. Cajetan is also thus far consistent with Geach, cited above by Burrell as an important corrective to "Thomistic" epistemology: like Cajetan, Geach understood "concepts" to be "mental capacities" the possession of which are "presupposed by acts of judgment," and the "abstractionism" criticized by Geach is in no way implied in Cajetan's understanding of concepts sketched here. Peter Geach, *Mental Acts: Their Content and Their Objects* (London: Routledge and Kegan Paul, 1957), 14 and *passim.*

40. Indeed, this medieval notion of the "*conceptus*" can easily be traced to the Greek tradition, as Sten Ebbesen has done, noting the connection between the classification of different kinds of equivocation (including analogy) on the one hand, and concept formation on the other. The Greek logical tradition's classification of different kinds of equivocals "can be understood as a classification of the reasons for choosing the same word to signify different concepts and things, deriving this classification from one that shows in how many ways concepts are formed." Sten Ebbesen, *Commentators and Commentaries on Aristotle's "Sophistici Elenchi": A Study of Post-Aristotelian Ancient and Medieval Writings on Fallacies,* vol. 1, *The Greek Tradition* (Leiden: Brill, 1981), 190. In this endeavor, the role of judgment ("*reasons for choosing* the same word to signify different concepts and things") is undeniable.

41. Nuchelmans clarifies that there are actually two senses of judgment one can consider: there is a kind of judging that is really an apprehension that forms a mental proposition (the "apprehensive proposition"), and there is a kind of judging that is the act of knowing, believing, or opining that this mental proposition is (or is not) true. Nuchelmans, *Late-Scholastic and Humanist Theories of the Proposition,* 74–76. But since the latter judgment requires the former apprehensive proposition, which in turn implies an apprehension of the terms of the apprehensive proposition, Nuchelmans's analysis only confirms that judgment is not opposed to, but rather presupposes, semantic considerations. As he puts it: "In general questions concerning acts of judging, knowing, and believing, and concerning objects of knowledge and belief, were treated by scholastic philosophers for other reasons than sheer curiosity about the semantics of declarative sentences. . . . But in dealing with the psychological and epistemological issues which were forced upon them by their theological interests or the pursuit of wider inquiries of a similar type, they were unavoidably faced with

problems which have a predominantly semantical character" (103). On the late-scholastic Thomist understanding of apprehensive propositions and the object of judgment, see 99–102, 111–12.

42. Cf. Étienne Gilson, *Linguistics and Philosophy: An Essay on the Philosophical Constants of Language*, trans. John Lyon (Notre Dame, Ind.: University of Notre Dame Press, 1988), 75–78, 187n25.

43. Cf. Étienne Gilson, *The Elements of Christian Philosophy* (New York: New American Library, 1963), 250.

44. "Les interlocuteurs ne parlent pas la même langue. . . . lorsqu'il rencontre l'analogie thomiste, on ne peut pas dire exactement que Duns Scot le réfute, on dirai plutôt qu'il ne peut pas y croire. . . . Évidement, ce serait perdre son temps que do vouloir concilier les deux doctrines et, tout autant, de réfuter l'une par l'autre." Gilson, *Jean Duns Scot*, 101–2.

45. Simon's article assumes, and never dissents from, Cajetan's treatment of analogy. Simon makes it clear he is using Cajetan's classification of analogous modes, and Cajetan's terminology for that classification (Simon, "On Order in Analogical Sets," 137); he agrees with Cajetan that "in [analogy of] attribution . . . the object signified by the analogical term exists intrinsically in only one" of the analogates (137); like Cajetan, Simon regards analogy of proper proportionality as the most genuine form of analogy (138ff.), and, as in Cajetan's theory, this is connected to the fact that in analogy of proportionality "the form designated by the analogical term exists intrinsically in each and every one of the analogates" (138; cf. 140); Simon defends Cajetan against the criticisms of F. A. Blanche (165–67n27); and he cites approvingly other unabashed Cajetanians (John of St. Thomas and James Anderson).

46. Simon might also be benefiting from John of St. Thomas's own reflections on this part of Cajetan's theory, in *Ars Logica*, p. 2, q. 13, a. 5, "Utrum in analogis detur unus conceptus ab inferioribus praecisus" (491a40–500b47). Simon was the chief translator of sections of the *Secunda Pars* of the *Ars Logica*, published (five years before Simon's "On Order in Analogical Sets") as *The Material Logic of John of St. Thomas: Basic Treatises* (Chicago: University of Chicago Press, 1955). At one point the translation renders the phrase "Analoga attributionis et analoga metaphorica" (491b21–22, literally: "analogues of attribution and metaphorical analogues") as "The terms of an *analogous set*, in analogy of attribution or of metaphor" (168, emphasis added).

47. *Contra* Burrell (*Analogy and Philosophical Language*, 203), Simon does take analogy of proper proportionality as the "normal form" or genuine kind of analogy.

48. All of this is why, in the previous chapter of *De Nominum Analogia*, Cajetan had already acknowledged that one must qualify the sense in which one may speak of an analogical concept (*DNA* §§36–37).

49. In this regard, we might say that Cajetan's treatment of analogy corroborates Gadamer's judgment: "The merit of semantic analysis, it seems to me, is that it has brought the structural totality of language to our attention and thereby has pointed out the limitations of the false ideal of unambiguous signs or symbols and of the potential of language for logical formalization." Hans-Georg Gadamer, "Semantics and Hermeneutics," trans. P. Christopher Smith,

in Hans-Georg Gadamer, *Philosophical Hermeneutics*, trans. and ed. David E. Linge (Berkeley: University of California Press, 1976), 83.

50. Simon, "On Order in Analogical Sets," 139. From his papers archived in the Jacques Maritain Center at the University of Notre Dame, we learn that Simon planned to take up just this question in a book on analogy with the working title "The Science of the Unknown," of which the paper "On Order in Analogical Sets" would constitute one chapter. Yves R. Simon Papers, 1920–1959, University of Notre Dame, box 2, folder 18.

51. L. M. de Rijk, *Logica Modernorum: A Contribution to the History of Early Terminist Logic*, vol. 1, *On the Twelfth Century Theories of Fallacy* (Assen: Van Gorcum, 1962), 22: "In the course of the present study it will become evident that the frequent occurrence of fallacies is not just a concomitant—as a reader of the *Summulae* might think—, but that the doctrine of fallacy forms the basis of terminist logic. For this logic developed as a result of the fact that, to a much greater extent than it had been done by Abailard and his contemporaries, the proposition was beginning to be subjected to a strictly linguistic analysis." However, elsewhere de Rijk does indicate that he believes that "the contextual approach" to language and "the doctrine of signification" are in tension; *vide* L. M. de Rijk, "The Origins of the Theory of the Properties of Terms," in *The Cambridge History of Later Medieval Philosophy* (Cambridge: Cambridge University Press, 1982), 161–73.

52. Alexander Broadie, *Introduction to Medieval Logic*, 2nd ed. (Oxford: Oxford University Press, 1993), 8–9.

53. Norman Kretzmann, "Semantics, History of," in *The Encyclopedia of Philosophy*, ed. Paul Edwards (New York: Macmillan, 1967), vol. 7, 371. Cf. Ashworth, "Logic, Medieval," §4: "Indeed, the avoidance of fallacy is at the heart of all new types of logical writing."

54. *DNA* §125: "Unde si quis falli non vult, solerter sermonis causam coniectet, et extremorum conditiones medio applicaturum se recolat; sic enim facile erit omnia sane exponere, et veritatem assequi."

55. The phenomenon really is ubiquitous, but one example of Cajetan's careful clarification of terms with respect to the role they play in the context of particular arguments is his commentary on *ST* Ia, q. 3, a. 3, which is discussed in Joshua P. Hochschild, "A Note on Cajetan's Theological Semantics," *Sapientia* 54 (1999): 367–76.

CHAPTER FOUR

1. Some examples, already cited in chap. 2: from Aquinas: Whatever is in potentiality is reduced to act by something actual; all things are brought into being by God; therefore, God is actual (*DPD* III.7.7, *corpus*, cited below, n. 5). From Cajetan: Every simple perfection is in God; wisdom is a simple perfection; therefore wisdom is in God (*DNA* §105). From Bochenski: Every being is good; God is a being; therefore God is good ("On Analogy," *The Thomist* [1948]: §16).

2. E. J. Ashworth, "Analogical Concepts: The Fourteenth-Century Background to Cajetan," *Dialogue* 31 (1992): 399–413.

3. Several scholars have noted Aquinas's concern that analogy avoid the fallacy of equivocation: James F. Ross, "Analogy as a Rule of Meaning for Religious Language," in *Inquiries into Medieval Philosophy: A Collection in Honor of Francis P. Clarke*, ed. James F. Ross, Contributions in Philosophy, no. 4 (Westport, Conn.: Greenwood, 1971), 37; Hampus Lyttkens, *The Analogy Between God and the World: An Investigation of Its Background and Interpretation of Its Use by Thomas of Aquino* (Uppsala: Almqvist and Wiksells Boktrycheri AB, 1952), 204; Patrick J. Sherry, "Analogy Today," *Philosophy* 51 (1976): 443; Ralph McInerny, "Scotus and Univocity," in *Being and Predication: Thomistic Interpretations* (Washington, D.C.: Catholic University of America Press, 1986), 161; Yves Simon, "On Order in Analogical Sets," in *Philosopher at Work: Essays by Yves R. Simon*, ed. Anthony O. Simon (Lanham, Md.: Rowman and Littlefield, 1999), 139; Vernon J. Bourke, "Cajetan, Cardinal," in *The Encyclopedia of Philosophy*, vol. 2, ed. P. Edwards (New York: Macmillan, 1967), 5–6. Cf. Michael P. Slattery, "Concerning Two Recent Studies of Analogy," *New Scholasticism* 31 (1957): 238. Garrigou-Lagrange also recognizes the importance of analogical terms in syllogisms, in *God: His Existence and Nature*, vol. 1, trans. Bede Rose (St. Louis: Herder, 1934, 1936), 224–27; he provides his own account of how this is possible in vol. 2, 203–21.

4. Thomas Aquinas, *Summa Theologiae* Ia.13.5.c: "Sed nec etiam [nomen de Deo et creaturis praedicatur] pure aequivoce, ut aliqui dixerunt. Quia secundum hoc ex creaturis nihil posset cognosci de Deo, nec demonstrari, sed semper incideret fallacia aequivocationis."

5. Thomas Aquinas, *Quaestiones disputatae de potentia Dei* III.7.7.c: ". . . cum omnis cognitio nostra de Deo ex creaturis sumatur, si non erit convenientia nisi in nomine tantum, nihil de Deo sciremus nisi nomina tantum vana, quibus res non subesset. Sequeretur etiam quod omnes demonstrationes a philosophis datae de Deo, essent sophisticae; verbi gratia, si dicatur, quod omne quod est in potentia, reducitur ad actum per ens actu, et ex hoc concluderetur quod Deus esset ens actu, cum per ipsum omnia in esse educantur; erit fallacia aequivocationis; et sic de omnibus aliis."

6. Thomas Aquinas, *Summa Contra Gentiles* I.33: "Quando unum de pluribus, secundum puram aequivocationem, praedicatur, ex uno eorum non possumus duci in cognitionem alterius. Nam cognitio rerum non dependet ex vocibus, sed ex ratione nominis. Ex his autem, quae in rebus aliis inveniuntur, in divinorum cognitionem pervenimus, ut ex dictis (c. 30 et 31) patet. Non igitur secundum puram aequivocationem dicuntur hujusmodi attributa de Deo et aliis rebus. . . . Aequivocatio nominis processum argumentationis impedit. Si igitur nihil diceretur de Deo et creaturis, nisi pure aequivoce, nulla argumentatio fieri posset, procedendo de creaturis ad Deum."

7. Thomas Aquinas, *Quaestiones disputatae de Veritate* 2.11.c: ". . . nec tamen potest dici quod omnino aequivoce praedicaetur quidquid de Deo et creatura dicitur; quia si non esset aliqua convenientia creaturae ad Deum secundum rem, sua essentia non esset creaturarum similitudo; et ita cognoscendo essentiam suam non cognosceret creaturas. Similiter etiam nec nos ex rebus creatis in cognitionem Dei pervenire possemus; nec nominum quae creaturis

aptantur, unum magis de eo dicendum esset quam aliud; quia ex aequivocis non differt quodcumque nomen imponatur, ex quo nulla rei convenientia attenditur."

8. Thomas Aquinas, *In duodecim libros Metaphysicorum expositio* IV, lect. 3 (§568 Cathala): "Non enim sequitur, quod si aliquid dicitur multipliciter, quod propter hoc sit alterius scientiae vel diversae. Diversa enim significata si neque dicuntur «secundum unum», idest secundum unam rationem, scilicet univoce, nec ratione diversa referuntur ad unum, sicut est in analogicis: tunc sequitur, quod sit alterius, idest diversae scientiae de his considerare, vel ad minus unius per accidens. . . . Haec autem omni referuntur ad unum principium. Sicut enim quae significantur per hoc nomen Unum, licet sint diversa, reducuntur tamen in unum primum significatum; similiter est dicendum de his nominibus, idem, diversum, contrarium, et hujusmodi."

9. Thomas Aquinas, *Scripta super libros Sententiarum* prol., q. 1, a. 2, obj. 2: ". . . una scientia est unius generis, sicut dicit Philosophus in I Posteriorum. Sed Deus et creatura, de quibus in divina doctrina tractatur, non reducuntur in unum genus, neque univoce, neque analogice. Ergo divina scientia non est una . . ."; ibid., ad. 2: ". . . dicendum quod Creator et creatura reducuntur in unum, non communitate univocationis sed analogiae."

10. Thomas Aquinas, *In Aristotelis Libros Peri Hermeneias et Posteriorum Analyticorum Expositio*, ed. Raymundi M. Spiazzi (Rome: Marietti, 1955), book 2, lectio 17, n. 4: ". . . ostendit investigare *propter quid* reducendo ad aliquod commune analogum; et dicit quod alius modus investigandi propter quid est eligere commune secundum analogiam, idest proportionem. Contingit enim unum accipere analogum quod non est idem secundum speciem vel genus; sicut os sepiarum, quod vocatur *sepion*, et spina piscium, et ossa animalium terrestrium. Omnia enim ista conveniunt secundum proportionem, quia eodem modo se habent spinae ad pisces sicut ossa ad terrestria animalia." Aristotle's example of the analogical relationship between bone, spine, and pounce will be invoked by Cajetan at *DNA* §§109, 117, and *De Conceptu Entis* §3, and Cajetan obviously finds it useful for answering questions about the role of analogical notions in scientific reasoning. Interestingly, Aquinas's comment on Aristotle quoted here is not among the texts collected by Klubertanz in *St. Thomas Aquinas on Analogy: A Textual Analysis and Systematic Synthesis* (Chicago: Loyola University Press, 1960), although Klubertanz's catalogue of texts does include another passage from later in the *Posterior Analytics* commentary (book 2, lectio 19, n. 3).

11. The *De fallaciis* describes three species of the fallacy of equivocation, and briefly mentions analogy in connection with the second: "secunda species est quando unum nomen principaliter unum significat, et aliud metaphorice sive transumptive. . . . et ad hanc speciam reducitur muliplicitas nominum analogorum quae dicuntur de pluribus secundum prius et posterius." *De fallaciis*, in *Opuscula philosophica*, ed. Raymundi M. Spiazzi (Rome: Marietti, 1954), c. 6. There is some doubt about whether Aquinas authored *De fallaciis*, but the text's teaching is such that the attribution to Aquinas is plausible. On this point about analogy and fallacy it is consistent with, and doesn't add anything to, Aquinas's remarks elsewhere.

12. *In Met.* IV, lect. 1, §535; XI, lect. 3, §2197; cf. Joseph Bobik, *Aquinas on Being and Essence: A Translation and Interpretation* (Notre Dame, Ind.: University of Notre Dame Press, 1965), 55–56.

13. Cf. Klubertanz, *St. Thomas Aquinas on Analogy*, 38: "Analogous intelligibles are neither exactly the same nor completely different; they are halfway between the two extremes. Though this is not an especially revealing description, it provides us with a minimum meaning which can be applied to all analogies."

14. Ibid., 37.

15. There are fifty-eight occurrences of the phrase in twenty-one works listed in Klubertanz, *St. Thomas Aquinas on Analogy*, 301. Klubertanz also notes several occasions of other terminology that also expresses priority and posteriority, p. 65. Aquinas was not the first to describe analogy as signification *per prius et posterius*; the scholastic use of the phrase is traced to the twelfth-century Latin translation of Avicenna. For some citations of this phrase in authors before Aquinas, cf. E. J. Ashworth, "Analogy and Equivocation in Thirteenth-Century Logic: Aquinas in Context," *Mediaeval Studies* 54 (1992): 107–8; Alain de Libera, "Les sources gréco-arabes de la théorie médiévale de l'analogie de l'être," *Les Études Philosophiques* (1989): 333; and H. A. Wolfson, "The Amphibolous Terms in Aristotle, Arabic Philosophy, and Maimonides," *Harvard Theological Review* 31 (1938): 151–73.

16. Ashworth, "Analogy and Equivocation in Thirteenth-Century Logic: Aquinas in Context," 125, and Ashworth, "Signification and Modes of Signifying in Thirteenth-Century Logic: A Preface to Aquinas on Analogy," *Medieval Philosophy and Theology* 1 (1991): 50; cf. McInerny, *Aquinas and Analogy* (Washington, D.C.: Catholic University of America Press, 1996), 70–74.

17. *SCG* I.32: "Quod praedicatur de aliquibus secundum prius et posterius, certum est univocum non praedicari."

18. E.g., *ST* I.5.6, ad 3.

19. Ralph McInerny, *The Logic of Analogy: An Interpretation of St. Thomas* (The Hague: Martinus Nijhoff, 1961), 79. Cf. McInerny, *Aquinas and Analogy*, 98: an analogous term "signifies a plurality of *rationes* which are related *per prius et posterius* . . ."

20. Klubertanz notes that Aquinas sometimes seems to deny that the *per prius et posterius* rule applies to analogy between God and creatures (*St. Thomas Aquinas on Analogy*, 29–30), yet later he discusses the rule as a "doctrinal constant" in Aquinas (64–69).

21. Yves Simon recognized the inadequacy of the *"per prius et posterius"* rule. Simon, "On Order in Analogical Sets," 148.

22. Thomas Aquinas, *Summa Theologiae* Ia 13.6.c: "in omnibus nominibus quae de pluribus analogice dicuntur, necesse est quod omni dicantur per respectum ad unum; et ideo illud unum oportet quod ponatur in definitione omnium." Cf. Aquinas, *Summa Theologiae* Ia 13.10: "in analogicis vero oportet quod nomen secundum unam significationem acceptum ponatur in definitione ejusdem nominis secundum alias significationes accepti." Cf. Aquinas, *Summa Contra Gentiles* I.32: "Quod praedicatur de aliquibus secundum prius et

posterius, certum est univoce non praedicari: nam prius in definitione posterioris includitur."

23. Silvestro Mazzolini, *Conflatum ex S. Thoma*: "regula decisiva totius quaestionis," quoted in Michael Tavuzzi, "Some Renaissance Thomist Divisions of Analogy," *Angelicum* 70 (1993): 110.

24. "... ad mentem Sancti Thomae, quod in omni modo analogiae verum est quod prius ponitur in definitione posterioris, inquantum analogice consideratur et significatur" (from Silvestri's commentary on *Summa Contra Gentiles*, quoted in Lyttkens, *The Analogy Between God and the World*, 226n7). For discussion see Lyttkens, *The Analogy Between God and the World*, 225–28, and Klubertanz, *St. Thomas Aquinas on Analogy*, 10–11.

25. E.g., McInerny, *Aquinas and Analogy*, 98; Bobik, *Aquinas on Being and Essence*, 53; Ian Wilks, "Aquinas on Analogy: The Distinction of Many-to-One and One-to-Another," *Modern Schoolman* 75 (1997): 37.

26. Klubertanz, *St. Thomas Aquinas on Analogy*, 32–34.

27. Cf. Joseph Owens, *The Doctrine of Being in the Aristotelian "Metaphysics": A Study in the Greek Background of Medieval Thought*, 3rd ed. (Toronto: Pontifical Institute of Medieval Studies, 1978), 118–23.

28. G. E. L. Owen, "Logic and Metaphysics in Some Early Works of Aristotle," in *Aristotle and Plato in Mid-Fourth Century*, ed. Ingemar Düring and G. E. L. Owen (Göteborg: Studia Graeca et Latina Gothoburgensia, 1960). Cf. McInerny, *Aquinas and Analogy*, 40: "What Owen calls focal meaning—a common predicate's having different but connected definitions in its different uses, the connection being provided by its primary sense on which the others depend—answers to what Thomas Aquinas calls an analogous name."

29. Cf., e.g., Aquinas, *De principiis naturae* 6: "Analogice dicitur praedicari quod praedicatur de pluribus, quorum rationes diversae sunt, sed attribuuntur alicui uni eidem."

30. Ross, "Analogy as a Rule of Meaning for Religious Language," 50. Yves Simon agrees, saying that in analogy of proper proportionality, "no first analogate needs to be included in the definition of the secondary analogates." Simon, "On Order in Analogical Sets," 138–39. Both Ross and Simon here are in agreement with Cajetan.

31. Aquinas himself raises this point at *De Veritate* 2.11., obj. 6. Nor is this point unique to *De Veritate*. In a parallel case, Aquinas denies that a term as predicated of God can be defined in terms of the meaning of that term as it refers to creatures ("God is good" cannot be taken to mean only that "God is the cause of good things," nor can it mean that "God is the cause of [creaturely] goodness"); *Summa Theologiae* I.13.2.c. When Aquinas does give a working definition of Divine goodness, it does make reference to creaturely goodness, but not as something *other* than God to which God is related, rather as something that itself pre-exists in a higher manner in God ("Cum igitur dicitur Deus est bonus, non est sensus Deus est causa bonitatis . . . , sed est sensus, id quod bonitatem dicimus in creaturis, praeexistit in Deo, et hoc quidem secundum modum altiorem"). Aquinas's point is that it is not essential to the goodness of God that

it be understood in terms of some other goodness ("non sequitur Deus competat esse bonum, inquantum causat bonitatem; sed potius, e converse, quia est bonus, bonitatem rebus diffundit").

32. Cajetan, *CDEE* §21: ". . . analogata primo modo [i.e., analogy of attribution] ita se habent, quod posterius secundum nomen analogum diffinitur per suum prius: puta accidens, inquantum ens per substantiam. Analogata vero secundo modo [i.e., analogy of proportionality] non: creatura enim inquantum ens non diffinitur per Deum."

33. Aquinas, *Summa Theologiae* Ia, 16.6.c: ". . . quando aliquid dicitur analogice de multis, illud invenitur secundum propriam rationem in uno eorum tantum, a quo alia denominantur . . ."

34. Aquinas, *Summa Contra Gentiles* I.32 : "Nam prius in diffinitione posterioris includitur." Cf. Aquinas, *Summa Theologiae* I.13.6: "Et quia ratio quam significat nomen est definitio, ut dicitur, necesse est quod illud nomen per prius dicatur de eo quod ponitur in definitione aliorum, et per posterius de aliis, secundum ordinem quo appropinquant ad illud primum."

35. McInerny, *Aquinas and Analogy*, 98. We should note that the rubric *"per prius et posterius"* does not have to be given the interpretation McInerny here gives it, as involving multiple *rationes* ordered to one. Signifying *"per prius et posterius"* could alternatively describe a common *ratio* that is unequally participated by its several analogates.

36. McInerny, *Aquinas and Analogy*, 114.

37. E.g., McInerny, *The Logic of Analogy*, 78: "The analogous name names one thing primarily, and others insofar as they relate in some way to what it principally names. The *rationes* of the secondary analogates will express their reference to the thing which perfectly saves the *ratio propria* of the word."

38. McInerny, *Studies in Analogy* (The Hague: Martinus Nijhoff, 1968), 75; McInerny, "The Analogy of Names Is a Logical Doctrine," in *Being and Predication*, 285; McInerny, "Scotus and Univocity," in *Being and Predication*, 162; McInerny, *Aquinas and Analogy*, 99.

39. McInerny, *Aquinas and Analogy*, 99–100; McInerny, "Can God Be Named by Us?" in *Being and Predication*, 274–75; McInerny, "Scotus and Univocity," 162–64.

40. McInerny, "The Analogy of Names Is a Logical Doctrine," 283: "St. Thomas will say that a term used analogously signifies the same *res significata* but has different *modi significandi*."; McInerny, *Aquinas and Analogy*, 103–4: "In a pithy text, Thomas compares univocals, equivocals and analogously named things. . . . Univocal terms have the same *res significata* and the same way of signifying it in all relevant uses; equivocal terms have different *res significatae*; things are named analogously when their common name has the same *res significata*, which is signified in different ways in each of the accounts."

41. *I Sent.* 22.1.3 ad 2: "dicendum quod aliter dividitur aequivocum, analogum et univocum. Aequivocum enim dividitur secundum res significatas, univocum vero dividitur secundum diversas differentias; sed analogum dividitur secundum diversos modos. Unde cum ens praedicetur analogice de

decem generibus, dividitur in ea secundum diversos modos. Unde unicuique generi debetur proprius modus praedicandi."

42. Ashworth, "Signification and Modes of Signifying," 60.

43. E.g., *I Sent.* 25.1.2 c: "Dicendum quod persona dicitur de Deo et creaturis non univoce nec aequivoce sed secundum analogiam; et quantum ad rem significatam per prius est in Deo quam in creaturis, sed quantum ad modum significandi est e converso, sicut est etiam de omnibus aliis nominibus quae de Deo et creaturis analogice dicuntur."

44. Ashworth, "Signification and Modes of Signifying," 60.

45. Ashworth, "Analogy and Equivocation," 122. Cf. Ashworth, review of McInerny, *Aquinas and Analogy*, in *Speculum* 74 (1999): 216. Cf. also Irène Rosier, *"Res significata* et *modus significandi*: Les implications d'une distinction médiévale," *Sprachtheorien in Spätantike und Mittelalter*, ed. Sten Ebbesen (Tübingen: Gunter Narr Verlag, 1995), 152–57. See also Seung-Chan Park, *Die Rezeption der mittelalterlichen Sprachphilosophie in der Theologie des Thomas von Aquin: Mit besonderer Berücksichtigung der Analogie* (Leiden: Brill, 1999), 128–67, 267–307.

46. In addition to McInerny, the view can be found in Mascall (*Analogy and Existence* [London: Longmans, Green, 1949], 100, 120), and is common in Copleston, although the latter's comments are always made in the context of a discussion of religious language. Cf. Fredrick Copleston, *A History of Medieval Philosophy* (New York: Harper and Row, 1972), 196–97; Copleston, *Aquinas* (Harmondsworth: Penguin, 1955), 129–35; and Copleston, *A History of Philosophy*, vol. 2, *Mediaeval Philosophy*, part 2, "Albert the Great to Duns Scotus" (Garden City, N.Y.: Image Books, 1962), 70. Before his more recent criticisms of the "classical" approach to analogy (in James F. Ross, *Portraying Analogy* [Cambridge: Cambridge University Press, 1981]), Ross apparently agreed that having one *res significata* and multiple *modi significandi* is a feature of analogy. Cf. Ross, "A Critical Analysis of the Theory of Analogy of St. Thomas Aquinas" (Ph.D. diss., Brown University, 1958), 102; Ross, review of McInerny, *The Logic of Analogy*, in *International Philosophical Quarterly* 2 (1962): 635; and Ross, "Analogy as a Rule of Meaning for Religious Language," 55–57. But Ross regarded this as only a necessary, not a sufficient, condition for language about God; to it Ross added the stipulation that there be "proportional similarity" of properties (Ross, "Analogy as Rule of Meaning for Religious Language," 62–63). Burrell appears to take a similar view, agreeing that the distinction between *res significata* and *modus significandi* is a part of Aquinas's analysis of analogy, at least with respect to religious language, but adding that the distinction is insufficient without the further stipulation that all predicates said analogously of God and creatures must be perfections. Cf. David Burrell, *Analogy and Philosophical Language* (New Haven: Yale University Press, 1973), 136. For that matter, McInerny also says that having a single *res significata* and diverse *modi significandi* is a necessary, but not a sufficient, condition of a term's being analogous (McInerny, *Aquinas and Analogy*, 104). Lyttkens is also willing to consider the role of *res significata* and *modi significandi* in Aquinas's understanding of analogy, though like Copleston, Ross, and Burrell he does so only in the context of discussion

about predicates said analogously of God and creatures (Lyttkens, *The Analogy Between God and the World*, 374–82, 468–71).

47. Ashworth, "Signification and Modes of Signifying," 56–57, 61.

48. McInerny, "Scotus and Univocity," 163. Cf. McInerny, *Aquinas and Analogy*, 104.

49. This attempted reconstruction of McInerny's analysis of analogy as involving one *res significata* and several *modi significandi* probably does not exhibit a Thomistic use of *modi significandi*. *Being a cause of something* and *being a sign of something* are not *modi significandi* in Thomas's sense, and a Thomistic analysis of the various senses of "healthy" would rather assign a different *res significata* to each sense of "healthy": *animal health*, *cause of animal health*, and *sign of animal health*.

50. Lyttkens observed, "We have no direct evidence of St. Thomas' own attitude to the question of the unity of the concept in the analogy of proportionality." Lyttkens, *The Analogy Between God and the World*, 471. Wilks frames the semantic issue felicitously: "For a word to retain the same meaning through successive uses is for it to remain linked to exactly the same *ratio* in each case. This is how univocity is to be understood; non-univocity will, conversely, involve successive uses with linkage to different *rationes*. Whether that non-univocity amounts to analogy or equivocation depends on the conceptual space that exists between the two *rationes*; the difference between them is capable of being greater or less, and if sufficiently less then the usage is said to be analogical." Then, Wilks says, "Aquinas gives us no theoretically comprehensive way of explaining what constitutes closeness of *ratio*." Of the rule that Wilks considers, viz., "that in each case one *ratio* constitutes part of another," he admits, "we cannot get a rigorous semantic account of analogy from this." Wilks, "Aquinas on Analogy," 37.

51. Ashworth, "Analogical Concepts"; Ashworth, "Analogy and Equivocation," 126.

52. *DNA* §7.

53. *DNA* §§14, 20. Elsewhere Cajetan says that this is not a rule for analogy as such, but a rule for determining of which thing a term is said *prius* (*CST* I.13.6, nn. i–ii), and Cajetan rejects it as a universal rule for analogy (*CST* I.13.6, n. iii: "dicit non esse verum universaliter quod primum analogatum poni debeat in rationibus aliorum analogatorum," citing Aquinas, *DV* 2.11).

54. *CST* I.16.6, n. vi: "illa regula de analogo tradita in littera, non est universalis de omni analogiae modo." Cf. John of St. Thomas, *Ars Logica*, p. 2, q. 13, a. 4 (490b28–491a22): ". . . respondetur, quod in illa universali loquitur S. Thomas non de omnibus analogis absolute, sed restrictive de analogis attributionis tantum. . . . In loco autem ex q. 16 non loquitur universaliter de omnibus analogis . . ." While it may seem bold for an interpreter to reject as universal rules what clearly appear to be formulated universally, there appear to be genuine inconsistencies in Aquinas; we must remember Klubertanz's inescapable conclusion about Aquinas's formulation of analogy rules, that "not every discussion that appears to be a general description applicable to all analogies is such

in actual fact." Klubertanz, *St. Thomas Aquinas on Analogy*, 37. Also, note that Cajetan will describe a way in which, even in analogy of proportionality, we can understand that the *ratio* of the analogue is wholly saved in one of the analogates but imperfectly in the others—yet he warns that this rule must be taken with a grain of salt. *DNA* §§100–101: ". . . in uno eorum, tota ratio divisi salvari dicatur; in alio autem imperfecte et secundum quid. Quod non est sic intelligendum quasi analogum habeat unam rationem, quae tota salvetur in uno, et pars eius salvetur in alio. Sed cum totum idem sit quod perfectum, et analogo nomine multae importentur rationes, quarum una simpliciter et perfecte constituit tale secundum illud nomen, et aliae imperfecte et secundum quid: ideo dicitur, quod analogum sic dividitur, quod non tota ratio eius in omnibus analogatis salvatur, nec aequaliter participant analogi rationem, sed secundum prius et posterius. Cum grano tamen salis accipiendum est, analogum simpliciter salvari in uno et secundum quid in alio."

55. *DNA* §1. The same three theories are listed again at *DNA* §71. For discussion of Cajetan's use of "indisjunction" at §1 and "disjunction" at §71, see Edward A. Bushinski and Henry J. Koren, *The Analogy of Names and the Concept of Being* (Pittsburgh: Duquesne University Press, 1953), 9n4, and Bruno Pinchard, *Metaphysique et semantique: La signification analogiques des termes dans les Principes Metaphysiques* (Paris: Vrin, 1987), 161.

56. Ashworth, "Analogical Concepts."

57. Ibid., 404–5. The distinction between objective and formal concepts will be explored in chap. 5, as a part of a more systematic presentation of Cajetan's semantic principles.

58. Ibid., 405. Ashworth's article discusses, in particular, historical disputes about the analogy of "being." Though this particular case of analogy was undoubtedly one of the most, if not the most, important case for the philosophers she discusses, it remains that the semantic problem is one for analogy generally, and not just for this particular analogical term. Cajetan does discuss the analogy of "being" in *DNA*, chap. 6, where he contrasts his view with the three rejected views (§71), but still it is clear that he is developing a logical or semantic theory of analogy generally, and not one specific to the case of "being," which he insists is used only as an example (§72).

59. Cf. Ashworth, "Analogical Concepts," 407. Note that Ashworth's exclusive alternatives presuppose particular semantic assumptions about the nature of objective and formal concepts, shared by all the authors she considers. If these assumptions are not shared, it would be possible to construe, e.g., "unity of order" and "unequal participation" as not mutually exclusive. This seems to be the position of McInerny in the following passage: "In things named analogically . . . the common notion signified by the name is not shared equally by all the things which receive the name; only one of the analogates is signified perfectly by the name. The others are signified imperfectly and in a certain respect, that is, insofar as they refer in some way to what is perfectly signified. . . . The analogous name signifies precisely an inequality of significations, but according to a certain order." McInerny, *The Logic of Analogy*, 76.

60. And with unknown authors: a late thirteenth-century commentator on the *Sophistici Elenchi* describes three kinds of analogy, of which one is the most genuine and involves a *ratio* that "non est aequaliter participata." Incertorum Auctorum, *Quaestiones super Sophisticos Elenchos,* ed. Sten Ebbesen (Copenhagen: Corpus Philosophorum Danicorum Medii Aevi, 1977), 317 (q. 823, l. 85).

61. Capreolus, *Defensiones theologiae,* vol. 1, ed. Paban and Pégues (1900), 135a, 142a–b (cited in Ashworth, "Analogical Concepts," 406).

62. Tavuzzi, "Some Renaissance Thomist Divisions of Analogy," 102.

63. Soncinas, *Super artem veterem* (Venice, 1499), f. 19r–v: "unam rationem in actu, sed inaequaliter participatum" (quoted in Tavuzzi, "Some Renaissance Thomist Divisions of Analogy," 99). Cf. Soncinas, *Quaestiones in XII Metaphysicorum* VI, q. 4, ad 1, 9, and *Epitomes quaestionum Ioannis Caprieoli, super libros sententiarum* I, d. 1, q. 2, 35, both also quoted in Tavuzzi, "Some Renaissance Thomist Divisions of Analogy," 101–2.

64. Ashworth, "Analogical Concepts," 406.

65. Dominic of Flanders, *Quaestiones super XII libros Metaphysicorum* (Frankfurt: Minerva, 1967 [reprint of Venice, 1499]), IV, q. 2, a. 1. Ashworth finds Dominic attributing the view to others; Ashworth, "Analogical Concepts," 406–7. Cf. Franco Riva, "L'analogia dell'ente in Dominico di Fiandra," *Rivista di Filosofia Neo-scolastica* 86 (1994): 289–90.

66. Ashworth, "Analogical Concepts," 402.

67. Ibid., 407.

68. John Versorius, *Quaestiones super metaphysicam Aristotelis* (Coloniae, 1494), f. 25v: "ens dicatur de omnibus entibus . . . de uno primo et principaliter et de aliis dicitur secundum quod unumquodque eorum habet habitudinem ad ipsum primum, ergo non est ibi pura aequivocatio sed est unitas analogiae." (Quoted in Tavuzzi, "Some Renaissance Thomist Divisions of Analogy," 96n11.)

69. Pinchard, Metaphysique et semantique, 161.

70. Ashworth, "Analogical Concepts," 408.

71. Dominic of Flanders, *Quaestiones super XII libros Metaphysicorum,* IV, q. 2, a. 6: "Utrum ens significet unum conceptum disiunctum?"

72. Ashworth, "Analogical Concepts," 408.

73. Stephen Brown, "L'unité du concept d'être au début du quatorzième siècle," in *John Duns Scotus: Metaphysics and Ethics,* ed. Ludger Honnefelder, Rega Wood, and Mechthild Dreyer (Leiden: Brill, 1996), 334–36.

74. Ibid. Cf. Ashworth, "Analogical Concepts," 408.

75. *DNA* §§1, 71.

76. Indeed, a further problem with the "disjunct concept" theory of analogy is that it allows any two things to be analogical, if we stipulate a word that signifies their alternative. This objection is raised by Bochenski, "On Analogy," *The Thomist* (1948): §16. However, Bochenski does prove that a term so analogous can be the middle term of a valid syllogism, if the *ratio* of the middle term of the major premise is the disjunction of the *ratio* of the middle term of the minor premise and some other *ratio* ("On Analogy," §15).

CHAPTER FIVE

1. Like many Thomists Cajetan also completed Aquinas's unfinished commentary on Aristotle's *De Interpretatione*. We could assume from this that Cajetan endorses the semantic principles articulated by Aquinas in that work, though Cajetan's semantic principles can be reconstructed without relying on Aquinas's commentary.

2. *CPA* 3: "... res incomplexae non adunantur et distinguuntur cum conditionibus, quas habent in rerum natura, sed ut sic acceptae per intellectum, id est ut stant sub simplici apprehensione intellectus, id est ut obiectae simplici apprehensioni intellectus, et res sic acceptae nihil aliud sunt quam res dictae verbis interioribus, vel (quod idem est) quam res conceptae conceptibus simplicibus, et res huiusmodi nihil aliud sint quam res significatae vocibus incomplexis, quondo voces sunt signa conceptuum et conceptus rerum."

3. In this and other respects Cajetan stands firmly in the *via antiqua* "realist" tradition, on which see Gyula Klima, "The Medieval Problem of Universals," in *The Stanford Encyclopedia of Philosophy* (Fall 2000 ed.), ed. Edward N. Zalta. URL = http://plato.stanford.edu/archives/fall2000/entries/universals-medieval/.

4. *CDEE* §84: "... est notandum, quod cum nomine naturae intelligatur id quod per diffinitionem significatur, nomen autem suppositi individuum habens illam quiditatem."

5. *CPA* 18: "... scito quod formae nomine in hac materia intelligimus omne id quo aliquid dicitur tale, sive illud sit secundum rem accidens, sive substantia, sive materia, sive forma." *CST* I.37.2, n. iv: "Omne denominans, ut sic, habet rationem formalis." Cf. *DNA* §§31–32: "... in nominibus tria inveniuntur, scilecet vox, conceptus in anima, et res extra, seu conceptus obiectivus. ... Vocatur autem in proposito *res*, non solum natura aliqua, sed quicumque gradus, quaecumque realitas, et quodcumque reale in rebus inventum." Cf. Aquinas, *Summa Theologiae* I.37.2.c: "... sciendum est quod, cum res communiter denominentur a suis formis, sicut album ab albedine, et homo ab humanitate, omne illud a quo aliquid denominatur, quantum ad hoc habet habitudinem formae. Ut dicam, iste est indutus vestimento, iste ablativus construitur in habitudine causae formalis, quamvis non sit forma." Cf. Aquinas, *Quaestiones disputatae de potentia Dei* 7.10, ad 8: "Dicendum est quod illud a quo aliquid denominatur non oportet quod sit semper forma secundum rei naturam, sed sufficit quod significetur per modum formae, grammatice loquendo. Denominatur enim homo ab actione et ab indumento, et ab aliis huiusmodi, quae realiter non sunt formae."

6. *CDEE* §8: "... nota quod sicut quid rei est quiditas rei, ita quid nominis est quiditas nominis. Nomen autem cum essentialiter sit nota earum quae sunt objective in anima passionum ex I Perihermenias, non habet aliam quiditatem nisi hanc quod est signum alicujus rei intellectae seu cogitatae: signum autem, ut sic, relativum est ad signatum. Unde cognoscere quid nominis nihil est aliud quam cognoscere ad quod tale nomen habet relationem ut signum ad signatum. Talis autem cognitio potest acquiri per accidentalia illius signati, per communia, per essentialia, per nutus et quibusvis aliis modis, sicut a Graeco quaerentibus

nobis quid nominis anthropos si digito ostendatur homo, jam percipimus quid nominis; et similiter de aliis. Interrogantibus ver quid rei, opertet assignare id quod convenit rei significatae in primo modo perseitatis adaequatae. Et haec est essentialis differnetia inter quid nominis et quid rei, scilicet quod quid nomis est relatio nomis ad signatum; quid rei vero est rei relatae seu significatae essentia. Et ex hac differentia sequuntur omnes aliae quae dici solent, puta quod quid nominis sit non entium complexorum, per accidentalia, per communia, per extranea; quid rei vero est entium incomplexorum per propria et essentialia: relatio enim vocis potest terminari ad non entia in rerum natura, et complexa, et declarari per accidentalia, et hujusmodi ; essentia autem rei non nisi per propria essentialia habetur de entibus incomplexis."

7. To be sure, considered as elements of Cajetan's particular philosophical psychology, which in turn depends on a certain metaphysical framework, one could take issue with Cajetanian "concepts." The only point here is that, considered in their general semantic and epistemological function, "concepts" are just what make possible signification and understanding.

8. The metaphysician might treat them as forms *analogically*, that is as not strictly speaking the same as, but nonetheless analogous to, really existing forms *in rerum natura*.

9. Cf. Gyula Klima, "The Semantic Principles Underlying Saint Thomas Aquinas's Metaphysics of Being," *Medieval Philosophy and Theology* 5 (1996): 106–7, 114–15.

10. Cf. Gyula Klima, "Ontological Alternatives vs. Alternative Semantics in Medieval Philosophy," in *Logical Semiotics*, special issue of *S-European Journal for Semiotic Studies* 3 (1991): 587–618.

11. The distinction between formal and objective concept is usually traced back to the fourteenth century, though many commentators have found Aquinas expressing, albeit without these technical names, the same distinction. It is not uncommon for it to be invoked in the Thomistic tradition; cf. Jacques Maritain, *Distinguish to Unite, or The Degrees of Knowledge*, trans. Gerald B. Phelan (New York: Charles Scribner's Sons, 1959): 387–417.

12. *CDEE* §14: ". . . nota quod conceptus est duplex: formalis et objectalis. Conceptus formalis est idolum quoddam quod intellectus possibilis format in seipso repraesentativum objectaliter rei intellectae: quod a philosophis vocatur intentio seu conceptus, a theologis vero verbum. Conceptus autem objectalis est res per conceptum formalem repraesentata in illo terminans actum intelligendi, verbi gratia: conceptus formalis leonis est imago illa quam intellectus possibilis format de quiditate leonina, cum vult ipsam intelligere; conceptus vero objectalis ejusdem est natura ipsa leonina repraesentata et intellecta. Nec putandum est cum dicitur nomen significare conceptum quod significet alterum tantum: significat enim leonis nomen conceptum utrumque, licet diversimode, est namque signum conceptus formalis ut medii, seu quo, et est signum conceptus objectalis, ut ultimi seu quod." In fact, Cajetan will in some contexts make even further distinctions about how the formal and objective concepts can be considered (cf. *CDEE* §48).

13. E.g., *DNA* §31.

14. *CDEE* §66: "Esse in intellectu contingit dupliciter, subjective et objective. Esse in intellectu subjective est inhaerere ipsi, sicut accidens suo subjecto, ut albedo superficiei. Esse in intellectu objective est terminare actum intellectus."

15. E.g., I. M. Bochenski, "On Analogy," *The Thomist* (1948).

16. E.g., E. J. Ashworth, "Signification and Modes of Signifying in Thirteenth-Century Logic: A Preface to Aquinas on Analogy," *Medieval Philosophy and Theology* 1 (1991): 51, 53.

17. E.g., Edward A. Bushinski and Henry J. Koren, *The Analogy of Names and the Concept of Being* (Pittsburgh: Duquesne University Press, 1953). Indeed, Bushinski's translation also renders "*ratio*" variously as "character," "notion," "nature," "definition," and "mode." This testifies to the difficulty of finding a single adequate word in English, but it also means that the centrality of this important notion is obscured by Bushinski's translation.

18. *CPA* 9: "Ly «ratio», licet multipliciter sumi possit, hic sumitur non pro diffinitione, quoniam res generalissimae aequivoca dici non possent, eo quod diffinitione carent, sed sumitur pro conceptu significato per nomen, qui in habentibus diffinitionem est diffinitio ipsa, in non habentibus vero diffinitionem ratio quam significat nomen vocatur, et nihil aliud est quam id quod directe significatur per nomen."

19. *CST* I.13.4, n. 3: "[ratio sumi potest pro] conceptionem et definitionem, sed diversimode. Conceptio enim mentalis ratio nominis dicitur, quia est id quo refertur nomen in significatum extra animam: definitio autem, quia est id quo explicatur nominis significatum." Cf. Aquinas, *Summa Theologiae* I.5.2. Cajetan is clarifying the sense of Aquinas's claim, "Ratio enim quam significat nomen, est conceptio intellectus de re significata per nomen." It is worth noting that in the context of this article Cajetan recommends taking "*ratio*" as the mental concept, not as the definition, and so his interpretation would apparently differ from that of Ashworth, who would translate "*ratio*" with "analysis." Ashworth, "Signification and Modes of Signifying in Thirteenth-Century Logic," 51, 53.

20. On the inherence theory of predication see L. M. de Rijk, *Logica Modernorum: A Contribution to the History of Early Terminist Logic*, vol. 1, *On the Twelfth Century Theories of Fallacy* (Assen: Van Gorcum, 1962), 37–38; Peter T. Geach, *Logic Matters* (Berkeley: University of California Press, 1980), 289–301; and Klima, "The Semantic Principles Underlying Saint Thomas Aquinas's Metaphysics of Being."

21. Cf., e.g., *CDEE* §63.

22. Ashworth explains the difference between what is predicated and what verifies the predication as the difference between the significate (*significatum*) and the thing signified (*res significata*). Ashworth, "Signification and Modes of Signifying in Thirteenth-Century Logic," 50–53. Her explanation is coherent and valuable with respect to the thirteenth-century authors she considers, but I do not notice Cajetan observing a strict technical difference between "*significatum*" and "*res significata.*"

23. In fact, this is the reason why in certain contexts Cajetan is reluctant to describe predication in terms of inherence, and instead describes what looks like the theory sometimes contrasted with the inherence theory of predication,

the identity theory (or "two-names theory") of predication. *CPA* 47: "Praedicari de aliquo cum nihil aliud importet quam inesse seu convenire illi de quo praedicatur, consequens est quod praedicari de aliquo secundum nomen nihil aliud sit quam nomen praedicati convenire subiecto, ita quod nomen praedicata sit etiam nomen subiecti; nec refert an tale nomen sit subiecti secundum substantiam aut secundum qualitatem, vel quodcumque aliud extraneum, Sufficit enim quod nomen illud eius aliquo modo nota sit essentialiter vel denominative intrinsece vel extrinsece; et similiter sequitur quod praedicari secundum rationem nihil aliud sit quam rationem praedicata convenire subiecto, ita quod ratio praedicati sit etiam ratio subiecti; nec refert an ratio praedicati sit tota ratio subiecti an sit pars rationis, dummodo sit pars intrinseca, quod dico propter ea quae cadunt in ratione ut addita, sicut subiectum est pars rationis accidentis et corpus animae." *CDEE* §9: ". . . veritas propositionis, quae est entis secundo modo significati, nihil aluid est quam compositio facta in secund operatione intellectus objecto conformis, verbi gratia, Sortes est caecus, ly est non significat inhaerentiam caecitatis in Sorte, eo quod caecitas omni inhaerentia caret, cum inhaerere realium accidentium sit, sed significat compositionem factam ab intellectu adequante seipsum per illam objecto, Sorti, scilicet, carente virtute visiva, unde V Metaph. in alia littera, dicitur quod ens significans veritatem propositionis significat quoniam propositio est vera." But cf. *CPI* 20–21: "Imaginandum enim est, quod intellectus videns Sortem habere albedinem, prima sua attentione format hanc propositionem mentalem: Sortes est albus in qua propositione tot terminos poscit, quot videt extra animam res; tria siquidem ibi videt, scilicet Sortem, albedinem et inhaesionem albedinis in Sorte." The point is that on Cajetan's semantics, in a true sentence the predicate-term and the subject-term both supposit for the same thing(s), because the predicate supposits for that in which the significate of the predicate inheres. Some articulations of the (realist) inherence theory, in emphasizing its contrast with the (nominalist) identity theory, have denied that in the realist theory the predicate supposits. On the supposition of the predicate in realist semantics, see Stephen Theron, "The Supposition of the Predicate," *Modern Schoolman* 77 (1999): 73–78.

24. Klima, "The Semantic Principles Underlying Saint Thomas Aquinas's Metaphysics of Being," carries out this project with respect to Aquinas, with results substantially the same as those we would expect from a similar analysis of Cajetan.

25. However, what cannot be avoided is that the different senses of "being" that are required to account for these different verification conditions are an instance of "the analogy of being." Since this outline of Cajetan's semantic assumptions was supposed to be preparatory for his semantic analysis of analogical signification, it might seem circular for a semantic analysis of analogy to presuppose semantic principles that in turn presuppose the analogy of "being." However, it is not circular. Cajetan's theory of analogy is not an attempt to prove that there is analogy, but rather an attempt to show that, given that there is analogy, we can make some sense of its semantic conditions. That these semantic conditions are themselves described in the context of a general semantic theory that in turn is articulated by means of terms that are analogical is no more circular than a presentation of the semantic conditions of univocity that assumes

the existence of (and makes use of) univocal terms. Furthermore, the occurrence of analogical terms even in Cajetan's basic framework of semantic principles should at least appease those who might otherwise fear that a semantic analysis of analogy is an attempt to analyze analogy away.

26. *CPA* 16: "non debet denominativum differre a nomine formae denominatis in significatione. . . . Differentia autem in modo significandi inventa inter denominativum et denominans non excluditur."

27. Otherwise, e.g., *"lapis"* (stone)—in the accusative *"lapidem"*—which was hypothesized to have been imposed from *"laedens pedem"* (foot-hurting), would have *foot-hurting* as its denominating form, when in fact it denominates stones on account of their nature, which could be called *"lapiditas."* Cf. the discussions of imposition in Klima, "The Semantic Principles Underlying Saint Thomas Aquinas's Metaphysics of Being," 110–11, and Ashworth, "Signification and Modes of Signifying in Thirteenth-Century Logic," 46–50.

28. In general, it is remarkable that there is so little explicit reflection and explanation of the notions of intrinsic or extrinsic denomination, both in modern scholarship and in the medieval authors. While the distinction has obvious precedents in Aquinas and before, it appears in technical terminology only later, and the examples and applications quickly become familiar, but even in a systematic work of logic such as the *Ars Logica* of John Poinsot's *Cursus Philosophicus* the notion of extrinsic denomination is taken for granted and neither fully defined nor explained.

29. E.g., Aquinas, *In octo libros Physicorum exposito* 3.5, §322; Aquinas, *Summa Theologiae* I.6.4.

30. For a discussion of the notion of extrinsic denomination in Aquinas, see Thomas J. Loughran, "Efficient Causality and Extrinsic Denomination in the Philosophy of St. Thomas Aquinas" (Ph.D. diss., Fordham University, 1969), 78–123.

31. The *Summa Totius Logicae* was also occasionally attributed to Peter of Spain. According to the hypothesis of Angel d'Ors, the author is one Gratiadeus of Asculo, a fourteenth-century Dominican logician, as attested by St. Antonio de Firenze (1389–1459) and Johannes Trithemius. See p. 238 of Angel D'Ors, "Petrus Hispanus O.P., Auctor Summularum (II): Further Documents and Problems," *Vivarium* 39 (2001): 209–54.

32. *Summa Totius Logicae* tr. 5, c. 6: "Dupliciter autem potest aliquid de alio praedicari denominative, sive illud denominare. Uno modo quod talis praedicatio seu denominatio fiat ab aliquo quod sit intrinsecum ei de quo fit talis praedicatio seu denominatio, quod videlicet ipsum perficiat sive per identitatem sive per inhaerentiam. . . . Secondo modo fit denominatio ab extrinseco, scilicet ab eo quod non est in denominato formali, sed est aliquod absolutum extrinsecum, a quo fit talis denominatio."

33. John P. Doyle, "Prolegomena to a Study of Extrinsic Denomination in the Works of Francis Suarez, S.J.," *Vivarium* 22 (1984): 122–23. Doyle is careful to offer this as a provisional description, not a definition of extrinsic denomination as that was understood by Suarez or other medieval philosophers.

34. *Summa Totius Logicae* tr. 5, c. 6: "Sciendum est autem, quod denominatio ab extrinseco requirit aliquem per se respectum inter extrinsecum

denominans et denominatum ab eo; quia oportet quod per se et ex conditione rerum talis modus denominandi consequatur res; et ideo oportet quod illud a quo fit talis denominatio, sit fundamentum per se alicujus habitudinis."

35. *CST* I.6.4, nn. 3, 8: "... denominatio est duplex, quaedam intrinseca, et quaedam extrinseca. Vocatur denominatio intrinseca, quando forma denominativi est in eo quod denominatur, ut album, quantum, etc.: denominatio vero extrinseca, quando forma denominativi non est in denominato, ut locatum, mensuratum, et similia. ... Dupliciter enim contingit aliquid dici tale ab aliquo extrinseco. Uno modo, ita quod ratio denominationis sit ipsa relatio ad extrinsecum, ut urina dicitur sana, sola relatione signi signi ad sanitatem. Alio modo, ita quod ratio denominationis sit, non relatio similitudinis, aut quaevis alia, sed forma quea est fundamentum relationis similitudinis ad illud extrinsecum; ut aer dicitur lucidus luce solari, ea ratione qua participat eam per formam luminis." It is not clear whether we can regard one of Cajetan's two alternatives as reducible to the other, insofar as a *relation* is only called extrinsic because its *foundation* is extrinsic.

36. Cf., e.g., Cajetan's discussion of the objects of understanding being extrinsically denominated as intelligible or as actually understood; *CDEE* §67.

37. This often seems to be the case in late medieval discussions of whether the "six principles" (the last six of the accidental categories) were real beings or not; it was often suggested that they were not, and that they were denominated extrinsically. Cf. *Summa Totius Logicae*, tr. 5, c. 6. For discussion of these debates and references, cf. William E. McMahon, "Some Non-Standard Views of the Categories," in *La tradition médiévale des Catégories (XIIe–XVe siècles): XIIIe symposium européen de logique et de sémantique médiévales*, ed. Joël Biard and Irène Rosier-Catach (Louvain: Peters, 2003), 53–67, and William E. McMahon, "The Categories in Some Post-Medieval Spanish Philosophers," in *Medieval and Renaissance Logic in Spain*, ed. I. Angelelli and P. Pérez-Ilzarbe (Hildesheim: Georg Olms Verlag, 2000), 355–70.

38. This is at least the case with what were called relatives *secundum esse*, as opposed to relatives *secundum dici*; the former signify a relation, the latter only imply a relation insofar as they signify something that is the foundation of a relation.

39. Aquinas, *Summa Theologiae* I–II.7.2, ad 1: "In his autem quae ad aliquid dicuntur, denominatur aliquid non solum ab eo quod inest, sed etiam ab eo quod extrinsicus adjacet."

40. Cf. *CPA* 4–5.

41. There are some conditions, at least, in which we would be willing to say that the eye sees itself, and not just that the eye sees only its reflection. Alternatively we could have considered the case in which Socrates is thinking about something, and what he is thinking about is his own intellect.

42. *CPA* 124: "Ly vero «ad aliquid» sive «relativa» potest accipi dupliciter scilicet: materialiter pro re illa quae relativa vel ad aliquid denominatur, et formaliter pro ipsa relatione seu re ut habet relatione, verbi gratia: dominus potest accipi pro illo homine qui denominatur dominus, et potest accipi pro illo in quantum dominium habet."

CHAPTER SIX

1. *CPA* 10: "Ly «diversa» non coartatur ad diversitatem simpliciter, sed communiter accipitur ut comprehendit sub se diversitatem simpliciter vel secundum quid, totaliter vel partialiter, ita quod aequivoca dicuntur et illa quorum ratio secundum illud nomen est penitus diversa, et illa quorum ratio secundum illud nomen commune est aliquo modo diversa."

2. *CPA* 10: "Et propter hoc cave ne dixeris hic esse diffinita tantum pure aequivoca, quae alio vocabulo dicuntur aequivoca a casu, sed dicito aequivoca in communi, ut comprehendunt analoga quae aequivoca a consilio sunt, et pure aequivoca diffiniri, et quod pure aequivocis convenit habere rationem substantiae diversam penitus, analalogis vero diversam aliquo modo."

3. Cf. *CST* I.13.5 n. 12: "analoga comprehenduntur sub aequivocis, quae in Praedicamentis definiuntur." Of course in finding analogy inchoately contained in the *Categories* discussion of equivocation, Cajetan is just following a long tradition, which includes Boethius and goes back at least to Porphyry. Boethius, *In Categorias Aristotelis Libri Quatuor*, in *PL* 64, 166B–167A. Porphyry, *In Aristotelis Praedicamenta per interrogationem et responsionem brevis explanatio*, in *Commentaria in Aristotelem Graeca*, IV.1, ed. A. Busse (Berlin: Reimeri, 1887), 65.16–67.34.

4. *CPA* 11: "Quot autem modis contingat variari analogiam et quomodo, nunc quum summarie loquimur, silentio pertransibimus, specialem de hoc tractatum, si Deo placuerit, cito confecturi."

5. One of the few studies to compare Cajetan's teaching on analogy in *CDEE* with that in *DNA* is Aloys Goergen, *Kardinal Cajetans Lehre von der Analogie; Ihr Verhältnis zu Thomas von Aquin* (Speyer a. Rh.: Pilger-Druckerei, 1938), 13–18, 20–22.

6. *CDEE* §21: "Univocata sunt, quorum nomen est commune, et ratio secundum illud nomen est eadem simpliciter. Pura aequivocata sunt, quorum nomen est commune, et ratio secundum illud nomen est diversa simpliciter. Analogata sunt quorum nomen est commune, et ratio secundum illud nomen est aliquo modo eadem, et aliquo modo diversa seu secundum quid eadem, et secundum quid diversa.... Unde analogum est medium inter purum aequivocum et univocum, sicut inter idem simpliciter et diversum simpliciter cadit medium idem secundum quid et diversum secundum quid."

7. *CDEE* §18: "...aliquid dupliciter contingit de aliquibus praedicari per prius et posterius. Uno modo secundum esse illius praedicati. Alio modo secundum propriam rationem ejusdem. Illud dicitur praedicari analogice secundum esse, quod perfectius habet esse in uno quam in alio et sic omne genus praedicatur per prius et posterius de suis speciebus, eo quod perfectius esse necessario habet in una specie, quam in alia."

8. *CDEE* §21: "Nota secundo quod duplicia sunt analogata: quaedam secundum determinatam habitudenem unius ad alterum; quaedam secundum proportionalitatem. Exemplum: Substantia et accidens sunt analogata primo modo sub ente; Deus autem et creatura secundo modo: infinita enim est distantia inter Deum et creaturam. Differunt autem haec plurimum: quoniam analogata

primo modo ita se habent, quod posterius secundum nomen analogum diffinitur per suum prius: puta accidens, inquantum ens per substantiam. Analogata vero secundo modo non: creatura enim inquantum ens non diffinitur per Deum."

9. *CDEE* §21: "Unde analogata primo modo habent nomen commune, et rationem secundum illud nomen secundum quid eadem et secundum quid diversam: per hoc quod analogum illud simpliciter, id est sine additione aliqua, de primo dicitur, et de aliis vero non nisi diversimode respiciendo primum, quod cadit in eorum rationibus sicut in exemplo de sano manifestum est: analogata vero secundo modo habent nomen commune et rationem secundum illud nomen alliquo modo eadem et aliquo modo diversam: non propter hoc, quod illud simplicitur dicatur de primo et de aliis relative ad primum, sed habent rationem eadem secundum quid propter identitatem proportionis, quae in eis invenitur, et secundum quid diversam, propter diversitatem naturarum suppositarum illius proportionibus. Exemplum: Forma et materia substantialis et forma et materia accidentium sunt analogata quaedam sub nominibus formae et materiae: habent enim nomen commune, puta formam et materiam, et rationem secundum nomen formae sive materiae eamdem et diversam hoc modo, quia forma substantialis ita se habet ad substantiam, sicut forma accidentalis ad accidens; similiter materia substantiae ita se habet ad substantiam, sicut materia accidentis ad accidens: utrobique enim salvatur identitas proportionum cum diversitate naturarum et unitate nominis. Hunc modum analogiae exprimit Commentator (XII Metaph., com. XXVIII), et clarius cum Aristotele (I Ethic., cap. VII)."

10. *CDEE* §21: "Ens analogice utroque modo analogiae dicitur de substantia et accidente."

11. The point cannot be, therefore, just that one mode of analogy is relevant to what some refer to as the "transcendental" predication of being (being as said of God and creatures) and another is relevant to "predicamental" predication (being said of the different categories). More will be said about Cajetan's treatment of such "mixed cases" later in this chapter.

12. We cannot rule out the possibility that Cajetan may have in mind here Aquinas's distinction between analogy *secundum esse* and analogy *secundum intentionem* in *I Sent*. 19.5.2 ad 1, even if he does not cite that text. But even if Cajetan does have that text in mind, we must note that he alters its terminology slightly and does not apply it consistently. Cajetan says: ". . . aliquid dupliciter contingit de aliquibus praedicari per prius et posterius. Uno modo secundum esse illius praedicati. Alio modo secundum propriam rationem ejusdem" (*CDEE* §18). But being predicated "per prius et posterius . . . secundum esse" is here sufficient to describe (what Cajetan will later call) analogy of inequality, although according to a parallelism with *I Sent*. 19.5.2 ad 1, *two* modes of analogy (Cajetan's analogy of inequality and analogy of proportionality) should be *per prius et posterius secundum esse*, and a sufficient description of inequality is that it is "secundum esse *et non secundum intentionem*." Furthermore, in discussing what will come to be called analogy of attribution and analogy of proportionality, Cajetan does not say that the former is analogy "secundum rationem et non secundum esse," nor does he say that the latter is analogy "secundum rationem

et secundum esse." Cajetan's terminology in these passages thus does not suggest that he is trying to justify his threefold distinction by basing it on implicit reference to the threefold distinction in *I Sent*. 19.5.2, ad 1.

13. *CDEE* §21: "... cum talis unitas apud Aristotelem (IV Metaph., text. com. II) sufficiat ad objectum scientiae, ens non oportet poni univocum ad hoc quod passiones habeat et contradictionem fundet, et reliqua hujusmodi habeant sibi convenientia." The reference to Aquinas's commentary on the *Metaphysics* is apparently to book 4, lect. 1 (§547 Cathala).

14. Cajetan presents the arguments of Scotus in *CDEE* §19.

15. Among those who have inaccurately claimed that Cajetan's distinction between modes of analogy is *based on* or *defined in terms of* the properties of extrinsic and intrinsic denomination are E. J. Ashworth, "Analogy and Equivocation in Thirteenth-Century Logic: Aquinas in Context," *Mediaeval Studies* 54 (1992): 126, and John D. Beach, "Analogous Naming, Extrinsic Denomination and the Real Order," *Modern Schoolman* 42 (1965): 201.

16. *DNA* §10–11; Cf. *DNA* §29.

17. *DNA* §4: "Analoga secundum inaequalitatem vocantur, quorum nomen est commune, et ratio secundum illud nomen est omnino eadem, inaequaliter tamen participata"; §8: "Analoga autem secundum attributionem sunt, quorum nomen commune est, ratio autem secundum illud nomen est eadem secundum terminum, et diversa secundum habitudines ad illum"; §23: "[A]naloga secundum proportionalitatem dici, quorum nomen est commune, et ratio secundum illud nomen est proportionaliter eadem."

18. The one apparent exception to this parallel is that Aristotle was careful to emphasize that he was not defining things *as they are*, but *as they are signified by our terms*. Thus, as has often been noted, Aristotle wrote that equivocals and univocals "*dicuntur*," rather than "*sunt*." Cajetan only follows this inconsistently; he uses "*sunt*" for analogy of attribution, but since he uses "*vocantur*" for analogy of inequality and "*dici*" for analogy of proportionality, I think we can assume that the deviation is not significant. On Cajetan's appreciation of Aristotle's use of "*dicitur*," see chap. 2, n. 16, above.

19. Ashworth, "Analogy and Equivocation in Thirteenth-Century Logic," 107. Cf. Cajetan's use of "*latere*" at *DNA* §108, quoting Aristotle (*Sophisticis Elenchis*, 182b22). Ramirez also cites remarks on genus in Aristotle's *Physics* in connection with analogy of inequality. Jacobus M. Ramirez, "De analogia secundum doctrinam Aristotelico-Thomisticam," *Ciencia Tomista* 24 (1921): 195.

20. *CDEE* §18: "Unde Commentator (XII Metaph., com. II) dicit quod prioritas et posterioritas specierum non impedit unitatem generis." *DNA* §7: "Perhibet quoque huic analogiae testimonium Averroës in XII Metaph., text. 2 dicens, cum unitate generis stare prioritatem et posterioritatem eorum, quae sub genere sunt."

21. The distinction also turns out to be the same as the distinction between the nature absolutely considered and the nature as it is in things. Cf. *CDEE* §55. This also helps us to make sense of why Cajetan can say that in analogy of inequality, "the analogates are the same in the *ratio* signified by that common name, but they are not the same in the being [*esse*] of that *ratio*" (*DNA* §6).

22. *DNA* §6: "Non solum enim planta est nobilior minera; sed corporeitas in planta est nobilior corporeitate in minera." While this formulation might seem to depend entirely on a specific version of Aristotelian hylomorphist metaphysics, even someone who rejects that metaphysics can understand the intuitive point that Cajetan is trying to express: that stone and plant are equally bodies, though they are not equal bodies. Cf. Aquinas, preparing us to understand how not all sins are equal, *Quaestiones disputate de malo*, II.9, ad 16: "Dicendum quod omnia animalia sunt aequaliter animalia, sed unam animal est altero maius et perfectus." In fact, while Cajetan's and Aquinas's language presupposes a *hierarchy* of species within a genus, all that matters for a genus term to signify by analogy of inequality is that there be a *diversity* of species. For a brief but common-sense discussion of analogy of inequality ("the pseudo-analogy, the stretched univocity called analogy of inequality by Cajetan") see Yves Simon, "On Order in Analogical Sets," in *Philosopher at Work: Essays by Yves R. Simon*, ed. Anthony O. Simon (Lanham, Md.: Rowman and Littlefield, 1999), 135–36, 138.

23. *DNA* §§5, 7.

24. *DNA* §3.

25. Cajetan also notes that this is why even though in this sense every genus term is analogous, they are not normally so called; *DNA* §5. Aristotle says that generic unity implies analogical unity in *Metaphysics* V.6 (1017a2).

26. Herbert Thomas Schwartz, "Analogy in St. Thomas and Cajetan," *New Scholasticism* 28 (1954): 127–44.

27. Frank R. Harrison also fails to understand Cajetan's comments on analogy of inequality because he fails to understand Cajetan's semantic principles; in his case, a Wittgensteinian inclination prevents him from understanding the semantic function of the *ratio*. Frank R. Harrison, "The Cajetan Tradition of Analogy," *Franciscan Studies* 23 (1963): esp. 185–86. Armand Maurer criticizes Cajetan's position on analogy of inequality, but in fact it is precisely the position that Maurer finds and agrees with in Aquinas: accepting it from the point of view of the natural philosopher, rejecting it from the point of view of the logician. Maurer, "St. Thomas and the Analogy of Genus," *New Scholasticism* 29 (1955): 127–44. Maurer complains that Cajetan's position is evidence of his "essentialism," as compared with the "existential" approach of Aquinas. Maurer is apparently reading Cajetan through the somewhat distorting lens of Étienne Gilson, "Cajétan et l'existence," *Tijdschrift voor Philosophie* 15 (1953): 267–86. For correctives to Gilson's interpretation of Cajetan see Laurence Dewan, "Étienne Gilson and the *Actus Essendi*," *Maritain Studies/Études Maritainiennes* 15 (1999): 70–96, and John P. Reilly, *Cajetan's Notion of Existence* (The Hague: Mouton, 1971). Riva discusses the allegations of Cajetan's "essentialism" in *Analogia e univocità in Tommaso de Vio "Gaetano"* (Milan: Vita e Pensiero, 1995), 65–82.

28. *DNA* §8: ". . . *sanum* commune nomen est medicinae, urinae et animali; et ratio omnium in quantum sana sunt, ad unum terminum (sanitatem scilicet), diversas dicit habitudines. Si quis enim assignet quid est animal in quantum sanum, subiectum dicet sanitatis; urinam vero in quantum sanam, signum sanitatis; medicinam autem in quantum sanam, causam sanitatis proferet." Cf. *DNA* §52.

29. More specifically, it is a relation *secundum esse*, not *secundum dici*; cf. chap. 5, n. 38, *supra*.

30. *CST* I.13.6, n. 4: "Quaedam enim significant ipsos respectus ad primum analogatum, ut patet de sano." This is confirmed in Ross's attempt to formulate definitions of the different modes of analogy, where it is clear that a word analogous by attribution, insofar as it signifies a secondary term, signifies a relation. James F. Ross, "Analogy as a Rule of Meaning for Religious Language" in *Aquinas: A Collection of Critical Essays*, ed. Anthony Kenny (Garden City, N.Y.: Anchor Books, 1969), 115.

31. *DNA* §10: "Attribuuntur autem huic analogiae multae conditiones, ordinate se cosequentes: scilicet quod analogia ista sit secundum denominationem extrinsecam tantum; ita quod primum analogatorum tantum est tale formaliter, caetera autem denominantur talia extrinsece."

32. Even Ashworth is imprecise on this point, referring to "Cajetan's notorious claim . . . that the supposed division between analogy of attribution and analogy of proper proportionality is based on the difference between intrinsic and extrinsic denomination." Ashworth, "Analogy and Equivocation in Thirteenth-Century Logic," 126.

33. *DNA* §11: "Sed diligenter advertendum est, quod haec huiusmodi analogiae conditio, scilicet quod non sit secundum genus causae formalis inhaerentis, sed semper secundum aliquid extrinsecum, est formaliter intelligenda et non materialiter: idest non est intelligendum per hoc, quod omne nomen quod est analogum per attributionem, sit commune analogatis sic, quod primo tantum conveniat formaliter, caeteris autem extrinseca denominatione, ut de sano et medicinali accidit; ista enim universalis est falsa, ut patet de ente et bono; nec potest haberi ex dictis, nisi materialiter intellectis. Sed est ex hoc intelligendum, quod omne nomen analogum per attributionem ut sic, vel in quantum sic analogum, commune est analogatis sic, quod primo convenit formaliter, reliquis autem extrinseca denominatione."

34. *DNA* §11: "Ens enim quamvis formaliter conveniat omnibus substantiis et accidentibus etc., in quantum tamen entia, omnia dicuntur ab ente subiective ut sic, sola substantia est ens formaliter; caetera autem entia dicuntur, quia entis passiones vel generationes etc. sunt; licet entia formaliter alia ratione dici possint."

35. E.g., cf. John Beach, "Analogous Naming, Extrinsic Denomination, and the Real Order," *Modern Schoolman* 42 (1965): 204, and Henry Chavannes, *The Analogy Between God and the World in Saint Thomas Aquinas and Karl Barth*, trans. William Lumley (New York: Vantage Press, 1992), 53–58. Masiello finds Cajetan's qualification an odd concession. Ralph J. Masiello, "The Analogy of Proportion According to the Metaphysics of St. Thomas," *Modern Schoolman* 35 (1958): 95–97. Jean-Luc Marion, *Sur la théologie blanche de Descartes*, 94n33, calls Cajetan's clarification "l'étrange précaution."

36. Ralph McInerny, *Aquinas and Analogy* (Washington, D.C.: Catholic University of America Press, 1996), 20. Cf. McInerny, *The Logic of Analogy: An Interpretation of St. Thomas* (The Hague: Martinus Nijhoff, 1961), 7–9.

37. Although this has been McInerny's interpretation for some time, in this most recent book on analogy it is accompanied by an unfortunate mistranslation

of part of Cajetan's qualification, which does indeed render that qualification nonsensical: "Although being belongs formally to all substances and accidents, etc., *insofar as they are called beings they are all denominated from the being which is a subject*, only substance is being formally; the others are called beings because they are properties or becomings of being, etc., although they can be called beings formally for other reasons" (McInerny, *Aquinas and Analogy*, 20, emphasis added). However, McInerny had earlier rendered the passage correctly: "For although *being* agrees formally with all substances, accidents, etc., nevertheless *insofar as all are denominated from being taken subjectively as such*, substance alone is being formally, and the others are called beings because they are qualities, activities, etc. of being. However, under a different aspect they could be called beings in a formal sense." Ralph McInerny, "The Logic of Analogy," *New Scholasticism* 31 (1957): 157 (emphasis added).

38. Cajetan also uses a reduplicative term when he describes analogy of attribution at *CDEE* §21: ". . . accidens, *inquantum ens* [diffinitur] per substantiam. . . . creatura enim *inquantum ens* non diffinitur per Deum." We are not surprised to find similar reduplicative phrases in other expositions of Cajetan's position. Thus Penido writes: "L'attribution *en tant qu'*attribution ne pose pas autre chose parce qu'ell est un pur rapport de dépendence" (emphasis added). M. T.-L. Penido, *Le rôle de l'analogie en théologie dogmatique* (Paris: Librairie Philosophique J. Vrin, 1931), 27. According to Anderson, followers of Cajetan "do not hold that there is nothing intrinsic to the secondary analogates but only that they do not realize *formally* the analogical notion *as such*" (second emphasis added). Anderson, *The Bond of Being: An Essay on Analogy and Existence* (St. Louis: Herder, 1949), 109–10. Cf. Yves Simon, "On Order in Analogical Sets," 165–66: "If the unity of a concept is analogical, its inferiors make up an ordered set, and . . . neither the unity of the set nor the meaning of each member, *considered qua member of the set*, is understood except in the system of relations of priority and posteriority . . ." (emphasis Simon's).

39. Harrison, "The Cajetan Tradition of Analogy," 191, maintains that Cajetan's theory couldn't account for the case of healthy skin.

40. A similar argument could be made for "healthy" as predicated of food. Some foods may have their own intrinsic health, although "healthy" is the traditional example of a term analogous by attribution which denominates food extrinsically. Cf. Aquinas, *De Veritate* 1.4, and Hampus Lyttkens, *The Analogy Between God and the World: An Investigation of Its Background and Its Use by Thomas of Aquino* (Uppsala: Almqvist and Wiksells Boktrycheri AB, 1952), 331. We have here also the material for a reply to Beach, who claims that Cajetan is unable to explain how a leech or oyster might be denominated healthy extrinsically, and yet still be intrinsically healthy. Beach, "Analogous Naming, Extrinsic Denomination, and the Real Order," 204.

41. *Log.* p. 2, q. 13, a. 4 (487b25–32): "possunt tamen in illis analogatis minus principalibus praerequiri aliqui respectus intrinseci, non quibus denominentur analogice et sub forma analoga constituantur, sed quibus respiciant illud principale analogatum, ut deinde denominentur extrinsece ab illo analogice."

42. Cajetanians have expressed the point in a variety of ways. Garrigou-Lagrange puts it this way: "Analogy of attribution never implies intrinsic

denomination in the various analogates, but does not necessarily exclude it." Reginald Garrigou-Lagrange, *God: His Existence and His Nature*, vol. 2, trans. Bede Rose (St. Louis: Herder, 1934, 1936), 207. Anderson, *The Bond of Being*, 112, describes mixed cases as "a kind of 'material coincidence' of attribution and proportionality." John of St. Thomas speaks of cases of proportionality which contain analogy of attribution "virtually": "Analogia entis ad decem praedicamenta non sufficienter explicatur dicendo, quod est transcendentiae, sed dicendum est quod est analogia proportionalitatis formaliter, licet virtualiter analogiam attributionis seu proportionis includet." John of St. Thomas, *Ars Logica* p. 2, q. 14, a. 3 (512b26–33). Cf. Ibid., q. 13, a. 4 (489b42–490a6): "Quodsi inquiras, quomodo ista duplex analogia possit eidem convenire, v.g. enti, cum habeant conditiones omnino oppositas. . . . Respondetur non dari utramque analogiam formaliter, sed alteram virtualiter." Joseph Owens arrives at a very similar treatment of the relationship between Aristotle's two kinds of equivocation (*pros hen* equivocation and analogy): "There is nothing in the Aristotelian text . . . to preclude the same things from being equivocal in both ways. . . . The two types, though clearly distinct, are not mutually exclusive. Just as things may be denominated univocally or equivocally by the same word, according as their nature demands, so things may be expressed by the same term [either] analogously or through reference, according as their nature allows." Joseph Owens, *The Doctrine of Being in the Aristotelian "Metaphysics": A Study in the Greek Background of Medieval Thought*, 3rd ed. (Toronto: Pontifical Institute of Medieval Studies, 1978), 125.

43. Suarez, *Disputationes Metaphysicae*, vol. 2, disp. 28, sect. 3, ¶¶14, 17; disp. 32, sect. 2, ¶14 (Paris, 1866; repr. Hildesheim: Georg Olms, 1965), 17, 19, 323; P. Pedro Descoqs, *Institutiones Metaphysicae Generalis* (Paris: Beauchesne, 1925), 260–69; Descoqs, *Praelectiones Theologiae Naturalis*, vol. 2 (Paris: Beauchesne, 1932),: 765; Giulio Righi, *Studio sulla Analogia in S. Tommaso* (Milan: Marzorati Editore, 1981), 97–106.

44. E.J. Ashworth, "Suárez on the Analogy of Being: Some Historical Background," *Vivarium* 33 (1995): 59–65; Ashworth, "Domingo de Soto (1494–1560) on Analogy and Equivocation," in *Studies on the History of Logic*, ed. Ignacio Angelelli and María Cerezo (Berlin: Walter de Gruyter, 1996), 122–23; Riva, *Analogia e univocità in Tommaso de Vio "Gaetano,"* 139–64.

45. Ashworth, "Suárez on the Analogy of Being," 59.

46. Anderson, *The Bond of Being*, 232.

47. Ibid., 232–33. Similarly, a review note by R. Bernard in *Bulletin Thomist* 1 (1924): 124–27, suggests that the different treatments of analogy by the Suarezian Blanche and the Cajetanian Ramirez might be attributed to the fact that the former considers analogy *in actu exercito*, while the latter considers analogy *in actu signato*. Cajetan does not invoke this distinction himself in this context, although he introduces the terminology at *DNA* §78–79; cf. *DNA* §72. On this distinction in general, a study by Nuchelmans confirms the sense invoked by Anderson and Bernard that it is the distinction between considering a form (or significate of a term) either "as concretely realized in some individual or as abstractly conceived of in an intellectual act of simple apprehension." Gabriel Nuchelmans, "The Distinction *Actus Exercitus/Actus Significatus*

in Medieval Semantics," in *Meaning and Inference in Medieval Philosophy*, ed. Norman Kretzmann (Dordrecht: Kluwer, 1988), 57–90.

48. Ironically, in the context of his criticism of Suarez, Jean-Luc Marion might be said to fall into this same Suarezian trap of failing to distinguish between the signification of an analogical term just as conceived by the intellect, and the signification as concretely realized in the analogates. Thus, after observing that Cajetan grants that accidents have intrinsic (or formal) being, and that even created beings have inherent goodness, Marion writes: "Mais, justement aux yeux de Cajetan, cet être formel et cette bonté inhérente aux analogués dérivés ne peuvent pas, sauf contradiction, appartenir aussi, *per prius* et formellement, au seul *analogum princeps*; il faut donc invoquer un *autre* être et une *autre* bonté qui, intrinsèques à l'*analogum princeps* et à lui uniquement, n'atteindront les autres analogués que par une dénomination extrinsèque. . . . Cajetan n'envisage jamais l'hypothèse que le même être, la même bonté *à la fois* constituent intrinsèquement, mais sur un mode déficient, les analogués seconds et relèvent intrinsèquement de Dieu qui les constitue" (Marion, *Sur la théologie blanche de Descartes*, 94). Of these two sentences, the latter is false, and the former is confused by an equivocation. Cajetan needs only to posit an *other* being and an *other* goodness "formally"—that is, as distinct semantic entities—to observe the difference between the way a term signifies by analogy of attribution and the way a term signifies by analogy of proportionality. But of course as a metaphysician, Cajetan entertains—indeed, regards as true—the hypothesis that the same being and the same goodness are intrinsic to God and creatures (provided Marion's qualification that they are in creatures only in a "deficient way," and provided the further qualification that the "sameness" here is not specific or generic but proportional).

49. E.J. Ashworth, "Equivocation and Analogy in Fourteenth Century Logic: Ockham, Burley and Buridan," in *Historia Philosophiae Medii Aevi: Studien zur Geschichte der Philosophie des Mittelalters*, vol 1, ed. Burkhard Mojsisch and Olaf Pluta (Amsterdam: Gruner, 1991), 28.

50. Ashworth, "Signification and Modes of Signifying in Thirteenth-Century Logic," 67. Cf. the many other comments by Ashworth on this theme, quoted and cited in chap. 3 above.

51. *DNA* §8; cf. §4 and §19.

52. And at *DNA* §12 Cajetan explains that this is true whether we consider the "one" universally or particularly.

53. *DNA* §14.

54. *DNA* §15.

55. *DNA* §19.

56. *DNA* §20.

57. *DNA* §7: "In huius modi autem analogis, quomodo inveniantur unitas, abstractio, praedicatio, comparatio, demonstratio et alia huiusmodi, non oportet determinare; quoniam univoca sunt secundum veritatem, et univocorum canones in eis servandi sunt."

58. *DNA* §22: "Quomodo autem de huiusmodi analogis sit scientia, et contradictiones et demonstrationes, et consequentiae et alia huiusmodi de eis fiant,

ex dictis, et consuetudine Aristotelis patet. Oportet enim significationes diversas prius distinguere (propter quod *ambigua* apud Arabes haec dicuntur), et deinde a primo ad alia procedere." It is commonly said that Cajetan preferred analogy of proportionality to analogy of attribution because the latter involves extrinsic denomination, while the former involves intrinsic denomination. This is only partially correct. It would be more fair to say that Cajetan prefers analogy of proportionality because it is more genuinely a mean between univocation and equivocation; analogy of attribution, as we see here, is logically speaking a form of equivocation, and although unified *secundum quid*—that is, with respect to the primary analogate, to which the secondary analogates are referred—it is not unified enough to avoid being treated like equivocation in all respects relevant to the logician—that is, insofar as abstraction, predication, and reasoning are concerned. But Cajetan's reasons for preferring proportionality will be taken up in greater detail in the next chapter.

CHAPTER SEVEN

1. *DNA* §23: "Ex abusive igitur analogis ad proprie analogiam ascendendo." Cf. *DNA* §21.

2. Cajetan also speaks of other "abusive" locutions at *DNA* §§51, 94, 121.

3. On Latin and Greek use of "*analogia*" see the introduction. Ashworth notes that fourteenth- and fifteenth-century authors often remarked on the distinction between Greek and Latin senses of "*analogia*." E. J. Ashworth, "Suárez on the Analogy of Being: Some Historical Background," *Vivarium* 33 (1995): 55–56.

4. *DNA* §2: ". . . multarum distinctionum adunatio si fieret, confusionem paret."

5. The exaggerated phrase is from John Deely, "The Absence of Analogy," *Review of Metaphysics* 55 (March 2002): 539. Cf. Ralph McInerny, *Aquinas and Analogy* (Washington, D.C.: Catholic University of America Press, 1996), 21, 24, interpreting Cajetan as accusing Aquinas of a "misuse" of language. A similar overinterpretation of "abusive" is found in Jean-François Courtine, *Inventio analogiae: Métaphysique et ontothéologie* (Paris: Vrin, 2005), 231–32.

6. Still, the sense of improper or abusive language should not be diminished too much; *DNA* §121 implies that a term's use can be extended so that its use is "quite broad and liberal" without being improper, but that if it is extended too much, it would become "abusive and false."

7. For examples of some playful metaphorical language in *De Nominum Analogia*, see Cajetan's use of '*expoliata*' in §111 and '*pater*' in §122.

8. *DNA* §23: "analoga secundum proportionalitatem dici, quorum nomen est commune, et ratio secundum illud nomen est proportionaliter eadem. Vel sic: Analoga secundum proportionalitatem dicuntur, quorum nomen commune est, et ratio secundum nomen est similis secundum proportionem."

9. Cf., e.g., Aristotle, *Metaphysics* 5.6 (esp. 1016b31–1017a2); Aquinas, *De principiis naturae* c. 6.

10. Of course, Aristotle clearly seemed to distinguish these two kinds of unity in the famous passage in *Nichomachean Ethics* I.6 (1096b27–29). Cajetan invokes this passage at *DNA* §28. On the difference between analogy and *pros hen* equivocation in Aristotle, cf. Joseph Owens, *The Doctrine of Being in the Aristotelian "Metaphysics": A Study in the Greek Background of Medical Thought*, 3rd ed. (Toronto: Pontifical Institute of Medieval Studies, 1978), 116–25.

11. *DNA* §23: "... quia sicut intelligere, rem animae offert, ita videre corpori animato."

12. *DNA* §§25–26: "Fit autem duobus modis analogia haec: scilicet metaphorice et proprie. *Metaphorice* quidem, quando nomen illud commune absolute unam habet rationem formalem, quae in uno analogatorum salvatur, et per metaphoram de alio dicitur. ... *Proprie* vero fit, quando nomen illud commune in utroque analogatorum absque metaphoris dicitur: ut principium in corde respectu animalis, et in fundamento respectu domus salvatur. Quod, ut Averroës in comm. septimo *I Ethic.* ait, proportionaliter de eis dicitur."

13. This is why in metaphor, as opposed to analogy of proper proportionality, what is secondarily (metaphorically) signified by the term is not understood without understanding also what is primarily (nonmetaphorically) signified by the term. Cf. *DNA* §75–76. More will be said on this in chap. 8, below.

14. A principled theoretical distinction between metaphor and analogy does not rule out hard cases in practice. Given the development of language, an extension of a term that is originally only metaphorical may come to be regarded as no longer (merely) metaphorical but rather more (analogically) literal. (E.g., it is not clear that English speakers regard speaking of the "leg" of a table as merely metaphorical, although it may once have been.) Indeed, at certain points in a language's history it may be difficult to determine whether given terms are being used metaphorically or properly analogically. (E.g., is it only metaphorically that we speak of "folders" on the "desktop" of a computer operating system?) Likewise, a term that is predicated of something analogically in one language may have a correspondingly close translation in another language whose predication of the same thing would be regarded as at best metaphorical. (E.g., while a support for a table is called a "leg" in English, the standard French translation of "leg" [*jambe*] would be predicated of a table support only metaphorically; in French, it would more properly be called a *pied* [English "foot"].) Indeed, analogical or metaphorical predications in one language may be completely nonsensical in another language, as is often the case with poetic expressions and figures of speech (idioms, colloquialisms, slang, etc.). That is why so much of learning a language involves coming to appreciate what metaphors and analogies are considered native to a language, and where certain terms are in the move from metaphor to proper analogy.

15. The formula is used especially in the debate between Penido and Descoqs, and from there is taken up by, e.g., Garrigou-Lagrange and Mascall. P. Pedro Descoqs, *Institutiones Metaphysicae Generalis*, vol. 1 (Paris: Beauchesne, 1925), 269–83; Descoqs, *Praelectiones Theologiae Naturalis*, vol. 2 (Paris: Beauchesne, 1932, 1935), 794–96; M. T.-L. Penido, *Le rôle de l'analogie en théologie dogmatique* (Paris: Vrin, 1931), 22–25, 65; Reginald Garrigou-Lagrange, *God:*

His Existence and His Nature, vol. 1, trans. Bede Rose (St. Louis: Herder, 1934, 1936), 218–20; E. L. Mascall, *Existence and Analogy* (London: Longmans, Green, 1949), 104–11, 120.

16. Austin Farrer frames the "two unknowns" objection, saying, "The scheme of proportionality looks as uninformative as it is unexceptionable . . . we cannot do the sum which the formula appears to propose to us." Austin Farrer, *Finite and Infinite: A Philosophical Essay* (Westminster: Dacre Press, 1943), 53. Likewise, Mascall frames the objection: "Our equation has . . . two unknowns and cannot be solved." Mascall, *Existence and Analogy*, 110.

17. Garrigou-Lagrange, *God: His Existence and His Nature*, vol. 1, 227. Cf. Ibid., vol. 2, 217–20.

18. James F. Anderson, *The Bond of Being: An Essay on Analogy and Existence* (St. Louis: Herder, 1949), 286–90. Anderson adds to this a further response to the two-unknowns objection: he says that the apparent equation actually contains only three terms, not four, since two of the four are analogically the same. This leads to an objection of circularity, as it seems the fourth term in an analogy is known only by analogy; the objection of circularity will be considered below.

19. To the objection that in analogy, "it is impossible [except in mathematical analogies] to ascertain the nature of one term from the other three," James F. Anderson agrees, saying, "But metaphysical analogy is not a means of 'calculating' or in any way ascertaining the nature of something from the known natures of other things. It is in our minds a way of seeing how things are, not of discovering what they are." Anderson, "Response to Comments," *Review of Metaphysics* 5 (1952): 470.

20. Hilary Putnam, "Thoughts Addressed to an Analytical Thomist," *The Monist* 80 (1997): 496–97.

21. Thus McInerny notes that Cajetan's definition of analogy of proportionality "could be trivialized by rephrasing it thus: 'those things are said to be analogous according to analogy which have a common name, and the notion signified by the name is the same according to analogy.'" McInerny, *Aquinas and Analogy*, 22.

22. Anderson, *The Bond of Being*, 289.

23. Mascall, *Existence and Analogy*, 104–5.

24. Ibid., 105–6. For a compressed version of the infinite regress objection, see Hampus Lyttkens, *The Analogy Between God and the World: An Investigation of Its Background and Interpretation of Its Use by Thomas of Aquino* (Uppsala: Almqvist and Wiksells Boktrycheri AB, 1952), 474.

25. Mascall, *Existence and Analogy*, 109–26.

26. David Burrell, *Analogy and Philosophical Language* (New Haven: Yale University Press, 1973), 13.

27. Ibid., 9.

28. Ibid., 10.

29. Ibid., 14.

30. Ibid.

31. Paul C. Hayner, "Analogical Predication," *Journal of the History of Philosophy* 55 (1958): 857, 860, 862.

32. Yves Simon, "On Order in Analogical Sets," in *Philosopher at Work: Essays by Yves R. Simon*, ed. Anthony O. Simon (Lanham, Md.: Rowman and Littlefield, 1999), 139.

33. One may object here that what Cajetan offers is rather an explanation of what it is for two *things* to be analogically related. Cajetan's definition speaks of analogues, after all, not analogous terms. In response, observe that Cajetan offers an explanation of what it is for things to be *said* to be analogous by analogy of proportionality: "analoga secundum proportionalitatem *dici*, quorum nomen est commune [&c.]." Given Cajetan's understanding of the nature of logic, this statement proves to be equivalent to the claim made here, that Cajetan offers an explanation of what it is for a term to be analogous by analogy of proportionality. Cf. *CPA* 4–5: "Idem enim est tractare de rebus ut conceptis simplici apprehensione, et de vocibus ut significant illas sic conceptas. . . . Quamvis autem sic intellecta intentio ista sustinenda sit, memores tame esse oportet eius quod optime ab Avicenna in principio suae Logicae dicitur, scilicet quod considerare de vocibus non est logici negocii ex intentione, sed necessitas ad hoc compulit, quoniam res sic conceptas nonnisi verbis exprimimus, docemus, adunamus et ordinamus. . . . Et propterea si quaeratur, de vocibus an de rebus principaliter hic tractetur, respondendum est quod de rebus non absolute sed incomplexe conceptis et consequenti necessitate significatis."

34. James F. Ross, "Analogy as a Rule of Meaning for Religious Language," in *Aquinas: A Collection of Critical Essays*, ed. Anthony Kenny (Garden City, N.Y.: Anchor Books, 1969), 131.

35. To Ross's hope for a "practicable criterion of similarity relations" it is tempting to respond with the words of Aristotle: "But the greatest thing by far is to be a master of metaphor. It is the one thing that cannot be learnt from others; and it is also a sign of genius, since a good metaphor implies an intuitive perception of the similarity in dissimilars" (*Poetics*, 22 [1459a5–8]). It was no doubt a failure to secure the kind of "practicable criterion" Ross was looking for that led to the different turn his work took with *Portraying Analogy*, although in giving up the search for such a "practicable criterion" Ross did not have to repudiate Cajetan and classical semantics.

36. More typical of Aristotelian commentators is to treat the ability to found a contradiction as a *feature* of univocal terms, e.g., Simplicius, *Commentary on Aristotle's "Categories, 34.7–11"* (*On Aristotle's "Categories 1–4*," trans. Michael Chase [Ithaca: Cornell University Press, 2003], 48). But for Simplicius and others this is still compatible with treating analogous terms as a mean between univocation and equivocation, exhibiting some features of both. Scotus may have been the very first to *define* univocity explicitly in terms of the ability to found a contradiction, an approach that became common among Scotists.

37. *DNA* §§3, 23, 27.

38. The priority of attribution in Aquinas is defended by Klubertanz, Montagnes, Lyttkens, and others. But the findings of Klubertanz also make clear how difficult it is to discern in Aquinas's works a coherent teaching on analogy in general, or on analogy of proportionality and analogy of attribution in particular. In this light it is somewhat surprising that those who most

faithfully remind us that Aquinas had no *ex professo* teaching should be the most adamant that Cajetan's teaching contradicts Aquinas's own teaching on analogy of attribution and analogy of proportionality.

39. George B. Klubertanz, *St. Thomas Aquinas on Analogy: A Textual Analysis and Systematic Synthesis* (Chicago: Loyola University Press, 1960), 92.

CHAPTER EIGHT

1. *DNA* §30: "Sed quoniam, ut dictum est, obscura et necessaria valde res haec est, accurate distincteque dilucidanda est per plura capitula."

2. A similar structural observation was made by Robillard, although he did not classify chap. 11 as pertaining to reasoning. Hyacinthe-Marie Robillard, *De l'analogie et du concept d'être de Thomas de Vio, Cajetan: Traduction, commentaires et index* (Montreal: Les Presses de l'Université de Montréal, 1963), 253.

3. *CPA* 8: "Aequivoca ergo diversis respectibus et nomina et res significare dicuntur. Dicitur enim nomen aliquod aequivocum, quia significat plura secundum diversas rationes, ut ly 'canis' significat caelestem, marinum atque terrestrem canem. Ipsae vero res significae dicuntur aequivocae, non quia significant, sed quia significantur unico vocabulo diversis rationibus, ut sydus illud et piscis et animal latrabile aequivoca appelantur. Unde ipsum nomen appelari consuevit aequivocum aequivocans, res vero aequivoca aequivocata."

4. *CPA* 11: "Est siquidem duplex univocum, scilicet univocans univocum etc."

5. *DNA* §31: "Et quia in nominibus tria inveniuntur, scilicet vox, conceptus in anima, et res extra, seu conceptus obiectivus: ideo singula perlustrando, dicendum est, quomodo analogum ab analogatis distinguatur."

6. *DNA* §33: "Unde inter univocationem et analogiam haec est differentia: quod res fundantes univocationem sunt sic ad invicem similes, quod fundamentum similitudinis in una est eiusdem rationis omnino cum fundamento similitudinis in alia: ita quod nihil claudit in se unius ratio, quod non claudat alterius ratio. Ac per hoc fundamentum univocae similitudinis, in utroque extremorum aeque abstrahit ab ipsis extremis. Res autem fundantes analogiam, sic sunt similes, quod fundamentum similitudinis in una, diversae est rationis simpliciter a fundamento illius in alia: ita quod unius ratio non claudit id quod claudit ratio alterius. Ac per hoc fundamentum analogae similitudinis, in neutro extremorum oportet esse abstractum ab ipsis extremis; sed remanent fundamenta distincta, similia tamen secundum proportionem; propter quod eadem proportionaliter vel analogice dicuntur."

7. *DNA* §34: "Et ut possint omnibus praedicta patere, declarantur exemplariter in univocatione huius nominis *animal,* et analogia huius nominis *ens.* Homo, bos, leo et caetera animalia, quia habent in se singulas naturas sensitivas, seu proprias animalitates, quas constat diversas secundum rem esse, et mutuo similes: sic quod in quocumque extremo, puta homine aut leone, consideretur secundum se animalitas, quae est similitudinis fundamentum, invenitur aequaliter abstrahens ab eo in quo est, et nihil includens in uno quod non in

alio. Ideo et in rerum natura fundant secundum suas animalitates similitudinem univocam, quae identitas generica vocatur; et in esse cognito adunantur non ad duas vel tres animalitates, sed unam tantum, quae animalis nomine in concreto per se primo significatur, et univoce vocatur communi nomine *animal.*"

8. *DNA* §34: "Substantia autem quantitas, qualitas etc., quia non habent in suis quidditatibus aliquid praedicto modo abstrahibile, puta entitatem, (quoniam supra substantialitatem nihil amplius restat), ideo nullam substantialem univocationem inter se compatiuntur."

9. *DNA* §35: "Et quia cum hoc, quod non solum eorum quidditates sunt diversae, sed etiam primo diversae; retinent similitudinem in hoc, quod unumquodque eorum secundum suam proportionem habet esse; ideo et in rerum natura non secundum aliquam eiusdem rationis in extremis sed secundum proprias quidditates, ut commensuratas his propriis esse fundant analogam idest proportionalem similitudinem. Et in intellectu adunantur ad tot res, quot sunt fundamenta, proportionis similitudine unitas, significatas (propter illam similitudinem) *entis* nomine, et analogice communi nomine vocantur *ens*. Differenter ergo res adunantur sub nomine Analogo et Univoco."

10. *Representatio* and *significatio* are not always the same, but here Cajetan's "*repraesentare*" is just a word for the natural signification of the objective concept (the object of the intellect) by the formal concept (the intellectual intention that mediates understanding). It does not imply the kind of problematic "representationalism" that has been rightly distinguished from genuine Thomistic philosophies of mind and language. See John O'Callaghan, *Thomistic Realism and the Linguistic Turn: Toward a More Perfect Form of Existence* (Notre Dame, Ind.: University of Notre Dame Press, 2003).

11. *DNA* §38: "conceptus unus repraesentans perfecte alterum analogatum ut sic, imperfecte repraesentat reliquum."

12. *DNA* §36: "analogo et suis analogatis respondet *unus* conceptus mentalis imperfectus" (emphasis added). Cf. *DNA* §38: "Analogi vero et analogatorum ut sic, plures necessario sunt conceptus perfecte ea repraesentantes, et unus est conceptus imperfecte repraesentans."

13. In fact, this seems to be Cajetan's position at *DCE* §7: "Et sicut in mente duplex conceptus imperfectus reperitur, ita res significata, extra potest obici dupliciter: imperfecte scilicet vel in uno explicite in quo caetera obiciuntur indeterminate; vel in nullo explicite, sed omnia implicite, in solo formalissimo significato explicite."

14. *DNA* §37: "Unde et analogum unum habere mentalem conceptum, et plures habere conceptus mentales: verum est diversimode; quamvis simpliciter loquendo, magis debeat dici, analogi esse plures conceptus; nisi loquendi occasio aliud exigat. Dico autem hoc: quoniam cum secundum dicentes, analoga omnino carere uno conceptu mentali, sermo est; unum eorum conceptum absolute dicere non est reprehendendum. Propter quod oportet solerti discretione lectorem uti quando invenitur scriptum, quod analogata conveniunt in una ratione, et quando invenitur dictum alibi, quod analogata non conveniunt in una ratione."

15. On the sense in which there is and is not a common concept in analogy, cf. John of St. Thomas addressing the question "utrum in analogis detur unus conceptus ab inferioribus praecisus" in *Ars Logica* p. 2, q. 13, a. 5, especially (492b49–493a7): "Analogia proportionalitatis propriae possunt habere conceptum unum respectu omnium analogatorum inadaequatum et imperfectum, nec praescindentem ab inferioribus per aliquid, quod in potentia illa includat et actu excludat, sed per aliquid quod actu non explicet, actu autem includat seu implicet."

16. *DNA* §§33, 34.

17. *DNA* §43: "[*abstrahere*] semper sonat intelligi unum, non intellecto altero."

18. *DNA* §44: "nihil aliud est agere de abstractione analogi ab analogatis quam inquirere et determinare, quomodo res significata analogo nomine intelligi possit, non cointellectis analogatis; et quomodo conceptus illius habeatur, absque conceptibus istorum."

19. *DNA* §46.

20. *DNA* §58.

21. *DNA* §47: "Unde concedi potest, rem analogam abstrahere, et non abstrahere ab analogatis diversimode. Abstrahit quidem, pro quanto abstrahit ab eis, quemadmodum res ut sic, idest ut res similis alteri proportionaliter abstrahit a se absolute sumpta. Non abstrahit vero, pro quanto res ut sic accepta seipsam necessario includit, et absque seipsa intelligi non potest. Quod de univocis dici non potest: quia res univoca, absque aliis quibus est univoce communis, intelligitur sic, quod res in suo intellectu nullo modo actualiter includit ea quibus est communis, ut patet de animali." Cf. *DNA* §56: "Sicque fit, ut in analogo secundum identitatem in se clausam, ad diversitatem rationum in se quoque clausam comparato, abstractio quaedam, quae non tam abstractio quam quidam abstractionis modus est inveniatur."

22. *DNA* §53.

23. David Burrell, *Analogy and Philosophical Language* (New Haven: Yale University Press, 1973), 14.

24. *DNA* §49: "De ratione siquidem unius proportionaliter est habere quatuor terminos (ut in *V Ethicorum* dicitur). Quoniam proportionalitas qua similitudo proportionum fit, inter quatuor ad minus, (quae duarum proportionum extrema sunt), necessario est; et consequenter unum proportione non unificatur simpliciter, sed distinctionem retinens, unum pro tanto est et dicitur, pro quanto proportionibus dissimilibus divisum non est. Unde sicut non est alia ratio quare unum proportionaliter non est unum absolute, nisi quia ista est eius ratio formalis; ita non est quaerenda alia ratio, cur a similibus proportionaliter non potest abstrahi res una; hoc enim ideo est, quia similitudo proportionalis talem in sua ratione diversitatem includit. Et accidit ulterius procedentibus, ut quaerant id, quod sub quaestione non cadit: ut quare homo est animal rationale, etc."

25. I. M. Bochenski, "On Analogy," *The Thomist* (1948): 425–77, §17. (I cite this work by section number as it has been reprinted, with corrections, in *Logico-Philosophical Studies*, ed. Albert Menne (Dordrecht: Reidel, 1962), and in

Inquiries into Medieval Philosophy: A Collection in Honor of Francis P. Clarke, ed. James F. Ross (Westport, Conn.: Greenwood, 1971), 99–122.

26. Cf. Bochenski, *A History of Formal Logic*, trans. Ivo Thomas (Notre Dame, Ind.: University of Notre Dame Press, 1961), 397, commenting on a discussion of "systematic ambiguity" from *Principia Mathematica*: "All the statements in question evidently share the same formal *structure*. We have in fact a case of isomorphy. It is remarkable that the name used for this kind of isomorphy, 'systematic ambiguity,' is an exact translation of the common Scholastic expression *aequivocatio a consilio*, synonymous with 'analogy'; for isomorphy is precisely analogy."

27. *DNA* §§33–34.

28. This is not just an *ad hoc* distinction, but one anticipated before the writing of *DNA*, as is evident from Cajetan's discussion of univocation in *CPA*. Commenting on Aristotle's definition of univocals, according to which there is "eadem ratio substantiae," Cajetan says of the word "*eadem*" that it "non dicit identitatem simpliciter vel secundum quid, sed identitatem simpliciter, ita quod licet ad aequivocationem sufficiat qualiscunque diversitas rationis secundum illud nomen, ad univocationem tamen non sufficit qualiscunque identitas rationis secundum illud nomen, sed exigitur quod ratio univocatorum, quae attenditur penes illud nomen in quo univocantur, sit totaliter eadem et nihil plus aut minus includat unum quam reliquum in ratione illius nominis" (*CPA* 11).

29. *DNA* §§67–68: "Fundatur enim superioritas super identitate rationis rei significatae, idest super hoc quod res significata invenitur non in hoc tantum, sed illamet non numero sed ratione invenitur in alio. Univocatio autem supra modo identitatis omnimodae scilicet identitate rationis rei significatae, idest super hoc quod ratio rei significatae in illo et in isto est eadem omnino. Quamvis enim in analogis hic identitatis modus non inveniatur, quem in univocis inveniri pluries dictum est, identitas tamen ipsa rationum invenitur. Est namque identitas proportionalis, identitas quaedam. Et ideo non minus analogum (puta ens) est praedicatum superius, quam univocum (puta animal), sed alio modo: analogum enim est superius proportionaliter, quia fundatur supra identitate proportionali rationis rei significatae; univocum autem praecise et simpliciter, quia supra omnimoda identitate rationis rei significatae eius superioritas fundatur."

30. Cajetan describes the same *sophisma consequentis* at *CST* I.13.5 nn. 9–10, this time explictly in response to Scotus's famous argument that a concept is univocal between God and creatures if it is not specific to one but applies commonly to both. Cajetan replies: "illud argumentum nihil aliud concludit nisi alietatem conceptus sapientiae, verbi gratia, in communi, a sapientia Dei et sapientia creaturae. Sed ex hoc inferre, *ergo univocus conceptus*, est sophisma Consequentis: quoniam conceptus analogus est etiam alius ab inferioribus. Non tamen eo alietatis modo, quo est alius conceptus univocus ab univocatis: quia hic est alius ut praecisus ab eis, ille vero ut continens eos, ut diffuse scripsimus in tractatu *De Nominum Analogia*."

31. *DNA* §69: "... obiectiones ad oppositum adductae in hoc peccant, quod inter identitatem et modum identitatis non distinguunt. Fatendum enim

est, quod ad hoc, quod aliquis terminus denominetur superior aut communior, oportet ut rem unam et eamdem in utroque ponat; sed sophisma consequentis committitur inferendo ex hoc: ergo oportet quod dicat rem unam et eamdem omnino. Et est semper sermo de identitate secundum rationem, seu definitionem. Identitas enim et unitas continent sub se non solum unitatem et identitatem omnimodam, sed proportionalem, quae in analogi nominis ratione salvatur."

32. *DNA* §1.

33. *DNA* §71: "Ex praedictis autem manifeste patet, quod analogum non conceptum disiunctum, nec unum praecisum inaequaliter participatum, nec unum ordine; sed conceptum unum proportione dicit et praedicat."

34. *DNA* §83: "Constat autem quod analogum nomen, puta ens aut bonum, non relationem identitatis aut similitudinis significat, sed fundamentum."

35. *CST* I.13.6, n. 4: "Quaedam enim significant ipsos respectus ad primum analogatum, ut patet de sano. Quaedam vero significant fundamenta tantum illorum respectuum; ut communiter invenitur in omnibus vere analogis, proprie et formaliter salvatis in ominbus analogatis."

36. *DNA* §79: "sicut animal dictum de homine et de equo importans univocationem in actu exercito, non praedicat de homine totum hoc, scilicet naturam sensitivam eamdem omnino secundum rationem naturae sensitivae equi et bovis, sed naturam sensitivam simpliciter; quam tamen ad hoc, quod univoca sit praedicatio, oportet omnino esse eamdem secundum rationem naturae sensitivae equi et bovis,—ita ens importans proportionalitatem in actu exercito, non praedicat de quantitate totum hoc, scilicet habens se ad esse sic proportionaliter sicut substantia, aut qualitas ad suum esse; sed habens se ad esse sic absque alia additione; quod tamen oportet, ad hoc quod analoga sit praedicatio, idem proportionaliter esse cum altero, sic se habere ad esse quod de substantia aut qualitate ens praedicat."

37. *DNA* §76: "analogum metaphorice sumptum, nihil aliud praedicat, quam hoc se habere ad similitudinem illius, quod absque altero extremo intelligi nequit."

38. *DNA* §75: "sed proprie sumptum, in ratione sui metaphorice sumpti claudi necesse est; quoniam impossibile est intelligere quid sit aliquid secundum metaphoricum nomen, nisi cognito illo, ad cuius metaphoram dicitur. Neque enim fieri potest, ut intelligam quid sit pratum in eo quod ridens, nisi sciam quid significet risus nomen proprie sumptum, ad cuius similitudinem dicitur pratum ridere."

39. To be sure, as Yves Simon pointed out, one *can* understand a metaphorical *predication*, and even know *that it is* a metaphorical predication, without knowing the primary (nonmetaphorical) analogate, and so without understanding *why* the subject of the metaphorical predication is a subject of *that* predicate—but then, in a crucial sense, one does not understand *the metaphor*. "Many people who know that 'crocodile tears' stand for demonstrations of feigned sadness do not know why such demonstrations are called crocodile tears. . . . I cannot say why feigned demonstrations of sadness are called crocodile tears unless

I know that in ancient legends crocodiles were reputed to imitate human sobbing in order to attract passersby and devour them." Yves Simon, "On Order in Analogical Sets," in *Philosopher at Work: Essays by Yves R. Simon*, ed. Anthony O. Simon (Lanham, Md.: Rowman and Littlefield, 1999), 167.

40. *DNA* §78.

41. *DNA* §82. Cf. *CST* I.13.6 n.7: "Huiusmodi nomina, quoad *rem significatam*, prius de Deo: quoad *impositionem nominis*, prius de creaturis dicuntur."

42. The question of an order of priority in proportionality was raised by Blanche. For citations and discussion see the long footnote in Simon, "On Order in Analogical Sets," 165–67n27.

43. *DNA* §67.

44. *DNA* §86: "Succumbitur autem difficultati huic, quia proprium comparationis fundamentum non consideratur. Fundatur enim super identitate seu unitate rei, in qua fit comparatio, et non super modo identitatis aut unitatis; sicut de intentione superioritatis praedictum est. Unde cum analogum ex dictis constet rem unam, licet proportionaliter, dicere; nihil prohibet in ipso comparari analogata, licet non eo modo, quo univoca fit comparatio."

45. Cajetan returns to the issue of comparison in analogy in *CST* I.13.5 nn. 9–10. To the Scotistic objection that "omnis comparatio est in aliqualiter univoco," Cajetan responds: "comparatio fit etiam in analogo, quod medium est inter univocum et aequivocum. . . . Cum enim dicitur, *Deus est perfectius ens creatura*, comparatio fit in ratione entis una secundum analogiam, et sic communi utrique, ut alibi docuimus."

46. *DNA* §46.

47. *DNA* §56.

48. *DNA* §57: "Sicque non sola significationum in voce confusio, analogo convenit, sed confusio quaedam conceptuum, seu rationum fit in identitate eorum proportionali, sic tamen ut non tam conceptus, quam eorum diversitas confundatur."

49. *DNA* §§98–100.

50. *DNA* §§102–3.

51. *DNA* §99.

CHAPTER NINE

1. *DNA* §105: "Verbi gratia: si ponamus *sapientiam* esse analogice communem Deo et homini, ex hoc quod sapientia, in homine inventa, secundum formalem rationem praecise sumpta, dicit perfectionem simpliciter: non potest concludi: ergo Deus est formaliter sapiens, sic arguendo: Omnis perfectio simpliciter est in Deo; sapientia est perfectio simpliciter; ergo etc. Minor enim distinguenda est: et si ly *sapientia* pro ratione sapientiae, quae est in homine stat, argumentum est ex quatuor terminis: quia in conclusione, sapientia stat pro ratione sapientiae quam ponit in Deo, cum concluditur: ergo sapientia est in Deo. Si autem pro ratione sapientiae in Deo, stat in minore; non concluditur, ex

perfectione sapientiae creatae, Deum esse sapientem; cuius oppositum et philosophi et theologi omnes clamant."

2. *DNA* §106: "Decipiuntur autem isti, Scotum (cuius est ratio haec *I Sent.* dist. 3, q. 1) sequentes: quia in analogo diversitatem rationum inspicientes, id quod in eo unitatis et identitatis latet, non considerant."

3. *DNA* §106: "eo quod quidquid convenit uni, convenit et alteri proportionaliter; et quidquid negatur de una, et de altera negatur proportionaliter: quia quidquid convenit simili, in eo quod simile, convenit etiam illi, cui est simile, proportionalitate semper servata."

4. Cf. *DNA* §36: "Quidquid assimilatur simili ut sic, assimilatur etiam illi, cui illud tale est simile." Cf. *DCE* §3: "quidquid est imago alicuius similis alteri, est etiam imago illius alterius quatenus primo assimilatur." It goes without saying that similarity, in addition to being transitive, is also symmetrical.

5. Even here a clarification is needed: if one did not call the picture cute *qua picture of that puppy*, but rather called it cute because of its artistic style, then it does not follow that one regards the depicted puppy as cute. But then this case also confirms Cajetan's principle.

6. *DNA* §107: "unitas analogiae non esset in coordinatione unitatum numeranda, nisi unum proportionaliter, unum esset affirmabile et negabile, et consequenter distribuibile et scibile, ut subiectum, et medium, et passio."

7. *DNA* §112: "Identitas siquidem tam rerum quam rationum, ut pluries replicatum est, ad identitatem proportionalem se extendit."

8. *DNA* §111: "Unde, cum fit huiusmodi processus: Omnis perfectio simpliciter est in Deo; sapientia est perfectio simpliciter; ergo etc.; in minore ly *sapientia* non stat pro hac vel illa ratione sapientiae, sed pro sapientia una proportionaliter, idest, pro utraque ratione sapientiae non coniunctim vel disiunctim; sed in quantum sunt indivisae proportionaliter, et una est altera proportionaliter, et ambae unam proportionaliter constituunt rationem."

9. Bochenski offers a formal proof of the validity of syllogisms using analogical middle terms, in "On Analogy," *The Thomist* (1948): §19. He defines analogy in terms of "isomorphy" (which is proportional similarity) (§17), and attributes this interpretation of analogy ("the isomorphic theory") not only to Cajetan (§16) but also to Aquinas (§12 and §17).

10. *DNA* §113: "Ex hoc autem apparet, Scotum in *I Sent.* dist. 3, q. 1, vel male exposuisse conceptum univocum vel sibi ipsi contradicere: dum, volens univocationem entis fingere, ait: «Conceptum univocum voco, qui ita est unus, quod eius unitas sufficit ad contradictionem, affirmando et negando ipsum de eodem». Et sic univocum vult esse ens. Si enim identitas sufficiens ad contradictionem, univocatio dicitur; constat quod, ponendo ens esse analogum, et secundum proportionalitatem tantum unum, satisfiet univocationi: quod scoticae doctrinae adversatur, tenenti ens habere conceptum unum simpliciter, et omnino indivisum, (ut de univocis diximus). Si autem non omnis talis identitas sufficit ad univocationem, non recte igitur univocatio conceptus declarata est esse eam, quae ad contradictionem sufficit, quasi proportionalis identitas ad hoc non sufficiat."

11. *DNA* §109.

12. DNA §108. "... ideo oportet, huiusmodi analogis nominibus utendo ex parte unitatis, semper modum proportionalitatis subintelligi; aliter in univocationem lapsus fieret. Nisi enim prae oculis haberetur proportionalitas, cum dicitur immateriale omne esse intellectuale, tamquam univoce dictum acciperetur, et latens aequivocatio non visa obreperet." Apparently the problem Cajetan has in mind in his example ("everything immaterial is intellectual") is that in concluding to God's intellectuality from his immateriality, we might wrongly attribute to his intellectuality what is proper only to creaturely intellectuality (e.g., that it is discursive).

13. *DNA* §115.

14. *DNA* §117. Cf. *DCE* §5.

15. *DNA* §118: "Cavendum tertio est, ne vocalis unitas rationis analogi nominis mentem involvat. Ex eo namque verbi gratia, quod principium dicitur esse id ex quo res fit, aut est, aut cognoscitur; et haec ratio in omnibus quae principia dicuntur, salvatur: principii nomen univocum creditur. Erratur autem, quia ratio ipsa non est una simpliciter, sed proportione et voce. Vocabula enim, ex quibus integratur, analoga sunt, ut patet; neque enim fieri, neque esse, neque cognosci, neque ly *ex* unius omnino est rationis, sed proportionalis salvatur. Et propterea ratio illa in omnibus utpote proportionalis salvatur: sicut et principii nomen proportionaliter commune dicitur."

16. *DNA* §119.

17. *DNA* §§120–22.

18. *DNA* §§123–24.

19. *DNA* §125: "Unde si quis falli non vult, solerter sermonis causam coniectet."

20. *CDEE* §14: "... idem est loqui de conceptu entis et de significatione ejus."

21. *DCE* §3; cf. *DNA* §§36, 106.

22. *DCE* §4.

23. *DCE* §5.

24. *DCE* §6.

25. *DCE* §7.

26. *DCE* §8.

27. *DCE* §9: "Ita quod (ut unico verbo rem absolvam): ens esse primo notum in quod fit omnis resolutio, in quod omnia addunt, per modum analogi interpretandum est: cum quo stare potest, quod ens secundum perfectum adaequatumque conceptum, non abstrahit a naturis praedicamentalibus, sicut nec aliquod analogum a fundantibus analogiam."

28. And it is compressed, despite Cajetan's polite claim to the contrary ("Plura nunc non mihi occurunt ad propositum dicenda, immo prolixior fui acutissimo ingenio tuo, quo ex unico verbo concepisses cuncta" [*DCE* §10]).

Bibliography

WORKS OF CAJETAN

Commentaria in De Ente et Essentia. 1495. Edited by M. H. Laurent. Turin: Marietti, 1934.
Commentaria in Porphyrii Isagogen ad Praedicamenta Aristotelis. 1497. Edited by I. Marega. Rome: Angelicum, 1934.
Commentaria in Praedicamenta Aristotelis. 1498. Edited by M. H. Laurent. Rome: Angelicum, 1939.
Commentaria in Summam Theologiae St Thomae. 1507–22. Rome: Leonine Commission, 1906.
De Conceptu Entis. 1509. Edited by N. Zammit. Rome, 1934. Revised by H. Hering. Rome: Angelicum, 1951.
De Nominum Analogia. 1498. Edited by N. Zammit. Rome, 1934. Revised by H. Hering. Rome: Angelicum, 1951. 2

TRANSLATIONS OF *DE NOMINUM ANALOGIA*

Bushinski, Edward A., and Henry J. Koren. *The Analogy of Names and the Concept of Being.* Pittsburgh: Duquesne University Press, 1953.
Pinchard, Bruno. *L'Analogie des Noms,* in *Metaphysique et semantique: La signification analogiques des termes dans les Principes Metaphysiques.* Paris: J. Vrin, 1987.
Robillard, Hyacinthe-Marie. *De l'analogie et du concept d'être de Thomas de Vio, Cajetan: Traduction, commentaires et index.* Montreal: Les Presses de l'Université de Montréal, 1963.

OTHER SOURCES

Anderson, James F. "Bases of Metaphysical Analogy." *Downside Review* 66 (1948): 38–47.

――――. *The Bond of Being: An Essay on Analogy and Existence.* St. Louis: Herder, 1949.

――――. "Mathematical and Metaphysical Analogy in St. Thomas." *Thomist* 3 (1941): 564–79.

――――. *Reflections on the Analogy of Being.* The Hague: Martinus Nijhoff, 1967.

――――. "Some Basic Propositions Concerning Metaphysical Analogy" (with comments and responses). *Review of Metaphysics* 5 (1952): 46

Ashworth, E. J. "Analogical Concepts: The Fourteenth-Century Background to Cajetan." *Dialogue* 31 (1992): 399–413.

――――. "Analogy and Equivocation in Thirteenth-Century Logic: Aquinas in Context." *Mediaeval Studies* 54 (1992): 94–135.

――――. "Analogy and Equivocation in Thomas Sutton, O.P." In *Vestigia, Imagines, Verba: Semiotics and Logic in Medieval Theological Texts (XIIth–XIVth Century)*, edited by Constantino Marmo, 289–303. Turnhout: Brepols, 1997.

――――. "Analogy, Univocation, and Equivocation in Some Early Fourteenth-Century Authors." In *Aristotle in Britain During the Middle Ages*, edited by John Marenbon, 233–47. Turnhout: Brepols, 1996.

――――. "Domingo de Soto (1494–1560) on Analogy and Equivocation." In *Studies on the History of Logic*, edited by Ignacio Angelelli and María Cerezo, 117–31. Berlin: Walter de Gruyter, 1996.

――――. "Equivocation and Analogy in Fourteenth Century Logic: Ockham, Burley and Buridan." In *Historia Philosophiae Medii Aevi: Studien zur Geschichte der Philosophie des Mittelalters*, vol. 1, edited by Burkhard Mojsisch and Olaf Pluta, 23–43. Amsterdam: Gruner, 1991.

――――. "Language, Renaissance Philosophy of." In *Routledge Encyclopedia of Philosophy*, vol. 5, 411–15. New York: Routledge, 1998.

――――. "Logic, Medieval." In *Routledge Encyclopedia of Philosophy*, vol. 5, 746–59. New York: Routledge, 1998.

――――. "Medieval Theories of Analogy." In *Stanford Encyclopedia of Philosophy*, edited by Edward N. Zalta, Winter 1999 ed. URL = http://plato .stanford.edu/archives/win1999/entries/analogy-medieval/.

――――. Review of McInerny, *Aquinas and Analogy. Speculum* 74 (1999): 215–17.

――――. "Signification and Modes of Signifying in Thirteenth-Century Logic: A Preface to Aquinas on Analogy." *Medieval Philosophy and Theology* 1 (1991): 39–67.

――――. "Suárez on the Analogy of Being: Some Historical Background." *Vivarium* 33 (1995): 50–75.

Aubenque, Pierre. "Les origines de la doctrine de l'analogie de l'être: Sur l'histoire d'un contresens." *Les Etudes Philosophiques* 33 (1978): 3–12.

Avicenna. *Liber de Philosophia Prima sive Scientia Divina I–IV & V–X*. Edited by S. Van Riet. 2 vols. Leiden: Brill, 1977, 1980.

Beach, John D. "Analogous Naming, Extrinsic Denomination, and the Real Order." *Modern Schoolman* 42 (1965): 198–213.

Bernard, R. Review note. *Bulletin Thomist* 1 (1924): 124–27.

Blanche, F. A. "L'analogie." *Revue de Philosophie* 30 (1923): 248–70.

————. "La notion d'analogie dans la philosophie de S. Thomas D'Aquin." *Revue des Sciences Philosophiques et Théologiques* 10 (1921): 169–93.

————. "Sur le sens de quelques locutions concernant l'analogie dans la langue de S. Thomas D'Aquin." *Revue des Sciences Philosophiques et Théologiques* 10 (1921): 52–59.

————. "Une théorie de l'analogie: Éclairissements et développements." *Revue de Philosophie*, nouvelle série 3 (1932): 37–78.

Bobik, Joseph. *Aquinas on Being and Essence: A Translation and Interpretation.* Notre Dame, Ind.: University of Notre Dame Press, 1965.

Bochenski, I. M. *A History of Formal Logic.* Translated by Ivo Thomas. Notre Dame, Ind.: University of Notre Dame Press, 1961.

————. "On Analogy." *The Thomist* (1948): 425–77. Reprinted with corrections in *Logico-Philosophical Studies*, edited by Albert Menne. Dordrecht: D. Reidel, 1962; and in *Inquiries into Medieval Philosophy: A Collection in Honor of Francis P. Clarke,* edited by James F. Ross, 99–122. Westport, Conn.: Greenwood, 1971.

Boethius. *In Categorias Aristotelis Libri Quatuor. Patrologia Latina*, vol. 64.

————. *Institution Arithmétique.* Edited and translated by Jean-Yves Guillaumin. Paris: Les Belles Lettres, 1995.

Bourke, Vernon J. "Cajetan, Cardinal." In *The Encyclopedia of Philosophy*, vol. 2, edited by Paul Edwards, 5–6. New York: Macmillan, 1967.

Broadie, Alexander. *Introduction to Medieval Logic.* 2nd ed. Oxford: Oxford University Press, 1993.

Brown, Stephen. "L'unité du concept d'être au début du quatorzième siècle." In *John Duns Scotus: Metaphysics and Ethics*, edited by Ludger Honnefelder, Rega Wood, and Mechthild Dreyer, 327-344. Leiden: Brill, 1996.

Burrell, David. *Analogy and Philosophical Language.* New Haven: Yale University Press, 1973.

————. "Aquinas and Scotus: Contrary Patterns for Philosophical Theology." In *Theology and Dialogue: Essays in Conversation with George Lindbeck*, edited by Bruce D. Marshall, 105–29. Notre Dame, Ind.: University of Notre Dame Press, 1990.

————. "Beyond the Theory of Analogy." *Proceedings of the American Catholic Philosophical Association* 46 (1972): 114–21.

————. "From Analogy of 'Being' to the Analogy of Being." In *Recovering Nature: Essays in Natural Philosophy, Ethics, and Metaphysics in Honor of Ralph McInerny*, edited by Thomas Hibbs and John O'Callaghan, 253–66. Notre Dame, Ind.: University of Notre Dame Press, 1999.

————. "A Note on Analogy." *New Scholasticism* 36 (1962): 225–32.

————. "Religious Language and the Logic of Analogy: Apropos of McInerny's Book and Ross' Review." *International Philosophical Quarterly* 2 (1962): 643–58.

————. Review of Ross, *Portraying Analogy. New Scholasticism* 59 (1985): 347–57.

Bushinski, Edward A., and Henry J. Koren, trans. *The Analogy of Names and the Concept of Being* [a translation of Cajetan, *De Nominum Analogia* and *De Conceptu Entis*]. Pittsburgh: Duquesne University Press, 1953.

Chavannes, Henry. *The Analogy Between God and the World in Saint Thomas Aquinas and Karl Barth.* Translated by William Lumley. New York: Vantage Press, 1992.

Copleston, Frederick C. *Aquinas.* Harmondsworth: Penguin, 1955.

———. *A History of Medieval Philosophy.* New York: Harper and Row, 1972.

———. *A History of Philosophy.* Vol. 2, *Mediaeval Philosophy.* Part 2, "Albert the Great to Duns Scotus." Garden City, N.Y.: Image Books, 1962.

———. *A History of Philosophy.* Vol. 3, *Late Mediaeval and Renaissance Philosophy.* Part 2, "The Revival of Platonism to Suarez." Garden City, N.Y.: Image Books, 1963.

Courtine, Jean-François. *Inventio analogiae: Métaphysique et ontothéologie.* Paris: Vrin, 2005.

Deely, John. "The Absence of Analogy." *Review of Metaphysics* 55 (March 2002): 521–50.

Descoqs, P. Pedro. *Institutiones Metaphysicae Generalis.* Vol. 1. Paris: Beauchesne, 1925.

———. *Praelectiones Theologiae Naturalis.* 2 vols. Paris: Beauchesne, 1932, 1935.

Dewan, Laurence. "Étienne Gilson and the *Actus Essendi.*" *Maritain Studies/ Études Maritainiennes* 15 (1999): 70–96.

———. "St. Thomas and Analogy: The Logician and the Metaphysician." In *Laudemus viros gloriosos: Essays in Honor of Armand Maurer,* edited by R. E. Houser, 132–45. Notre Dame, Ind.: University of Notre Dame Press, 2007. Also appears as chap. 6 in Dewan, *Form and Being: Studies in Thomistic Metaphysics.* Washington, D.C.: Catholic University of America Press, 2006.

Dominic of Flanders. *Quaestiones super XII libros Metaphysicorum.* Venice, 1499. Reprint, Frankfurt: Minerva, 1967.

D'Ors, Angel. "Petrus Hispanus O.P., Auctor Summularum (II): Further Documents and Problems." *Vivarium* 39 (2001): 209–54.

Doyle, John P. "Prolegomena to a Study of Extrinsic Denomination in the Works of Francis Suarez, S.J." *Vivarium* 22 (1984): 121–60.

Duns Scotus. *Commentaria Oxoniensia.* Edited by Marius Fernandez Garcia. Florence: Collegii S. Bonaventurae, 1912.

———. *In Libros Elenchorum Quaestiones.* Paris: Vives, 1891.

———. *In Librum Praedicamentorum Quaestiones.* In *Opera omnia,* vol. 1. Lyon, 1639. Reprint, Hildesheim: Georg Olms Verlag, 1968.

Ebbesen, Sten. *Commentators and Commentaries on Aristotle's "Sophistici Elenchi": A Study of Post-Aristotelian Ancient and Medieval Writings on Fallacies.* Vol. 1, *The Greek Tradition.* Leiden: Brill, 1981.

Flannery, Kevin, S.J. Review of Ralph McInerny, *Aquinas and Analogy. Fellowship of Catholic Scholars Quarterly* 20 (1997): 34–36.

Gadamer, Hans-Georg. "Semantics and Hermeneutics." Translated by P. Christopher Smith. In *Philosophical Hermeneutics,* edited and translated by David E. Linge, 82–94. Berkeley: University of California Press, 1976.

Gargan, Luciano. *Lo studio teologico e la biblioteca dei Domenicani a Padova nel tre e Quattrocento.* Padua: Editrice Antenore, 1971.

Garrigou-Lagrange, Reginald. *God: His Existence and His Nature*. Translated by Bede Rose. 2 vols. St. Louis: Herder, 1934, 1936.

———. *The One God: A Commentary on the First Part of St. Thomas' Theological Summa*. Translated by Bede Rose. St. Louis: Herder, 1943.

———. *La synthèse Thomiste*. Nov. ed. Paris: Desclée de Brouwer and Cie., 1950.

Geach, Peter T. *Logic Matters*. Berkeley: University of California Press, 1980.

———. *Mental Acts: Their Content and Their Objects*. London: Routledge and Kegan Paul, 1957.

Gilson, Étienne. *Being and Some Philosophers*. 2nd ed. Toronto: Pontifical Institute of Medieval Studies, 1952.

———. "Cajétan et l'existence." *Tijdschrift voor Philosophie* 15 (1953): 267–86.

———. *The Christian Philosophy of St. Thomas Aquinas*. Translated by L.K. Shook. New York: Random House, 1956.

———. *The Elements of Christian Philosophy*. New York: New American Library, 1963.

———. *Jean Duns Scot: Introduction à ses Positions Fondamentales*. Paris: Librairie Philosophique J. Vrin, 1952.

———. *Linguistics and Philosophy: An Essay on the Philosophical Constants of Language*. Translated by John Lyon. Notre Dame, Ind.: University of Notre Dame Press, 1988.

———. *Le Thomisme: Introduction a la philosophie de Saint Thomas d'Aquin*. 5th ed. Paris: Vrin, 1944.

Goergen, Aloys. *Kardinal Cajetans Lehre von der Analogie; Ihr Verhältnis zu Thomas von Aquin*. Speyer a. Rh.: Pilger-Druckerei, 1938.

Gunten, André F. von. "Cajétan et Capreolus." In *Jean Capreolus et son temps (1380–1444)*, edited by Guy Bedouelle, Romanus Cessario, and Kevin White. *Mémoire Dominicaine* special no. 1, 213–38. Paris: Les Éditions du Cerf, 1997.

Harrison, Frank R. "The Cajetan Tradition of Analogy." *Franciscan Studies* 23 (1963): 179–204.

Hayner, Paul C. "Analogical Predication." *Journal of the History of Philosophy* 55 (1958): 855–62.

Hesse, Mary. "Aristotle's Logic of Analogy." *Philosophical Quarterly* 15 (1965): 328–40.

———. *Models and Analogy in Science*. Notre Dame, Ind.: University of Notre Dame Press, 1966.

Hochschild, Joshua P. "A Note on Cajetan's Theological Semantics." *Sapientia* 54 (1999): 367–76.

Incertorum Auctorum. *Quaestiones super Sophisticos Elenchos*. Edited by Sten Ebbesen. Copenhagen: Corpus Philosophorum Danicorum Medii Aevi, 1977.

Klima, Gyula. "The Medieval Problem of Universals." In *The Stanford Encyclopedia of Philosophy* (Fall 2000 ed.), edited by Edward N. Zalta. URL = http://plato.stanford.edu/archives/fall2000/entries/universals-medieval/.

———. "Ontological Alternatives vs. Alternative Semantics in Medieval Philosophy." In *Logical Semiotics*, special issue of *S-European Journal for Semiotic Studies* 3 (1991): 587–618.

————. "The Semantic Principles Underlying Saint Thomas Aquinas's Metaphysics of Being." *Medieval Philosophy and Theology* 5 (1996): 87–141.

Klubertanz, George P. "Analogy." In *New Catholic Encyclopedia*, vol. 1, 461–65. New York: McGraw Hill, 1967.

————. *St. Thomas Aquinas on Analogy: A Textual Analysis and Systematic Synthesis.* Chicago: Loyola University Press, 1960.

Krauze, Andrej. *Zur Analogie bei Cajetan und Thomas von Aquin: Eine Analyse.* Halle: Hallescher Verlag, 1999.

Kretzmann, Norman. "Semantics, History of." In *The Encyclopedia of Philosophy*, edited by Paul Edwards, vol. 7, 358–406. New York: Macmillan, 1967.

Kuntz, Paul G. "The Analogy of Degrees of Being: A Critique of Cajetan's *Analogy of Names.*" *New Scholasticism* 56 (1982): 51–79.

Lakoff, George, and Mark Johnson. *Metaphors We Live By.* Chicago: University of Chicago Press, 1980.

Leszl, Walter. *Logic and Metaphysics in Aristotle: Aristotle's Treatment of Types of Equivocity and Its Relevance to His Metaphysical Theories.* Padua: Editrice Antenore, 1970.

Libera, Alain de. "Les sources gréco-arabes de la théorie médiévale de l'analogie de l'être." *Les Études Philosophiques* (1989): 319–45.

Lloyd, G. E. R. "Analogy in Early Greek Thought" In *Dictionary of the History of Ideas*, edited by Philip W. Wiener, vol. 1, 60–63. New York: Charles Scribner's Sons, 1968.

————. *Polarity and Analogy: Two Types of Argumentation in Early Greek Thought.* Cambridge: Cambridge University Press, 1966.

Lonergan, Bernard. *Insight: A Study of Human Understanding.* 3rd ed. New York: Philosophical Library, 1970.

————. *Verbum: Word and Idea in Aquinas.* Edited by David Burrell. Notre Dame, Ind.: University of Notre Dame Press, 1967.

Lonfat, Joël. "Archéologie de la notion d'analogie d'Aristote à saint Thomas d'Aquin." *Archives d'Histoire Doctrinale et Littéraire du Moyen Age* 71 (2004): 35–107.

Loughran, Thomas J. "Efficient Causality and Extrinsic Denomination in the Philosophy of St. Thomas Aquinas." Ph.D. diss., Fordham University, 1969.

Lubac, Henri de. *The Discovery of God.* Translated by Alexander Dru. New York: P. J. Kennedy and Sons, 1960.

Luna, C. "Paronymie, Homonymie πρὸς ἕν et Analogie: A propos d'un article de J. Hirschberger." Appendix 2 in *Simplicius: Commentaire sur les Catégories*, edited by Ilsetraut Hadot. Philosophia Antiqua 51, fasc. 3, 153–59. Leiden: Brill, 1990.

Lyttkens, Hampus. *The Analogy Between God and the World: An Investigation of Its Background and Interpretation of Its Use by Thomas of Aquino.* Uppsala: Almqvist and Wiksells Boktrycheri AB, 1952.

Mahoney, Edward P. "Cajetan (Thomas de Vio)." In *Routledge Encyclopedia of Philosophy*, vol. 2, 171–75. New York: Routledge, 1997.

Marion, Jean-Luc. *God Without Being: Hors-Texte.* Translated by Thomas A. Carlson. Chicago: University of Chicago Press, 1991.

————. *Sur la théologie blanche de Descartes: Analogie, création des vérités éternelles et fondement.* Paris: Presses Universitaires de France, 1981.

Maritain, Jacques. *Distinguish to Unite, or The Degrees of Knowledge.* Translated by Gerald B. Phelan. New York: Charles Scribner's Sons, 1959.

Mascall, E. L. *Existence and Analogy.* London: Longmans, Green, 1949.

Masi, Michael. *Boethian Number Theory: A Translation of the "De Institutione Arithmetica" (with Introduction and Notes).* Amsterdam: Rodopi, 1983.

Masiello, Ralph J. "The Analogy of Proportion According to the Metaphysics of St. Thomas." *Modern Schoolman* 35 (1958): 91–105.

Maurer, Armand. "Cajetan's Notion of Being in His Commentary on the 'Sentences.'" *Mediaeval Studies* 28 (1966): 268–78.

————. *Medieval Philosophy.* 2nd ed. Toronto: Pontifical Institute of Medieval Studies, 1982.

————. "St. Thomas and the Analogy of Genus." *New Scholasticism* 29 (1955): 127–44.

McCanles, Michael. "Univocalism in Cajetan's Doctrine of Analogy." *New Scholasticism* 42 (Winter 1968): 18–47.

McInerny, Ralph. "Analogy and Foundationalism in Thomas Aquinas." In *Rationality, Religious Belief, and Moral Commitment: New Essays in the Philosophy of Religion*, edited by Robert Audi and William J. Wainwright, 271–88. Ithaca: Cornell University Press, 1986.

————. "The Analogy of Names Is a Logical Doctrine." In McInerny, *Being and Predication*, 279–86.

————. *Aquinas and Analogy.* Washington, D.C.: Catholic University of America Press, 1996.

————. "Being and Predication." In McInerny, *Being and Predication*, 173–28.

————. *Being and Predication: Thomistic Interpretations.* Washington, D.C.: Catholic University of America Press, 1986.

————. *Boethius and Aquinas.* Washington, D.C.: Catholic University of America Press, 1990.

————. "Can God Be Named by Us?" In McInerny, *Being and Predication*, 259–78.

————. "The Logic of Analogy." *New Scholasticism* 31 (1957): 149–71.

————. *The Logic of Analogy: An Interpretation of St. Thomas.* The Hague: Martinus Nijhoff, 1961.

————. "Saint Thomas on *De hebdomadibus.*" In *Being and Goodness: The Concept of the Good in Metaphysics and Philosophical Theology*, edited by Scott MacDonald, 74–97. Ithaca: Cornell University Press, 1991.

————. "Scotus and Univocity." In McInerny, *Being and Predication*, 159–64.

————. *Studies in Analogy.* The Hague: Martinus Nijhoff, 1968.

McMahon, William E. "The Categories in Some Post-Medieval Spanish Philosophers." In *Medieval and Renaissance Logic in Spain*, edited by I. Angelelli and P. Pérez-Ilzarbe, 355–70. Hildesheim: Georg Olms Verlag, 2000.

————. "Some Non-standard Views of the Categories." In *La tradition médiévale des Catégories (XIIe–XVe siècles): XIIIe symposium européen de logique et de sémantique médiévales*, edited by Joël Biard and Irène Rosier-Catach, 53–67. Louvain: Peters, 2003.

Meagher, Robert E. "Thomas Aquinas and Analogy: A Textual Analysis." *The Thomist* 34 (April 1970): 230–53.

Mondin, Battista. *The Principle of Analogy in Protestant and Catholic Theology.* 2nd ed. The Hague: Martinus Nijhoff, 1968.

Montagnes, Bernard. *La doctrine de l'analogie de l'être d'après Saint Thomas d'Aquin.* Louvain/Paris: Publications Universitaires/Béatrice-Nauwelaerts, 1963. Published in English as *The Doctrine of the Analogy of Being According to Thomas Aquinas.* Translated by E. M. Macierowski. Milwaukee: Marquette University Press, 2004.

Moody, Ernest A. "The Medieval Contribution to Logic." In *Studies in Medieval Philosophy, Science, and Logic: Collected Papers, 1933–1969,* 371–92. Berkeley: University of California Press, 1975. Reprinted from *Studium Generale* 19 (1966): 443–52.

Moyer, Anne. *The Philosopher's Game: Rithmomachia in Medieval and Renaissance Europe.* Ann Arbor: University of Michigan Press, 2001.

Murdoch, John E. "*Mathesis in Philosophiam Scholasticam Introducta*: The Rise and Development of the Application of Mathematics in Fourteenth Century Philosophy and Theology." In *Arts Libéraux et Philosophie au Moyen Âge,* 215–49. Paris: Vrin, 1969.

———. "The Medieval Language of Proportions: Elements of the Interaction with Greek Foundations and the Development of New Mathematical Techniques." In *Scientific Change: Historical Studies in the Intellectual, Social and Technical Conditions for Scientific Discovery and Technical Invention, from Antiquity to the Present,* edited by A. C. Crombie, 237–71. New York: Basic Books, 1963.

Muskens, G. L. *De vocis ἀναλογίας significatione ac usu apud Aristotelem.* Groningen: Wolters, 1943.

Nuchelmans, Gabriel. "The Distinction *Actus Exercitus/Actus Significatus* in Medieval Semantics." In *Meaning and Inference in Medieval Philosophy,* edited by Norman Kretzmann, 57–90. Dordrecht: Kluwer, 1988. Reprinted in *Studies on the History of Logic and Semantics, 12th–17th Centuries,* edited by E. P. Bos. Aldershot: Variorum, 1996.

———. *Late-Scholastic and Humanist Theories of the Proposition.* Amsterdam: North Holland, 1980.

O'Callaghan, John. *Thomistic Realism and the Linguistic Turn: Toward a More Perfect Form of Existence.* Notre Dame, Ind.: University of Notre Dame Press, 2003.

O'Donovan, Leo. "Methodology in Some Recent Studies of Analogy." *Philosophical Studies* (Dublin) 16 (1967): 63–81.

Osborne, Thomas. "The Concept as Formal Sign." *Semiotica* (forthcoming).

Owen, G. E. L. "Logic and Metaphysics in Some Early Works of Aristotle." In *Aristotle and Plato in Mid-Fourth Century,* edited by Ingemar Düring and G. E. L. Owen, 163–90. Göteborg: Studia Graeca et Latina Gothoburgensia, 1960.

Owens, Joseph. *The Doctrine of Being in the Aristotelian "Metaphysics": A Study in the Greek Background of Medieval Thought.* 3rd ed. Toronto: Pontifical Institute of Medieval Studies, 1978.

Padovan, Richard. *Proportion: Science, Philosophy, Architecture*. London: Spon, 1999.

Park, Seung-Chan. *Die Rezeption der mittelalterlichen Sprachphilosophie in der Theologie des Thomas von Aquin: Mit besonderer Berücksichtigung der Analogie*. Leiden: Brill, 1999.

Penido, M. T.-L. *Le rôle de l'analogie en théologie dogmatique*. Paris: Librairie Philosophique J. Vrin, 1931.

Phelan, Gerald B. *St. Thomas and Analogy*. Milwaukee: Marquette University Press, 1941.

Philippe, M.-D. "*Analogon* and *Analogia* in the Philosophy of Aristotle." *The Thomist* 33 (1969): 1–74.

Pinborg, Jan. *Medieval Semantics: Selected Studies in Medieval Logic and Grammar*. Edited by Sten Ebbesen. London: Variorum Reprints, 1984.

———. "A Note on Some Theoretic Concepts of Logic and Grammar." In *Medieval Semantics*. Reprinted from *Revue Internationale de Philosophie* (Brussels) 29:113 (1975): 286–96.

———. "Some Problems of Semantic Representations in Medieval Logic." In *Medieval Semantics*. Reprinted from *History of Linguistic Thought and Contemporary Linguistics*, edited by H. Parret, 254–78. Berlin: Walter de Gruyter, 1976.

———. "Some Syntactical Concepts in Medieval Grammar." In *Medieval Semantics*. Reprinted from *Classica et Mediaevalia (Francisco Blatt dedicata)*, Dissertationes IX, 496–509. Copenhagen: Gyldendal, 1973.

Poinsot, John (John of St. Thomas). *Ars Logica*. Edited by B. Reiser. Turin: Marietti, 1930.

Porphyry. *In Aristotelis Praedicamenta per interrogationem et responsionem brevis explanatio*. In *Commentaria in Aristotelem Graeca* IV.1, edited by A. Busse. Berlin: G. Reimeri, 1887.

Prentice, Robert. "Univocity and Analogy According to Scotus's *Super Libros Elenchorum Aristotelis*." *Archives d'Histoire Doctrinale et Littéraire du Moyen Age* 35 (1968): 39–64.

Przezdziecki, Joseph J. "Thomas of Sutton's Critique of the Doctrine of Univocity." In *An Etienne Gilson Tribute*, edited by Charles J. O'Neil, 189–208. Milwaukee: Marquette University Press, 1959.

Pseudo-Augustine. *Categoriae Decem. Patrologia Latina*, vol. 32.

Putnam, Hilary. "Thoughts Addressed to an Analytical Thomist." *The Monist* 80 (1997): 487–99.

Ramirez, Jacobus M. *De Analogia*. In *Opera omnia*, tom. 2. 4 vols. Madrid: Instituto de Filosofia "Luis Vives," 1970.

———. "De analogia secundum doctrinam Aristotelico-Thomisticam." In *Ciencia Tomista* 24 (1921): 20–40, 195–214, 337–57; 25 (1922): 17–38.

———. "En torno a un famoso texto de Santo Tomas sobre analogia." In *Opera omnia* 2.4: 1811–50. Reprinted from *Sapientia* 8 (1953): 166–92.

Reilly, John P. *Cajetan's Notion of Existence*. The Hague: Mouton, 1971.

Revue Thomist 39. Special issue, *Cajetan* (Nov. 1934–Feb. 1935).

Reynolds, Philip L. "Analogy of Names in Bonaventure." *Mediaeval Studies* 65 (2003): 117–62.

————. "Bonaventure's Theory of Resemblance." *Traditio* 58 (2003): 219–55.

Righi, Giulio. *Studio sulla Analogia in S. Tommaso.* Milan: Marzorati Editore, 1981.

Rijk, L. M. de. *Logica Modernorum: A Contribution to the History of Early Terminist Logic.* Vol. 1, *On the Twelfth Century Theories of Fallacy.* Assen: Van Gorcum, 1962.

————. "The Origins of the Theory of the Properties of Terms." In *The Cambridge History of Later Medieval Philosophy*, 161–73. Cambridge: Cambridge University Press, 1982.

Riva, Franco. *Analogia e univocità in Tommaso de Vio "Gaetano."* Milan: Vita e Pensiero, 1995.

————. "L'analogia dell'ente in Dominico di Fiandra." *Rivista di Filosofia Neoscolastica* 86 (1994): 287–322.

————. *L'analogia metaforica: Una questione logico-metafisica nel tomismo.* Milan: Vita e Pensiero, 1989.

————. "Il Gaetano e l'ente come «primum cognitum»." *Rivista di Filosofia Neo-scolastica* 85 (1993): 3–20.

————. *Tommaso Claxton e l'analogia della proporzionalità.* Milan: Vita e Pensiero, 1989.

Rocca, Gregory Philip. *Speaking the Incomprehensible God: Thomas Aquinas on the Interplay of Positive and Negative Theology.* Washington, D.C.: Catholic University of America Press, 2004.

Rolnick, Philip A. *Analogical Possibilities: How Words Refer to God.* Atlanta: Scholars Press, 1993.

Rosier, Irène. "Évolution des notions d'*equivocatio* et *univocatio* au XIIe siècle." In *L'ambiguité: Cinq études historiques*, edited by Irène Rosier, 103–66. Lille: Presses Universitaires de Lille, 1988.

————. "*Res significata* et *modus significandi*: Les implications d'une distinction médiévale." In *Sprachteorien in Spätantike und Mittelalter*, edited by Sten Ebbesen, 135–68. Tübingen: Gunter Narr Verlag, 1995.

Ross, James F. "Analogy as a Rule of Meaning for Religious Language." In *Inquiries into Medieval Philosophy*, edited by James F. Ross, 35–74. Reprinted from *International Philosophical Quarterly* 1 (1961): 468–502; reprinted also in *Aquinas: A Collection of Critical Essays*, edited by Anthony Kenny, 93–138. Garden City, N.Y.: Anchor Books, 1969.

————. "A Critical Analysis of the Theory of Analogy of St. Thomas Aquinas." Ph.D. diss., Brown University, 1958.

————, ed. *Inquiries into Medieval Philosophy: A Collection in Honor of Francis P. Clarke.* Contributions in Philosophy, no. 4. Westport, Conn.: Greenwood, 1971.

————. "A New Theory of Analogy." *Proceedings of the American Catholic Philosophical Association* 49 (1970): 70–85.

————. *Portraying Analogy.* Cambridge: Cambridge University Press, 1981.

————. Review of McInerny, *The Logic of Analogy. International Philosophical Quarterly* 2 (1962): 633–42.

Schwartz, Herbert Thomas. "Analogy in St. Thomas and Cajetan." *New Scholasticism* 28 (1954): 127–44.

Sherry, Patrick J. "Analogy Today." *Philosophy* 51 (1976): 431–46.

Shields, Christopher. *Order in Multiplicity: Homonymy in the Philosophy of Aristotle*. Oxford: Oxford University Press, 1999.

Simon, Yves. "On Order in Analogical Sets." In *Philosopher at Work: Essays by Yves R. Simon*, edited by Anthony O. Simon, 135-71. Lanham, Md.: Rowman and Littlefield, 1999. Reprinted from *New Scholasticism* 34 (1960): 1–42.

Simplicius. *On Aristotle's "Categories 1–4."* Translated by Michael Chase. Ithaca: Cornell University Press, 2003.

Slattery, Michael P. "Concerning Two Recent Studies in Analogy." *New Scholasticism* 31 (1957): 237–46.

———. "The Three-fold Division of Analogy." *Philosophical Studies* (Dublin) 15 (1966): 131–54.

Spade, Paul Vincent. "The Semantics of Terms." In *The Cambridge History of Later Medieval Philosophy*, 188–98. Cambridge: Cambridge University Press, 1982.

———. *Thoughts Words and Things: An Introduction to Late Medieval Logic and Semantic Theory*. Version 1.0. URL = http://pvspade.com/Logic/docs/thoughts.pdf.

Stern, Josef. Review of Ross, *Portraying Analogy*. *Journal of Philosophy* 84 (1987): 392–97.

Suarez, Francisco. *Disputationes Metaphysicae*. 2 vols. Hildesheim: Georg Olms Verlag, 1965. Reprinted from Suarez, *Opera omnia*, vols. 25 and 26. Paris: Vives, 1866.

Summa Totius Logicae [*De Totius Logicae Aristotelis Summa*]. In Thomas Aquinas, *Opera omnia*, vol. 17, 32–117. Parma: Fiaccadori, 1864.

Sutton, Thomas. *Quaestiones Ordinariae*. Edited by Johannes Schneider. Munich: Verlag der Bayerischen Akademie der Wissenschaften, 1977.

Tavuzzi, Michael. "Hervaeus Natalis and the Philosophical Logic of the Thomism of the Renaissance." *Doctor Communis* 45 (1992): 132–52.

———. *Prierias: The Life and Works of Silvestro Mazzolini da Prierio, 1456–1527*. Durham, N.C.: Duke University Press, 1997.

———. "Some Renaissance Thomist Divisions of Analogy." *Angelicum* 70 (1993): 93–121.

Theron, Stephen. *Africa, Philosophy and the Western Tradition: An Essay in Self-Understanding*. Frankfurt: Peter Lang, 1995.

———. "The Resistance of Thomism to Analytical and Other Patronage." *The Monist* 80 (Oct. 1997).

———. "The Supposition of the Predicate." *Modern Schoolman* 77 (1999): 73–78.

Thomas Aquinas. *In Aristotelis Libros Peri Hermeneias et Posteriorum Analyticorum Expositio*. Edited by Raymundi M. Spiazzi. Rome: Marietti, 1955.

———. *In duodecim libros Metaphysicorum expositio*. Rome: Marietti, 1971.

———. *De fallaciis*. In *Opuscula philosophica*, edited by Raymundi M. Spiazzi. Rome: Marietti, 1954.

———. *De principiis naturae*. In *Opera omnia*, vol. 43. Rome: Leonine Commission, 1976.

———. *Quaestiones disputatae de potentia Dei*. Edited by M. Pession. Rome: Marietti, 1953.

———. *Quaestiones disputatae de Veritate*. In *Opera omnia*, vol. 23. Rome: Leonine Commission, 1970–76.

———. *Scripta super libros Sententiarum*. Edited by P. Mandonnet. 2 vols. Paris: Lethielleux, 1929.

———. *Summa Contra Gentiles*. In *Opera omnia*, vols. 13–15. Rome: Leonine Commission, 1918–30.

———. *Summa Theologiae*. In *Opera omnia*, vols. 4–12. Rome: Leonine Commission, 1888–1906.

Tracy, David. *The Analogical Imagination: Christian Theology and the Culture of Pluralism*. New York: Crossroad, 1981.

Weisheipl, James A. "Cajetan (Tommaso de Vio)." In *New Catholic Encyclopedia*, 2nd ed., edited by Bernard L. Marthaler et al., vol. 2, 852–55. Detroit: Gale/Catholic University of America Press, 2003.

Wilks, Ian. "Aquinas on Analogy: The Distinction of Many-to-One and One-to-Another." *Modern Schoolman* 75 (1997): 35–53.

Wippel, John F. *The Metaphysical Thought of Thomas Aquinas: From Finite Being to Uncreated Being*. Washington, D.C.: Catholic University of America Press, 2000.

Wolfson, H. A. "The Amphibolous Terms in Aristotle, Arabic Philosophy, and Maimonides." *Harvard Theological Review* 31 (1938): 151–73.

Index

abstraction, 54–55, 59, 143, 148–53,
158–59, 168–69, 175–76, 195n39
analogia: Greek vs. Latin meanings,
5–11, 179n9
analogical unity, 54–55, 59, 66, 77,
109, 131, 139, 216n25. *See also*
proportional unity
analogy of attribution, 11–12, 17, 20,
23, 45, 71–72, 77, 98, 124, 153–54,
156
  in Cajetan's *De Ente et Essentia*
  commentary, 25, 104–5, 214n12
  defined, 36, 106–7, 110
  in *De Veritate*, 139–40
  functions logically as equivocation,
  118–21
  mixed cases, 112–17, 141, 218n38,
  218n40, 218n42
  only "abusively" a form of analogy,
  123
  secondary analogates denominated
  extrinsically, 20, 23, 26, 111–17,
  141
  signifies a relation, 111, 113, 118
  Yves Simon on, 196nn45–46
  See also analogy of proportionality
analogy of inequality, 11, 17, 81, 99,
101–4, 107–10, 153, 214n12,
215n21, 216n22, 216n27
  before Cajetan, 108, 215n19

  in the *De Ente et Essentia*
  commentary, 25, 102–4
  defined, 36, 107–8
  logically equivalent to univocation,
  37, 81, 109, 118–21, 142
  only "abusively" a form of analogy,
  123
analogy of proportionality
  and abstraction, 144–51, 167–68
  in Aquinas, 18–20, 23, 103, 105,
  139–40, 182n22, 199n10, 204n50,
  214n12, 224n38
  circularity objection, 126, 131–34,
  223n21
  in the *De Ente et Essentia*
  commentary, 25, 102–6
  defined, 36, 106–7, 124–25
  and intrinsic denomination, 20,
  23–24, 26, 98, 111, 140, 220n58
  most genuine mode of analogy, 12,
  139–42, 220n58
  priority and posteriority, 156–58,
  230n42
  proper vs. metaphor, 11–12,
  125–29, 156, 222nn13–14
  signifies the foundation of a
  relation, 154–55
  as true mean between univocation
  and equivocation, 139–42,
  173–74, 220n58

analogy of proportionality (*cont.*)
two unknowns objection, 129–31,
223n16, 223nn18–19
and valid reasoning, 45, 105–6, 125,
161–64
See also metaphor; *proportio*;
proportionalitas
Anderson, James F., 19, 116, 130,
180n20, 184n48, 196n45, 218n38,
218n42, 223nn18–19
Aristotle
and analogy of inequality, 108,
215n19, 216n25
associated meaning vs. nongeneric
likeness, 4–6, 178n4
Categories, 35, 86, 90, 92, 99–100,
187n4, 215n18
in *De Nominum Analogia,* 24–26,
104–5, 164–66, 199n10, 215n19
on metaphor in cognition and
language, 177n1, 224n35
on use of analogy in syllogism, 42,
44, 67, 106, 164
why being is not a genus, 159
Ashworth, E. J., 20, 28–29, 31–32,
41, 43, 47–51, 69, 74–79, 108,
115–17, 205n59, 209n19, 209n22,
217n32
associated meaning
in Aquinas, 9–10
in Aristotelian commentary, 6–7
in Aristotle, 4–6, 178n4
in Boethius and scholasticism, 8–9
defined, 2–3
in *De Nominum Analogia,* 12–13,
37, 173
relation to nongeneric likeness,
3–4, 179n10
Averroës, 24–26, 102–5, 108, 186n1

Bochenski, I. M., 42, 150, 176, 187n9,
190n35, 191n37, 206n76, 228n26,
231n9
Boethius, 7–9, 11, 41, 85
Bonaventure, 9

Broadie, Alexander, 60
Brown, Stephen, 79
Burrell, David, 21, 43, 53–55, 59,
133–35, 149–50, 181n8, 196n47,
203n46
Bushinski, Edward A., 19, 38, 209n17

concept, 36, 117
Cajetan on, 56–60, 86–91
criticism of Cajetan's attention to,
20, 27, 47–56
formal vs. objective, 34, 38, 77–78,
89–91, 108, 119, 144–45, 151–52,
167–68, 176, 194n37, 208nn11–
12, 226n10
part of semantic triangle, 34, 38–41,
86–91
perfect vs. imperfect, 144–48, 151,
158, 162–63, 168–69, 175
question of abstraction in analogy,
55, 59, 148–51, 169
question of how unified in analogy,
28–29, 35, 43–45, 48, 100, 169
Scotus on, 43–44
See also ratio

De Conceptu Entis, 166–68
De Ente et Essentia, Cajetan's
commentary on, 25, 39, 44, 57,
62, 99–106, 108, 168
denomination
defined, 92–93
extrinsic vs. intrinsic, 12, 23, 26,
93–98, 211n28, 220n58
Descoqs, P. Pedro, 19–20, 222n15
Dominic of Flanders, 28, 30, 44,
78–79, 185n61, 185n72
Doyle, John, 94

equivocation, 3–4, 6–9, 36, 40–45. *See
also* fallacy of equivocation; *pros
hen* equivocation

fallacy of equivocation, 42–45, 60,
65–81, 101, 118, 121, 125, 138–39,

143–44, 154, 162–65, 190n31,
190n35, 199n11
focal meaning, 4, 70. *See also pros hen*
equivocation
Francesco Securo da Nardò, 30
Francesco Silvestri da Ferrara, 70

Geach, Peter, 54, 195n39
Gerard of Bologna, 79
Gilson, Étienne, 20, 51–55, 57–59,
216n27
Goergen, Aloys, 18, 21

Hayner, Paul, 134–35
Henry of Ghent, 29, 79
hermeneutics, 12, 61–64, 165–66
Hervaeus Natalis, 28, 79

isomorphy, 150–51, 176, 228n26,
231n9. *See also analogia*;
nongeneric likeness;
proportionalitas; proportional
unity

Johannes Capreolus, 28, 78, 184n51
Johannes Versor (John Versorius),
78–79, 185n72
John Duns Scotus, 20, 31, 45, 63, 72,
102
arguments against analogy, 42–43,
60, 143, 173, 215n14
attention to concepts, 52–54, 58
Cajetan's response to, 44, 56, 101,
138–39, 152, 162–64, 170,
228n30
definition of univocity, 43, 224n36
John of Jandun, 28, 79
John of St. Thomas (John Poinsot),
xiv–xv, xvi, 114–15, 196n46,
211n28, 218n42, 227n15
judgment, 20, 51–55, 60–61, 124,
151–60, 195n41

Klubertanz, George P., 19–21, 68, 70,
141, 199n10

Kretzmann, Norman, 61
Kuhn, Thomas, 22, 26

Lyttkens, Hampus, 20–21, 203n46,
204n50

Marion, Jean-Luc, 20, 184n48, 220n48
Mascall, E. L., 132–33
Maurer, Armand, 51–52, 216n27
McInerny, Ralph, 21, 37, 70, 73–75,
112, 204n49, 205n59, 217n37
Meagher, Robert, 24, 37
metaphor, xx, 3–5, 8, 11–12, 123,
126–29, 156, 170, 177n1, 221n7,
222nn13–14, 224n35, 229n39
Mondin, Battista, 21, 192n14
Montagnes, Bernard, 19–21, 29,
185n67

nongeneric likeness
in Aquinas, 9–10
in Aristotle, 4–5, 178n4
defined, 1–2
as proportionality, 12, 125, 128, 138,
174
relation to associated meaning, 3–4,
179n10
See also proportionalitas;
proportional unity

Paulus Soncinas, 28, 30, 44, 78–79,
184n51, 185n72
Penido, M. T.-L., 18, 21
per prius et posterius, 8–9, 25, 68–70,
73, 77, 80, 101–2, 123, 157–58,
200n15, 200n21, 202n35
Peter Aureol, 28, 79
Pinchard, Bruno, 79, 188n15
Porphyry, 7, 62, 85, 179n11, 187n4,
213n3
proportio, 7
proportionalitas, 7–8
in Boethius, 7–8
See also analogia; nongeneric
likeness

proportional mean, 8–9
proportional unity, 59–60, 105, 125,
    129, 136–39, 141–42, 148, 154,
    158–59, 163–64, 169–71, 174,
    176, 222n10. *See also analogia*;
    analogical unity; nongeneric
    likeness
pros hen equivocation, 4, 6–9, 13,
    70–71, 136, 174, 187n4, 218n42,
    222n10
Putnam, Hilary, 131

Ramirez, Jacobus, 19–20, 219n47
ratio, 7, 36, 39, 68, 70–81, 90–91,
    209n17, 209n19
    in Cajetan's definitions of analogy,
        36, 107
    how signified in metaphor, 126–27
    of one analogate in the definition of
        others, 70–72, 77–78
    proper only in one analogate,
        72–74, 77–78
    proportional sameness of in
        syllogistic reasoning, 162–64
    See also concept
resolution, 157–59, 168
Rijk, L. M. de, 60–61, 197n51
Riva, Franco, 28–32, 115, 186n75,
    186n80, 190n25, 190n30
Ross, James, 43, 50–52, 54, 71, 137,
    191n37, 203n46, 217n30, 224n35

Schwartz, Herbert, 110
semantic triangle, xx, 34, 38, 40–42,
    86–91, 145–47
Sherry, Patrick, 52, 191n36
signification, 37, 45, 48–51, 57, 63,
    85–91, 117, 119, 124, 138, 167,
    170, 193n23, 194n38, 197n51,
    208n7, 220n48, 226n10

res significata vs. *modi significandi*,
    68, 74–76, 203n46, 204n49,
    209n22
Silvestro Mazzolini, 70
Simon, Yves, 18, 54–55, 59–60,
    135–36, 149, 181n8, 196nn45–46,
    197n50, 200n21, 201n30, 229n39
Simplicius, 7, 79, 179n11, 187n4,
    224n36
Suarez, Francisco, xiv, 20, 115–16,
    141, 219n47, 220n48
Sutton, Thomas, 44, 185n67
syllogistic reasoning, 42–44, 56–57,
    60, 67, 75–76, 162–64, 190n35,
    197n1, 206n76, 231n9

Tavuzzi, Michael, 28–32, 185n72
Thomas Aquinas, 9–10
    characterizations of the unity of
        analogical signification, 66–76
    Commentary on the Sentences,
        18–20, 23, 25, 30, 78, 105, 184n51,
        186n73, 214n12
    De Veritate, 18–19, 23, 25–26, 30,
        105, 140, 198n7, 201n31, 204n53
    logical vs. metaphysical approach
        to analogy, 9–10, 20, 37–38
    question of relation to Cajetan's
        analogy theory, xvi, 17–22, 24,
        27–32, 139–40, 176
    role of judgment in analogy, 51–55,
        57–59
    Summa Theologiae, 66, 70, 72,
        201n31
Thomas Claxton, 185n67
Thomas Sutton, 44, 185n67

Vincenzo Merlini da Venezia, 30

Wippel, John F., 21

Joshua P. Hochschild

is associate professor of philosophy and Dean of the College
of Liberal Arts at Mount St. Mary's University.